DISTINGUISHING PSYCHOLOGICAL FROM ORGANIC DISORDERS

Robert L. Taylor, MD, is a consulting psychiatrist and lecturer.

After completion of his psychiatric training at Stanford, he has held a number of academic, administrative, and clinical positions. He has been a psychiatry training specialist with the National Institutes of Mental Health; *Associate Clinical Professor* of Family Medicine, Stanford University School of Medicine; *Program Chief,* Marin County Community Mental Health Services; Consulting Psychiatrist for state mental health programs in California and Texas; Director, Student Health Services, California State University, Northridge; and Medical Director, Austin-Travis County Mental Health Mental Retardation Center and Charter Behavioral Health System of Austin.

Dr. Taylor is the author of *Mind or Body* (1982) and *Health Fact, Health Fiction* (1990).

DISTINGUISHING PSYCHOLOGICAL FROM ORGANIC DISORDERS

SECOND EDITION

Screening for Psychological Masquerade

Robert L. Taylor, MD

 Springer Publishing Company

Springer Publishing Company, Inc.
536 Broadway
New York NY 10012-3955

Acquisitions Editor: Bill Tucker
Production Editor: Helen Song
Cover design by James Scotto-Lavino

00 01 02 03 04 / 5 4 3 2 1

Library of Congress Cataloging-In-Publication Data

Taylor, Robert L., 1942–
      Distinguishing psychological from organic disorders : screening for psychological masquerade / Robert L. Taylor.—2nd ed.
            p.   cm.
      Includes bibliographical references and index.
      ISBN 0-8261-1329-X (hardcover)
      1. Mental illness—Physiological aspects. 2. Psychological manifestations of general diseases.   3. Diagnosis, Differential.
      4. Neuropsychiatry.   I. Title.
      [DNLM: 1. Delirium, Dementia, Amnestic, Cognitive Disorders—diagnosis.   2. Brain Diseases—diagnosis.
      3. Diagnosis, Differential. 4. Mental Disorders—diagnosis.
      WM 141 T244d 2000]
      RC455.4.B5 T38 2000
      616.89'075—dc21
                                                                        99-059688

Printed in the United States of America

To
Lester and Mary Lou Taylor

and to
Vanessa and Abbott

CONTENTS

PREFACE

Personal encounters in our everyday lives can produce striking changes in the way we think, feel, and act. Such changes, however, are not always the product of external events. Sometimes they are reflections of underlying physical disease. In these instances, despite their psychological appearance, the symptoms reflect problems in the brain itself.

Distinguishing masquerading medical conditions from psychological reactions is a challenge to all physicians, therapists, and counselors. The stakes are high. Mistakes lead to patient frustration, inappropriate therapy, and, in the most tragic cases, residual disability or even death. There are few clinical moments more distressing than when a health professional discovers that symptoms that have been construed as expressions of psychological conflict, are, in fact, manifestations of a brain tumor, seizure disorder, or some other organic condition.

This book is a practical guide to the clinical recognition of psychological masquerades arising from various organic mental disorders. Instead of an encyclopedic detailing of every medical disease known to cause psychiatric symptoms, the reader will find a clinical strategy that reduces the chances of mistaking organic disorders for psychological problems. Throughout the book illustrative case histories—drawn primarily from published accounts—are interwoven with general principles.

I want to express special thanks to Larry Koran, who several years ago set me to seriously thinking about the subject of this book and who thoughtfully reviewed the early draft chapters.

I am grateful to Barbara Arons and the staff of the inpatient psychiatric service at Santa Clara Valley Medical Center (San Jose,

California), from whom I learned invaluable lessons with respect to the clinical recognition of psychological masquerade.

For their published accounts of masquerading organic disorders I am also indebted to various authors, most of whom I have never met. Finally, the book has been improved considerably in response to comments from Frank Benson, Pat Jordan, Bev Abbot, David Lam, Linda Olvera-Perales, Lenore Morell, and Merna McMillan.

PREFACE TO THE SECOND EDITION

The passage of ten years since this book's original publication has not altered its basic premise: Psychological symptoms are not always best explained psychologically. A host of medical conditions continue to have a nasty habit of masquerading as psychiatric disorders. An active index of suspicion remains the clinician's most effective defense. Entertaining the possibility of psychological masquerade can transform subtle clues into compelling evidence. The greatest diagnostic pitfall remains the "obvious" psychological problem. In order to detect such masquerades, the clinician must be able to suspend judgment long enough to look beyond the most logical explanation. It is with the hope of aiding clinicians in this enterprise that this book has been written and revised.

Chapter 1

Appearances Can Be Deceiving

Difficulties lie in our habits of thought rather than in the nature of things.   —André Tardieu

Psychiatric symptoms are not always best explained psychologically. The same mental and emotional changes associated with various problems in living can also be caused by certain medical disorders. For the clinician, this dual origin of "psychological" symptoms raises critical diagnostic questions. Is the patient depressed because of problems on the job or at home, or is his depression a manifestation of hormonal imbalance, brain tumor, or epilepsy?

Psychological masquerade is the "flip side" of the psychosomatic symptom. Just as individuals with problems in living sometimes seek medical care, persons with medical disorders sometimes seek cures from psychotherapists. Like it or not, all mental health professionals are confronted with the task of clinically distinguishing organic medical conditions from psychological reactions. As we shall see, these misleading presentations are not uncommon; to complicate matters, they often occur in the context of what turns out to be an unrelated personal problem.

The task of detecting psychological masquerade cannot be avoided. Clear distinctions between medical and nonmedical responsibility occur only on organizational charts and in the pages of job descriptions. In the everyday world, the boundaries are blurred. Mastering the clinical skills and knowledge necessary to minimize the chances of misinterpreting organic mental disorders is the responsibility of all mental health professionals. They owe this to themselves as professionals and, more importantly, to their patients.

1

Detecting psychological masquerade does not require an in depth knowledge of neurology. While arriving at a specific medical diagnosis is the role of medical specialists, the initial clinical challenge is to suspect "organicity," so that referral for further medical evaluation can be made. It is at this critical juncture that the most glaring clinical mistakes are made.

THE STORY OF TWO LANGUAGES

Throughout this book, psychological reactions are contrasted with organic mental disorders. At times this distinction may seen overly simplistic. In reality, human problems are neither organic nor psychological! It is the explanatory language we use that is "organic" or "psychological." If our knowledge of human behavior were complete, one all-encompassing language would suffice. As it is, we are stuck with various "partial" languages (or models) to explain problems. In trying to explain human behavior, we rely primarily on two different languages. For convenience we'll call them Language I and Language II.

Mechanistic in character, Language I is used in the physical and biological sciences due to its greater specificity. Language II, in contrast, is much more subjective and metaphorical. It is more compatible with the demands of the arts and social sciences, mainly for its capacity to capture more subjective aspects of human experience such as motivation, meaning, and feeling.

Psychological reactions to problems in living are more easily described in Language II than in Language I. Explanations are characteristically framed as psychological hypotheses as opposed to mathematical equations or mechanistic relationships. The man is depressed because he did not get the advancement he was expecting at work. The loss is a blow to his self-esteem, resulting in a sense of despondency. This explanation suggests non-biological remedies, such as finding another job or pursuing psychotherapy.

But language II is not nearly as useful describing other kinds of problems. Take, for example, the problem of abdominal pain associated with acute appendicitis. Formulating this symptom in terms of childhood rejection is of limited utility compared to a physiological explanation rendered in Language I, which makes surgical intervention the treatment. Ultimately, the choice of explanatory language should be determined on the basis of which one better fits the problem at hand. Compare acute appendicitis and grief. Stated in biochemical terms (Language I), an explanation of human grief, while having some validity, is cumbersome and limited in the practical insights it can generate; not so with Language II. Its vocabulary lends itself to describing grief in ways that are more amenable to practical intervention. In short, any human problem can be explained in either organic (Language I) or psychological (Language II) terms. The choice comes down to which language, given current states of knowledge, provides the most productive solutions. This book focuses on symptoms, which—though often best explained psychologically—sometimes require biological explanation. Errors in the choice of explanatory language set the stage for treating brain tumor as a personality disturbance, thyroid disease as an anxiety disorder, and brain seizure as psychosis.

A college senior experienced a sensation of pressure in her head. Following graduation, she found herself becoming easily upset about minor problems arising in her new job as a schoolteacher. She had no appetite and in a short time had lost 15 pounds. She sought the help of a psychiatrist, who diagnosed her as suffering from schizophrenia.

When she experienced fainting episodes, vomiting, and unexplained fever, this diagnosis was reconsidered. She underwent a complete medical evaluation, but no physical basis for her symptoms was found.

Although her physical symptoms gradually disappeared without treatment, the woman began to act strangely. Despite electroconvulsive treatment, she became increasingly delusional and, finally, was admitted to a psychiatric hospital. She was described as "silly," alternating between periods of euphoric excitement and withdrawn depression. On occasion she expressed concern over what she feared was her impending death.

Her admitting psychiatric diagnosis was hebephrenic schizophrenia. (Rubert & Remington, 1962)

Subsequently, the diagnosis was changed in the face of rapidly developing neurological findings. At surgery the woman was found to have a large frontal lobe brain tumor. Even though the tumor was not malignant, it could not be successfully removed because of its advanced stage. The patient died shortly afterwards. Failure to appreciate this psychological masquerade resulted in a death that could have been avoided had the organic cause been suspected earlier.

PSYCHOLOGICAL MASQUERADERS: HOW COMMON ARE THEY?

Over the years, various researchers have tried to determine the frequency of psychological masquerade. One well-designed research investigation took a careful look at 658 consecutive psychiatric outpatient cases for evidence of "medical disorders productive of psychiatric symptoms." Although all the individuals had sought help for what they believed to be psychological problems, 9%, as it turned out, had an organic disorder that fully accounted for their "psychological" problems. The researchers concluded that "Psychiatric symptoms are nonspecific and commonly occur in medical as well as psychiatric disease" (Hall, Popkin, DeVaul, Faillace, & Stickney, 1978).

Another, somewhat larger study of 2,090 psychiatric outpatients turned up an even higher incidence of masquerading medical problems: 18% of the patients had symptoms directly attributable to organic disease. The author of the report emphasized the importance of persistent vigilance by clinicians: "The examiner must continually entertain the question: What other than the obvious might be the cause of or a contributing factor to the presenting symptom?" (Koranyi, 1979).

More recently (1983–1984), under a contract with the California Department of Mental Health, Dr. Lorrin Koran of Stanford University's Department of Psychiatry and his colleagues used a mobile evaluation unit to examine 529 patients drawn from the state's public mental health system (Koran et al., 1989). Underlying organic conditions either *causing* or *significantly exacerbating* the mental or emotional symptoms were found in 173 of the cases. Roughly half of the subjects approached, however, were not included in the study. They refused or were too violent or psychotic to cooperate, or they had a primary diagnosis of alcoholism. In their report of these findings to the California Department of Mental Health, these authors summarized nine additional studies and concluded that the average occurrence of psychological masquerade was 19%.

Using a reverse approach, another group of researchers focused on 395 patients with well-documented neurological disease and posed this question: Initially, how many of these cases were erroneously thought to represent psychological reactions? To find an answer, the researchers conducted an extensive review of the medical records. It showed that 53 (13%) of these patients had originally been misdiagnosed. The mistaken diagnoses included hysteria, schizophrenia, hypochondriasis, psychopathic personality, obsessive compulsive neurosis, anxiety, and somatization. On average, these false diagnoses had been maintained for 4 years. At one time or another, *all* of these patients had received psychotherapy for symptoms eventually accounted for on a neurological basis (Tissenbaum, Harter, & Friedman, 1951).

In light of new evidence, certain symptoms traditionally characterized as "psychological" require closer scrutiny. For example, it was not too long ago that mental health professionals were taught that male sexual impotence was a psychological problem. This turns out not to be the case. More often than not, this problem has a biological basis.

In a report published in the *Journal of the American Medical Association*, roughly 75% of 105 men studied for the symptom of sexual impotence were found to have causative physical diseases. Diabetes mellitus, sex-hormone imbalance, and various addictions ranked high on the list (Spark, White, & Connolly, 1980). Of the 34 men with hormonal problems who accepted treatment, 33 had a return of sexual potency. In an attempt to correct the problem, 14 of these men had undergone psychotherapy unsuccessfully.

"Hysteria" is another psychological characterization not to be applied prematurely. One investigation followed 85 persons who under the examining eyes of experienced physicians were presumed to have hysteria, characterized by somatic complaints without demonstrable organic disease and thought to be the manifestation of psychological conflict (Slater, 1965). But when these patients were followed for periods ranging from 7 to 11 years, more than one-third proved to have physical diseases that explained their "hysterical" symptoms.

Psychological masquerades congregate in psychiatric inpatient populations. A review of "100 patients of lower socioeconomic class" admitted to a state hospital showed that 46% had medical illnesses that "directly caused or greatly exacerbated their symptoms." This determination was made on the basis of an extensive diagnostic evaluation, including physical, psychiatric, and neurological examinations along with an automated blood analysis and complete blood count, urinalysis, electrocardiogram, and sleep-deprived electroencephalogram. An additional 34% were found to have a previously unrecognized physical illness, that (although not causative of psychiatric symptoms) "would have routinely been treated by a general physician if its presence were known" (Hall, Gardner, Stickney, LeCann, & Popkin, 1980).

These selected studies make it clear that psychological masquerade is not a rare occurrence. Conservatively, one can assume that among psychiatric outpatients, roughly 5 to 10% of persons seen for psychological symptoms suffer from a causative physical disease. (Hall, Beresford, Blow, & Hall, 1990.) The figure increases as we move from outpatient to inpatient and emergency settings. Similarly, it is greater in certain high-risk populations, such as the elderly, and in certain diagnostic categories such as hysteria, sexual impotence, and drug/alcohol problems.

These findings do not change the basic fact that the majority of cases exhibiting mental or emotional symptoms are appropriately explained psychosocially. They do indicate, however, that mental health professionals actively engaged in clinical work can expect to see a significant number of masquerading medical conditions over the course of a career.

HOW *NOT* TO DETECT PSYCHOLOGICAL MASQUERADE

A sound approach to clinical assessment starts with the understanding that organic mental disorders and psychological reactions are *not* distinguishable on the basis of the mental and emotional symptoms themselves. It is the broader context—the client's history as well as other clinical observations—that provides the basis for detecting psychological masquerade.

Consider the following case:

> Against his wishes, a 42-year-old proprietor of a small grocery store was brought for psychiatric treatment by his wife and brother. They stated that he had become highly irresponsible, engaging in impulsive and extravagant business deals.
>
> Previously, the man had been a respected member of his community. Although described as having his faults, such as boasting and occasional ostentatious spending, he had been a responsible husband-provider with no history of mental illness. Over the preceding year, however, his wife had noticed several changes. He had become extremely forgetful and prone to spells of unexplained anger. At other times, his mood would shift abruptly from depression to euphoria. He indulged in wild spending sprees and became preoccupied with fantastic schemes. Neglecting his grocery business, he took up much of his time driving about the countryside looking for new places to build bigger stores. Finally, when he impulsively purchased an automobile and solicited a large loan from the town banker, his wife decided he needed professional help. As her husband had tried to persuade the banker of the merits of his proposal, he had gotten quite excited, to the point of becoming incoherent.

> A clinical evaluation confirmed the man's inappropriate euphoria. He also showed a notable inability to perform simple math problems and to understand commonly used proverbs. (Hofling, 1968)

The changes could have been psychological. Here was a man in his middle forties, possibly confronting the meaning of his life, unable to avoid the inevitability of aging and eventual death. Construing this man's problem as a midlife crisis would not have been unreasonable. Irrational, impulsive behavior sometimes occurs in response to stress. On closer examination, however, a psychological explanation seemed unlikely. There were several important clues: his difficulty performing simple calculations (particularly unexpected in a man who owned a grocery store) and the absence of a previous history of manic behavior. Additionally, on medical examination, the man's pupils were found to be abnormally constricted and barely reactive to light. A blood test for syphilis was strongly positive, leading to a diagnosis of syphilitic brain disease. Additional history confirmed an untreated chancre sore during adolescence. He was treated with high doses of intramuscular penicillin and after 6 weeks showed virtually complete recovery, a fortunate and somewhat unusual therapeutic response for someone with advanced (tertiary) syphilis.

The man's manic behavior was no different than that experienced by persons with bipolar disorder or as a side effect of certain medications. The key to suspecting a psychological masquerade was not his euphoric, impulsive behavior but rather it was the associated cognitive deficit—his inability to solve simple math problems. This was the most telling clinical finding before a medical evaluation confirmed the organic nature of his problem.

WE SEE WHAT WE LOOK FOR

Distinguishing between organic and psychological disorders is complicated by our fixed patterns of perception—our mind set. While words and concepts help to organize the world around us, they also powerfully circumscribe what we perceive. For example, it is said that people who live most of their lives in snow country learn to distinguish many different kinds of snow, whereas a visitor from the sun belt has difficulty discerning more than a single variety. This phenomenon is at work as we evaluate problems clinically. All clinicians develop favorite explanations. We become attached to them, sometimes to the extent that they adversely limit our clinical observations. Evidence supporting preconceived ideas may be selectively observed while contradictory findings are ignored. Both forms of distortion often occur outside our awareness. If this tendency is exaggerated, it is not long before we are viewing all cases as variations of "repressed anger" or "primary narcissism" or "neurotransmitter imbalance." Although clinical hypotheses serve a valuable function by allowing us to organize our clinical observations, they also create blind spots (Abercrombie, 1960).

In G.K. Chesterton's story "The Invisible Man," one of the characters, sensing that a murder may be about to happen, sends four men to keep watch over the home of the intended victim (Chesterton, 1972). Despite these precautions, the murderer manages to enter the house unseen and to carry out his homicidal plan. Each of the four observers denies seeing the murderer come and go. At the conclusion of the story, it is made clear that the killer had been "invisible" to these men because he was the *postman*. The story illustrates how the same mind set that helps arrange our experiential world conveniently can also blind us to unanticipated findings.

The clinical settings in which we practice—the type of service provided, the typical clientele, the consensus viewpoint of clinicians who work together—fashion a powerful context capable of distorting clinical observations. This effect was dramatically illustrated in a now famous research study of eight "pseudopatients" admitted to one of twelve different mental treatment facilities (Rosenhan, 1973). The eight individuals who volunteered for the study included a graduate student, a housewife, a painter, three psychologists, a psychiatrist, and a pediatrician, none of whom had had any history of psychiatric problems. Individually, they presented themselves to various treatment facilities with the standard complaint "I have been hearing voices. They go empty, hollow, thud." Real names and occupations were not given; otherwise, the pseudopatients were truthful in reporting their lives. All of them were admitted for treatment, and all but one received a diagnosis of schizophrenia!

The research protocol prohibited these individuals from giving fictitious complaints subsequent to their hospital admission; in fact, they were required to speak of their admitting complaint as though it were a thing of the past. This had little effect on the length of their hospitalizations. They were retained for periods ranging from 7 to 52 days, with an overall average of 19 days. During the course of their various hospitalizations, collectively, they received a total of 2,100 pills, which in most instances they managed to dispose of without detection. Upon discharge all retained the diagnosis of schizophrenic in remission.

The study's most telling finding surfaced during follow-up interviews. Professional staff and patients were questioned about suspicions they might have had concerning the real identities of the pseudopatients. Whereas none of the professionals had any suspicion, several patients had guessed that these were not actual patients. The designer of the study commented: "The hospital itself imposes a special environment in which the meanings of behavior can easily be misunderstood" (Rosenhan, 1973).

Psychological masquerade is no respecter of persons.

In the late 1930s George Gershwin, the great American composer, suffered bouts of fatigue and pounding headaches. His friends found him uncharacteristically moody and overly critical of others. At the time this seemed understandable, given the mounting stress in the composer's frenetic life. After early musical successes, he had made a film in Hollywood, *Shall We Dance*, which had received less than rave reviews. Additionally, Gershwin and his brother, Ira, had agreed to work on a pet project of Samuel Goldwyn's known as the *Goldwyn Follies*, a 3-hour song and dance extravaganza. Gershwin found the project distasteful and did not like having to cater to the whims of its producer.

At about the same time, Gershwin fell in love with a woman considerably younger than himself. He contemplated marriage. It all added up to considerable stress. His friends thought, as he did, that it was just a little too much for him. His headaches and moodiness appeared to be the understandable result.

But the symptoms progressively worsened. Finally, Gershwin admitted himself to the Cedars of Lebanon Hospital in Los Angeles. He was subjected to extensive medical testing by an army of specialists. Despite this exhaustive medical evaluation, he was discharged 26 days later with the notation that the problem was "most likely hysteria."

At home, Gershwin found light painful to his eyes (photophobia). He drew the blinds to keep out sunlight. He became unsteady on his feet. Still, his friends and acquaintances persisted in their belief that it was all in George's mind. On one occasion he fell while walking along a sidewalk. One of the women accompanying him was heard to comment, "Leave him there. All he wants is attention."

His brother persisted in referring to the problem as a "nervous disorder." Gershwin continued to deteriorate, his headaches now unrelenting. He had trouble holding onto things. Finally, he was readmitted to the hospital and within a few days fell into a coma. An x-ray showed a mass compressing the right ventricle of the brain. Initially, at surgery, the mass was thought to be a benign brain cyst, but the elation quickly faded when a highly malignant glioblastoma was found beneath the cyst. It was inoperable. Gershwin died the following day at age 39 (Jablonski, 1987).

Our increasing sophistication about psychosomatic stress reactions ironically sets the stage for overlooking psychological masquerade. The key to avoiding such mistakes lies in the maintenance of a clinical orientation "porous" enough to register unanticipated clues to the existence of organic mental disorders. We must be able to sift through the obvious in order to view the hidden. The challenge is to resist attending only to those observations that confirm our favorite clinical explanations. Given that psychiatric symptoms are often best explained psychologically, we continually run the risk of being lulled into insensitivity regarding organic mental disorders. The objective of this book is to render the reader less susceptible to this oversight.

BRIEF PREVIEW

In the next chapter we consider the design of the nervous system with an emphasis on the structural basis of organic mental disorders.

Chapter 3 presents several clinical misconceptions that create blind spots for the clinician and predispose to failure to recognize psychological masquerade.

Chapters 4 and 5 discuss basic guidelines. Brain syndrome serves as a critical starting point for reviewing the most important clinical clues.

In Chapter 6, a practical method is outlined for efficiently organizing the search for psychological masquerade in the clinical interview.

Four masqueraders are reviewed in Chapter 7. These four medical disorders—brain tumors, epilepsy, endocrine diseases, and AIDS—commonly give rise to organic mental disorders easily misconstrued as psychological reactions.

Chapter 8 considers psychological masquerades induced by drugs (including medications). Chemical substances taken into the body are the number one cause of organic mental disorders.

Somatization is taken up in Chapter 9 as a means of alerting the reader to findings that are *inconsistent* with a psychosomatic explanation of physical symptoms. When applied too loosely, the clinical hypothesis that physical symptoms reflect psychological conflict can produce tragic results.

Chapter 10 focuses on psychological masquerade in children and the elderly.

A brief summary of the major points of this book and a self-test section of fifteen clinical case histories are provided in Chapter 11.

Finally, there is an annotated bibliography containing selected references relevant to the clinical detection of psychological masquerade.

REFERENCES

Abercrombie, J. (1960). *The anatomy of judgment.* New York: Basic Books.

Chesterton, C. K. (1972). The invisible man. In *Selected stories.* London: Kingsley Amis.

Hall, R., Popkin, M., DeVaul, R. A., Faillace, L., & Stickney, S. (1978). Physical illness presenting as psychiatric disease. *Archives of General Psychiatry, 35,* 1315–1320.

Hall, R., Gardner, E., Stickney, S., LeCann, A., & Popkin, M. (1980). Physical illness manifesting as psychiatric disease: II. Analysis of a state hospital inpatient population. *Archives of General Psychiatry, 36,* 414–419.

Hall, R., Beresford, T, Blow, F., & Hall, A. (1990). Differentiating physical from psychiatric disorders. In M. Thase et al. (eds.), *Handbook of Outpatient Treatment of Adults.* New York: Plenum Publishing.

Hofling, C. (1968). *Textbook of Psychiatry for Medical Practice (Second Edition).* Philadelphia: J. B. Lippincott, 292–298.

Jablonski, E. (1987). *Gershwin.* New York: Doubleday.

Koran, L, Sox, H., Marton, K., Moltzen, S., Kraemer, H., Kelsey, T., Levin, L, Imai, K. Rose, T., & Chandra, S. (1989). Medical evaluation of psychiatric patients: 1. Results in a state mental health system. *Archives of General Psychiatry, 46,* 733–740.

Koranyi, E. (1979). Morbidity and rate of undiagnosed physical illnesses in a psychiatric clinic population. *Archives of General Psychiatry, 36,* 414–419.

Rosenhan, D. (1973). On being sane in insane places. *Science, 179,* 250–258.

Rubert, S., & Remington, F. (1962). Why patients with brain tumors come to a psychiatric hospital: A 30-year survey. *American Journal of Psychiatry, 119,* 256–257.

Slater, E. (1965). Diagnosis of "hysteria." *British Medical Journal, 1,* 1395–1399.

Spark R., White, R., & Connolly, R. B. (1980). Impotence is not always psychogenic. *Journal of the American Medical Association, 243,* 750–755.

Tissenbaum, M., Harter, H., & Friedman, A. (1951). Organic neurological syndrome diagnosed as functional disorders. *Journal of the American Medical Association, 147,* 1519–1521.

Chapter 2

Design of the Nervous System

Man seems to be a rickety poor sort of thing. . . . A machine that was as unreliable as he is would have no market. —Mark Twain

The human nervous system is a complex communication network. Messages from the outside world, in the form of light (vision), chemical reactions (taste, smell), and mechanical stimulation (touch, vibration, sound) are received by specialized sensory detectors. They are then transmitted over peripheral channels to a central processing area for analysis and interpretation. Outgoing messages are generated and, in turn, translated into various responses: muscle action, speech, emotional response, glandular activity, contemplation, and many others. Through this arrangement, the nervous system maintains contact with the outside world as well as with the other systems of the human body upon which it is vitally dependent. This communication network allows the nervous system to plan and direct the essential activities of protection, maintenance, growth, and creation.

Skill in clinical assessment is enhanced by an understanding of the design of the nervous system—not so much a detailed understanding of neurophysiology or neuroanatomy as an appreciation of the big picture. This chapter highlights the most likely "break points" in the nervous system—those most at risk of going awry and producing organic mental disorder.

THE BRAIN AND ITS HOUSING

Brain substance is not very durable; in fact, it is only a little firmer than gelatin or tofu. A rigid, bony covering—the skull and spinal vertebrae—and three layers of soft coverings provide an element of protection. In addition the brain and spinal cord are insulated by cerebrospinal fluid contained within the surrounding coverings. The central nervous system is an island surrounded by its own private lake.

This protective arrangement, however, is not invincible. For example, while guarding the brain against external trauma, the rigid stone casing predisposes it to other dangers. If fluid collects within the brain (as sometimes occurs with infection or bleeding) or if there is a growing tumor, the only possible outcome is inward encroachment on brain substance.

Another potential problem relates to the fluid in which the brain is suspended. Cerebrospinal fluid not only surrounds the brain and spinal cord but also flows through the brain by way of a series of small canals known as *ventricles*. These passageways are relatively narrow and can be obstructed by aberrant growth, swelling, or hemorrhage, with an outcome similar to that after the damming of a river. Since it cannot be dissipated outward, pressure gradually builds behind the site of obstruction, compressing the brain substance until dysfunction or even death ensues. In newborn infants—because the skull has not yet ossified into bone—blockage of one of these fluid channels results in outward enlargement of the cartilaginous skull, resulting in the enormous head size seen in hydrocephalus. Eventually, however, the limits of accommodation are reached, and increased intracranial pressure is transmitted inward. Severe mental retardation or other developmental problems are common outcomes.

As for the soft coverings (meninges) of the brain, while they provide a degree of protection, they are also susceptible to infection. Characteristically manifested by stiff neck and headache, meningitis can also cause confusion, bizarre behavior, and even personality changes. The invading infectious agents, particularly viruses, attack the brain and cause encephalitis. The resulting clinical picture ranges from subtle headache and fatigue to gross aberrations in thought, emotion, and behavior. Psychiatric symptoms are sometimes the initial manifestation.

MESSAGE TRANSMISSION

The basic unit of the human nervous system is the neuron. Billions of these microscopic cells are intricately woven together to form an amazing communication network. Each neuron is composed of three elements: a cell body, an axon, and dendrites. Through a chemical language, messages are conveyed from one neuron to another.

The neurons do not make actual physical contact, since they are microscopically separated by spaces known as *synapses.* These "gaps" are the sites where messages are transmitted from one neuron to another in the form of chemicals called *neurotransmitters* (Omenn, 1976). The chemical messengers are released at the end of one neuron and, through chemical diffusion and more active pump-like mechanisms, they reach the adjacent neuron, delivering messages, either positive or negative (excitatory or inhibitory), to *neuroreceptors.* The state of the nervous system is the ongoing summation of these positive and negative messages across billions of neurons. Out of this neurochemical process, human experience emerges.

Hundreds of different chemical messengers convey brain messages. Some are highly concentrated in certain brain sites, while others are more generally distributed throughout the nervous system. A potential problem shared by all neurotransmitters is saturation. Once a neurotransmitter has communicated its message to an adjacent neuron, the chemical messenger must be deactivated in order to prevent clogging of the communicative channel. In other words, the signal previously sent must be erased before a new message can be sent. Communication within the nervous system is dependent on neurotransmitters and their receptors, the chemicals that erase them, and their relative proportions.

What is the clinical significance of this chemical brain language? Neurotransmitters and their erasers are similar in their actions to a variety of drugs. This sets the stage for the striking behavioral changes that drugs are capable of inducing as a result of chemical "jamming." Drugs, including medications, can cause mental disturbances by upsetting the chemical balance essential to normal brain communication. (We will consider this problem at greater length in a chapter on drug-induced mental disorders.)

Neurons are wrapped in supportive sheaths made of myelin. Certain diseases selectively compromise these protective coverings and by doing so cause something akin to electrical "short-circuiting." This is the problem, for example, in *multiple sclerosis*, a disease with considerable masquerading potential. The demyelinization occurs episodically in patches scattered across the nervous system, the exact location determining the nature of the symptoms.

> After 24 hours of nonstop, frenetic activity, a 34-year-old secretary was arrested for stealing a motorbike. The evening before, she had gone to her employer's home, assaulted his son, and made off with his motorcycle. As far as anyone could surmise, there was no precipitating circumstance.

The woman was sent to a hospital, where she was described as speaking in a rapid, rhythmic speech pattern that, at times, deteriorated into clanging word associations. She appeared both grandiose and paranoid, and she was sexually provocative. Although alert and oriented, her concentration was poor, and she had no insight as to how disturbed she was. A neurological examination was normal.

One year earlier, she had experienced sudden blindness in her left eye, along with peculiar sensations in her left leg. The symptoms rapidly disappeared, leaving no residual deficit. Four weeks later, she was hospitalized for a prolonged spending spree. Reportedly, she had been overactive, and talking in rapid-fire fashion. She told her boss he did not know how to do his job, insisting that the firm would be better off if he put her in charge of all investments.

Based on the earlier episode of sudden neurological deficits combined with the results of a lumbar puncture showing lymphocytes (white blood cells) in the cerebrospinal fluid, a diagnosis of multiple sclerosis was made. The patient's "manic attack" was presumed to be a psychiatric expression of her demyelinating disease. She was treated for 10 days with haloperidol and lithium.

After a gradual recovery, she returned to work and did well until her second attack a year later leading to her arrest for stealing the motorbike. (Kwentus, Hart, Calabrese, & HeKnati, 1986)

BRAIN SPECIALIZATION

The brain contains scattered areas of specialization that coordinate various brain functions. When disturbed, they produce rather distinctive neurological symptoms. Other areas involved in interpretation, integration, and introspection, however, can have less obvious symptomatic presentations. Deficits in these associative areas manifest as cognitive, behavioral, or emotional changes rather than paralysis or loss of sensation.

The following brief descriptions are of brain areas that when disordered, are prone to cause psychological masquerade.

Frontal Lobes

The frontal lobes are the most recently evolved part of the human brain. As the name implies, this area is located in the front part of the skull (bilaterally), representing approximately 50% of the brain's total surface area. A large area of the frontal lobes is not involved in motor movement and sensation, thus its characterization as a "silent area." For this reason, it is possible for frontal lobe disease to progress without the appearance of obvious neurological symptoms. The earliest signs may be more subtle changes in mood or personality (Heilman, 1979).

The frontal lobes are essential to abstract thinking. For example, a person with frontal lobe disease might have trouble grasping the commonality shared by a plum, an orange, and an apple. When asked how they are similar, he might ignore the fact that they are all fruits and focus on the more peripheral similarity of rounded shape.

Simple problem solving also is often compromised in frontal lobe disease. The person is confounded by hypothetical questions such as what he should do if he lost his house keys or came across a stamped and addressed letter lying in the street. Similarly, he finds simple math problems impossible to solve.

Impulse control is yet another important frontal lobe activity. It is as though this part of the brain constrained primitive urges, ensuring their translation into more acceptable social expressions. When impulse control is compromised, personal habits deteriorate and inappropriate sexual and aggressive behaviors emerge without regard for social impropriety.

Depending on their precise location, frontal lobe disorders compromise motivation to the point of apathy. The apathetic, unmotivated person withdraws from activities and loses the capacity for pleasure and humor. This can be mistaken for psychological depression. On occasion, frontal lobe dysfunction becomes so severe that the person is immobilized and unable to initiate speech, a condition resembling catatonic schizophrenia. In the opposite direction, frontal lobe dysfunction can cause wild impulsivity, similar to the manic behavior associated with bipolar disorder. The person appears driven and unable to concentrate and relates in a sociopathic manner, without regard for the feelings or welfare of others, even close friends.

Despite the relatively "silent" nature of the frontal lobes, certain changes in motor and sensory function sometimes occur in advanced stages of disease. Because of connections with other parts of the brain, a decrease in the size of the steps the person takes and a deterioration in balance can develop. Bladder dysfunction, starting with a recurrent sense of urgency and progressing to complete loss of control, is also observed. Urinary incontinence must never be ignored in persons with a recent onset of psychiatric symptoms.

Finally, as a result of the anatomical juxtaposition of the optic and olfactory nerves at the underside of the frontal lobes, visual disturbances or a diminished sense of smell can signal frontal disease long before other symptoms appear. In rare instances, tumors arising from neurosensory cells of the olfactory mucosa impinge on the frontal lobes and cause behavioral changes consistent with a "frontal lobe syndrome."

> After several months, the friends and coworkers of a 55-year-old male executive encouraged him to see a psychiatrist because of striking changes in his personality. Previously energetic and full of life, the man seemed to lose interest in everything. Pleasurable aspects of his life were drudgery. He was apathetic to the point of neglecting his own hygiene; his sexual interest disappeared completely. He was often late for work and during the day frequently fell asleep. In his initial interview with a psychiatrist, he downplayed the changes, insisting that his family was overreacting, but he also reported that he had started antidepressant medication 2 weeks earlier.
>
> After a general physical and neurological examination revealed no abnormalities, cranial computed tomography (CT) turned up a large soft tissue mass in the nasal cavities, extending back through the orbital areas and into both frontal lobes of the brain. Treatment involved surgical resection and radiation, followed by chemotherapy. The tumor was officially diagnosed as an esthesioneuroblastoma. (Griffith, & James, 1995)

Temporal Lobes

The way we *perceive* the world is critically shaped by the temporal lobes. One of their main tasks is to integrate the various sensory inputs received by the brain; thus, it is not surprising that temporal lobe disorders often involve strange perceptual distortions (Benson & Geschwind, 1975). Unpleasant smells, weird visual imagery, and even musical sounds are experienced. The distortions sometimes take the form of illusions, as when everything suddenly appears to grow large or shrink or seem far away. New surroundings suddenly seem familiar, or the opposite may occur, as well-known places, without warning, suddenly defy recognition. It is easy to see how such distortions could be mislabeled as "schizophrenic" or "hysterical."

On the dominant side of the brain (the left side for most of us), a language area is located at the margin of the temporal and parietal lobes. Normal functioning of this area is essential for speech. Temporal lobe disorders give rise to bizarre language aberrations that are suggestive of the rambling, incoherent verbal productions seen in psychotic disorders when, in actuality, they are manifestations of a neurological condition known as *aphasia*. (More about this later.)

At their inner margins, the temporal lobes merge into the limbic system, the ancient brain, seat of primitive emotions. This is why temporal lobe disorders sometimes unleash powerful emotions, such as panic.

> After 2 years of "panic attacks," a 69-year-old schoolteacher sought psychiatric treatment. She described episodes of unprovoked anxiety that would suddenly sweep over her. Feeling out of control, she became severely depressed. Antidepressant medication was prescribed (maprotiline, 50 to 75 mg/day); within a few months, the patient's depression was much improved. But the panic attacks persisted, and she began to have other symptoms. For brief moments, she experienced an overwhelming sense of unreality. Eventually, she thought that people's faces changed when she looked at them.
>
> After a few more months, these bizarre visual experiences stopped, but the panic attacks continued, particularly in the afternoons. Finally, one day, in the midst of a conversation with her sister, she became unresponsive, staring at the wall. For 10 minutes, she appeared totally unaware. Afterwards, although she was again able to speak, she was confused and unable to answer simple questions. She could not recall her address or her husband's work telephone number.
>
> After being taken to an emergency room, the patient had a second staring attack, during which she was described as having a terrified look on her face. She was also noted to exhibit strange movements of her lips. A CT scan revealed a right temporal lobe meningioma (confirmed by a carotid angiogram). The tumor was removed surgically, and the patient was started on antiseizure medication along with an antidepressant. After 8 months, she had had no more "spells." (Ghadirian, Gowthier, & Bertrand, 1986)

Somewhat unexpectedly, dysfunction in the temporal-limbic areas often gives rise to hyperspirituality. Some persons with epileptic foci in this part of the brain gradually become obsessed with religious matters and write prodigiously about them. In certain instances the religious preoccupation evolves into frank psychosis.

> A young woman who was an "A" student in college began having mystical experiences. At first they came on like spells. She heard voices and saw visions. There was an overwhelming sense of familiarity. Eventually, she became convinced that she was possessed by the devil. He told her to do terrible things; at times, she heard his loud laughter inside her head.
>
> After the Catholic hierarchy became convinced of the authenticity of the woman's experiences, a priest was authorized to perform a rite of exorcism. She failed to improve. Her condition remained a mystery

until an electroencephalogram (EEG) revealed abnormal brain-wave patterns over both temporal lobes. Her diagnosis was complex partial seizures. (Rhawn, 1996)

Associative Cortical Areas

Located as islands in the brain are areas essential to object recognition and to understanding how to carry out specific movements, like putting on one's clothes. Disruptions in these *associative areas* produce a variety of bewildering symptoms—for example, *agnosia*, the failure to grasp the significance of objects. The person is simply unable to recognize commonplace things that should be familiar. To an outside observer, this bewildering deficit has the appearance of the bizarre if not of psychosis.

In his intriguing book *The Man Who Mistook His Wife for a Hat*, the neurologist/writer Oliver Sacks describes a music instructor who became unable to recognize faces (Sacks, 1998). When students arrived for their lessons, Dr. P. could not recognize any individual until he or she spoke. The voices were familiar, but the faces that went with them were foreign. Even more bewildering, Dr. P. would see faces where there were none. On the street, reminiscent of the famous Mr. Magoo character, he patted the heads of water hydrants and parking meters, mistaking them for the heads of children. Inside his home, things were not much better. On occasion he spoke amiably to the carved knobs on the furniture, only to grow perplexed when they failed to answer.

At first, these odd mistakes were laughed off. The problem, whatever it was, did not detract from Dr. P's dazzling musical ability. He did not feel ill. It was 3 years later, after the onset of diabetes, that Dr. P's strange affliction was finally diagnosed. Knowing that diabetes could affect his eyes, Dr. P. consulted an ophthalmologist. After a careful history and eye examination, he was told there was nothing wrong with his eyes but that the visual part of his brain was not working correctly. Consultation with a neurologist revealed that Dr. P. suffered from degeneration of the visual associative area. He lived several more years and continued teaching music right up to the end.

One rare form of agnosia, known as *anosognosia*, leaves a person strangely unaware of one side of his body.

A young man was admitted to the hospital for medical tests. He felt fine, but at the conclusion of the first day of tests he was tired and fell asleep in his hospital room. Upon awakening with a sense of apprehension, he abruptly flung himself onto the floor, seemingly in a struggle with his own leg. Finally, he agreed to be placed back in bed. As this was done, he was asked where his own left leg was. He blanched pale. "I don't know," he said, "I have no idea."

Later, he told a medical student of this strange experience. He had first found "someone's leg" in his bed; a severed leg, he had thought to himself, put in the bed beside him while he was sleeping. He described being both amazed and disgusted. When he felt the limb, it was cold and "peculiar." Since it was New Year's Eve, he convinced himself that it was all part of a sick joke played by a drunken nurse. Angry but relieved, he hurled the disgusting limb onto the floor. Unfortunately, much to his dismay, it was attached to him! This is how he had come to be lying in the middle of the floor holding onto his own left leg. (Sacks, 1985)

This is a graphic example of the bizarre perceptual distortions that may be caused by dysfunction of the brain's parietal lobe.

Apraxia is the inability—despite normal muscle strength and function—to carry out a desired action. Although fully aware of what he wants to do, the apraxic person cannot translate his intention into the appropriate action. Common tasks, like getting dressed, defy completion despite intense effort. After repeated failure to accomplish routine tasks, the person becomes understandably perplexed and frustrated. Difficulty in copying simple geometric figures signals a different version of apraxia. In attempting to copy triangles, squares, or rectangles, the person produces distorted angles and lines.

Limbic System

From an evolutionary perspective, the limbic system is a much older part of the brain than the cerebral cortex. It is the center of survival activities upon which life depends, at both the individual and species levels. (MacLean, 1964). One researcher summarized these functions as the "four F's of the limbic system": feeding, fighting, fleeing, and the "undertaking of mating activity" (MacLean, 1958). Given its vital role, it is not surprising that the limbic area, in the face of threat, is the initiator of powerful and primitive emotions such as rage and terror. These feelings have been elicited from the limbic brain by electrical brain stimulation, which can also induce dramatic changes in mood, sometimes of psychotic proportion, and primitive sexual urges. Normally, limbic impulses are modulated by higher cortical centers, but their expression goes unchecked in various disease states.

In a famous study of monkeys, the bilateral removal of portions of the limbic brain gave rise to a bizarre constellation of behavioral changes (Kluver & Bucy, 1937). The animals became extremely docile. They no longer experienced fear, as demonstrated when they played casually with snakes that previously had terrified them. In addition, they engaged in indiscriminate sexual behavior and were given to compulsive chewing, licking, and sucking. It is little wonder that limbic dysfunction is frequently mistaken for emotional disorder.

When it invades the nervous system, the herpes simplex virus preferentially attacks the limbic area. The following case shows how easily this condition can be misinterpreted as a psychiatric problem.

Unable to tell a coherent story, a 30-year-old divorced woman was accompanied by her mother to the hospital. "I'm crazy—maybe I have been crazy all my life," she said. She said she had been "living in a dream." For the past several weeks, things had seemed "unreal." The woman's mother described her as having been agitated and despondent. Her daughter's appetite was poor, and she had great difficulty falling asleep. In a 2-week period, she had lost 10 pounds and was becoming increasingly disorganized and confused.

Further history revealed that she had had a serious love affair with her employer, whom she had fully expected to marry after he was free from his wife. Shortly before the onset of her symptoms, the man had taken his wife and family on an expensive vacation to the "island paradise" where the patient had anticipated living with him after they were married. Her mother said, "She acted like her dreams were shattered."

In the hospital, the woman appeared frightened. Most of her responses to questions, particularly those pertaining to where she was and the time of day, were flippant, circumstantial, or inappropriate. At times her speech was incoherent, but there were no obvious hallucinations or delusional thoughts. Her neurological examination was normal, as—with the exception of a slightly raised pulse rate of 104—were her vital signs. All admission laboratory work was normal. The provisional diagnosis was acute schizophreniform episode precipitated by severe personal stress.

Despite tranquilizer medication, the woman's condition worsened. She became mute and suffered obvious neurological deficits, including altered speech and leg paralysis. Finally, when she was found to have a marked elevation in antibodies to the herpes virus, a diagnosis of herpes simplex encephalitis was made.

The patient eventually recovered, at a follow-up visit a year later, however, she continued to have difficulty walking. (Wilson, 1976)

Autonomic Nervous System

Outside our awareness, the autonomic nervous system (ANS)carries out functions essential to body maintenance and response to stress. Arising deep within the brain in the hypothalamus, the ANS divides into two segments—sympathetic and parasympathetic. The parasympathetic division is conservation-oriented, acting in the interest of body maintenance and repair. Under its influence, the heart rate slows and the blood pressure drops. Blood is diverted from the muscles to the gut as a means of promoting the absorption of vital nutrients. The pupils are constricted; the body temperature is slightly lowered. Energy is conserved.

In contrast, the sympathetic division directs the body's emergency response. Heart rate increases and blood pressure rises. Blood is selectively directed to the muscles in preparation for action. The pupils are dilated; body temperature rises with increased sweating. Energy is expended as the body mobilizes.

The two divisions of the ANS depend on different chemical communicators (neurotransmitters), which various drugs can enhance or block. The effects of ANS activity, easily observed by the alert clinician, often provide valuable clues to drug intoxication. For example, widely dilated pupils are caused by stimulants, such as cocaine or "speed." A similar effect occurs when the parasympathetic division has been *suppressed* by an anticholinergic substance, common among prescription and nonprescription medications as well as street drugs.

The ANS controls the body's vital signs (respiration, heart rate, blood pressure, and temperature). Sustained alterations in these measures can be an important tipoff to underlying physical disease.

Basal Ganglia

Located in the midbrain, the basal ganglia are aggregates of neurons crucial to coordinated movement. As with the ANS, the functioning of the basal ganglia depends on a proper neurotransmitter balance. When there is an excess of *acetylcholine,* a pervasive stiffness and rigidity results. This is the basic problem in Parkinson's disease. Huntington's disease illustrates the other side of the coin. A balance between neurotransmitters is essential to normal movement.

This same neurotransmitter balance is also essential to higher brain functioning having to do with rational thought and emotional expression. Treatment of psychosis with traditional neuroleptic medications improves a disturbed ratio of brain neurotransmitters at higher cortical levels, but, simultaneously, causes an imbalance within the basal ganglia with resulting parkinsonian symptoms. Several "movement disorders" characteristically involve mental and emotional changes. Huntington's disease is a degenerative neurological disease affecting the basal ganglia and the cerebral cortex and is characterized by explosive, involuntary writhing, with muscle jerks and twitches and declining mental ability. Antisocial behavior, poor impulse control, hypersexuality, and frank psychosis are often part of the clinical picture. These psychological changes sometimes overshadow the abnormal movements.

> After a period of adolescent delinquency involving theft, drunkenness, and assault, a young man, aged 22, experienced the onset of unexplained physical awkwardness. In a short while he was also exhibiting strange facial grimaces that gave him a menacing appearance.
>
> At age 24 he married. Later, his wife related how extremely demanding he was, particularly sexually, insisting on frequent intercourse at inconvenient times and in inappropriate situations. If denied, he became vindictive and sometimes violent.
>
> Three years after the marriage, the man was committed to a criminal asylum after a vicious attack on his wife. By this time there was also an extensive history of brutality toward his children. He was diagnosed as having a psychopathic personality.
>
> Further investigation, however, revealed that the patient's mother had died at age 42 of Huntington's chorea. A neurological evaluation confirmed that the patient had the same disease. He showed severe unsteadiness in walking, and his arms and legs flung wildly about. His speech was slurred, and he had a serious memory problem.
>
> His condition progressed relentlessly until he died at the age of 32 of bronchopneumonia. (Dewhurst, 1970)

For reasons not completely understood, the integrity of the basal ganglia and psychological well-being are linked. All mental health professionals should be sensitized to the association of organic mental disorders and abnormalities of movement.

THE SUPPORTING CAST

Unlike simple life forms that carry out all life activities within a single cell, the human animal is highly specialized, requiring the integration of many different organ systems to conduct the day-to-day business of living. As highly evolved organisms far from their ancient beginnings, humans are confronted with the complex task of maintaining a stable internal environment reminiscent of the primordial sea (Simeons, 1960). Slight variations in body temperature, oxygen saturation, or electrolyte concentrations become life-threatening. Levels of various chemicals in the body must remain within a narrow range lest vital processes begin to fail, and waste products of life-sustaining energy consumption must be eliminated regularly if death due to "internal pollution" is to be avoided.

Although the brain directs this complicated array of life-support processes, it is, like most bosses, dependent on the work of its subordinates. When the supporting cast fails, problems in brain functioning are not far behind. The emergence of psychiatric symptoms in a person with known medical disease should always alert the clinician to the possibility of brain disturbance *secondary to a failing support system*. This is why individuals with chronic diseases are particularly susceptible to psychological masquerade. Secondary support problems are often more subtle in presentation than are primary diseases of the nervous system. *Secondary brain failure* is an important concept to keep in mind.

Heart, Lungs, and Blood

The brain is vitally dependent on an uninterrupted supply of oxygen. Sudden loss of oxygen produces coma in less than 60 seconds and death within a matter of minutes. For oxygen to reach the brain, the lungs must remove it from the air and transfer it to the blood. In turn, the heart must maintain a continuous flow of oxygen-laden blood by uninterrupted pumping. Alterations in the rhythm of the heart compromise its pumping effectiveness and rapidly lead to brain dysfunction, loss of consciousness, and death unless the problem is immediately corrected. Certain arrhythmias, while not life-threatening, can cause behavioral changes. Consider the following case:

> A widowed woman, age 54, became guilt-ridden and anxious. At times her heart beat rapidly, and she felt fearful and tense. Her children (adult) attributed these changes to her having "taken up" with her dead husband's former associate. Although she resisted this interpretation, she reluctantly agreed to see a psychiatrist.
>
> When the woman entered the psychiatrist's office, he noticed that she was unsteady on her feet and that her ankles were swollen. These observations, along with the patient's story of heart palpitations, led to a diagnosis of paroxysmal atrial tachycardia, a heart condition characterized by sudden, explosive episodes of rapid heart action.

Further investigation confirmed the diagnosis and established the precise cause: a defective heart valve (mitral stenosis). After corrective surgery, the woman had no further attacks of anxiety or guilt despite the continuation of her new relationship. (Shulman, 1977)

In addition to adequate heart pumping, the transporting of nutrient-rich blood to the brain requires that the "pipelines" be open. These arterial vessels running from the heart to the nervous system can become obstructed by clot formation, bleeding, or tumor. The resulting blockage produces what is commonly known as a "stroke." The specific disability depends on the precise location of the obstruction. If, for example, the blockage occurs in an artery supplying the motor cortex on the left side of the brain, the person will likely experience a weakness or complete paralysis of his right arm, leg, or both. But not all strokes have such obvious physical consequences.

Without any explanation, a 61-year-old banker failed to go to work one morning. Despite his wife's questioning, he gave no reason. He never again returned to work or even so much as mentioned the bank where he had been employed for years.

Several physicians examined the man but could find "nothing wrong." His wife, however, continued to be troubled by the changes she had observed. Much of her husband's charm and wit had disappeared. Seemingly overnight, this once capable and dynamic man had been transformed into an apathetic, dull, and sexless person. He no longer assumed responsibilities, made decisions, or did any reading. He also exhibited peculiar behaviors. On one occasion his wife watched him walk into a wall, as though he did not see it. Another time he suddenly fell to the floor and lost consciousness. Although he recovered quickly, he was, for a moment, unable to speak clearly. Eventually, he became confused and began to have difficulty shaving and dressing himself.

Several years later, another medical evaluation led to the diagnosis of stroke. It was thought that the man had suffered a series of small strokes, accounting for the striking changes in his personality and the decline in his overall competence. (Alvarez, 1966)

Many strokes are catastrophic events, easily recognized as medical emergencies, but the clinician is sometimes faced with more subtle presentations. When the brain's oxygen supply is slowly compromised, a diversity of "psychiatric" symptoms may result, alone or in various combinations, including irritability, confusion, apathy, depression, suspiciousness, and bizarre behavior.

Because of changes at the interface between the lungs and capillaries, chronic lung disease reduces the amount of oxygen diffusing into the bloodstream. Likewise, widespread tuberculosis or cancer of the lung can produce the same effect. Cancer of the lung is the most common cancer in American men; its incidence among women is rapidly rising. Before lung cancer is medically detectable, mental symptoms may appear. In some cases this reflects the early spread of the disease to the brain; in others, the mental manifestations stem from a compromise in lung function itself due to the invading tumor cells. The lungs become unable to "breathe" properly, creating a relative deprivation of oxygen. The clinical result may be quite unlike that anticipated for lung disease.

> The patient in this case, a man strong of body and mind, was a bricklayer, 53 years of age. Although rarely given to drink, he was a heavy smoker, consuming 40 cigarettes a day. He was described by friends as full of nervous energy, restless, often worried, sometimes depressed, but never bad-tempered.
>
> Over a 6-month period, he changed. His appetite failed and he slept poorly. He appeared vacant, gradually becoming less outgoing. He was frequently and irrationally quarrelsome.
>
> During a holiday, he suddenly became excited, burst out of his house, and ran across the field in the early morning hours, shouting that he had to go to work. He calmed down after being reassured by his family. For several months, there were no further manifestations until he began to make demands on his wife to meet him in strange places. When she arrived, he would not be there; if he did appear, he might then wander off without explanation.
>
> He became religiously preoccupied and eventually violent. On one occasion he locked himself in a room with his wife and one of his children and read to them loudly from the Bible. He called out to "Lord Jesus" and scribbled strange sayings on the walls. When the police arrived, he threw the Bible on the fire and, in front of the officers, grabbed a handful of hot coals from the fireplace and rubbed them across his face, sustaining burns on his forehead.
>
> The man was taken to the local hospital and admitted to the psychiatric ward, where he was diagnosed as suffering from paranoid schizophrenia. After improving enough to be discharged, he returned to work. Shortly afterwards, he suffered a severe vacant attack and was readmitted to the hospital, irrational, pacing, and talking nonsense.
>
> His condition deteriorated rapidly and he died 12 days later. At autopsy the cause of his "paranoid schizophrenia" was found—cancer of the lung. (Charaton & Brierly, 1956)

Heavy smokers are at risk for emphysema and chronic bronchitis as well as lung cancer. Unexplained "psychological symptoms" in this high-risk population necessitate a thorough assessment of pulmonary function (as well as close scrutiny of the medications these patients take, which are often numerous).

Gastrointestinal Tract

The brain and gastrointestinal tract are derived from common embryological material. Perhaps this accounts for the close association between psychological stress and gastrointestinal dysfunction, such as irritable bowel syndrome (spastic colon), ulcerative colitis, and ulcers of the stomach and duodenum. The stomach, intestines, pancreas, liver, and gallbladder are essential to proper digestion and absorption of food. When they become dysfunctional, psychological symptoms are often part of the clinical picture. For example, in certain cases (ulcer, inflammation, drug effects), the stomach and intestines become sources of occult (hidden) blood loss. As this slow hemorrhaging occurs, the person may experience fatigue secondary to anemia. When he or she complains of having no energy, the clinician may conclude depression.

The liver is the site of hundreds of enzymatic reactions. It plays an important role in maintaining proper blood sugar levels and is responsible for detoxifying the waste products of normal metabolism. When the liver fails, the brain is quick to suffer, as in severe cases of acute viral hepatitis or in hepatic failure associated with alcoholic cirrhosis. Lethargy and difficulty concentrating may progress to full-blown brain delirium and psychosis.

Unlike other parts of the body, the brain has but one source of energy: glucose. Its continuous availability is essential to normal brain functioning. The brain is completely dependent on other organ systems to secure this vital source of energy. Because the ingestion of glucose is episodic, a storage reservoir is necessary to guarantee the presence of glucose at all times. The liver serves as the warehouse where glucose is stored as glycogen for future use. When blood glucose drops, glycogen is broken down and diffuses into the blood to become available to the rest of the body and, most importantly, to the brain, which takes a disproportionate share. Conditions that impair liver function make a person more vulnerable to hypoglycemia with its dramatic cognitive and behavioral changes.

> Against her will, a 69-year-old black woman was brought by the police to a psychiatric emergency service. Agitated and inattentive, she was unable to give a coherent story. Her speech was rambling and loose. She was disoriented in time and space, insisting that she was in jail.

Physical examination showed an enlarged liver. Blood for a serum glucose level was drawn, and the patient was found to be profoundly hypoglycemic. Within seconds of receiving 50 mL of 50% glucose intravenously, the patient became coherent and attentive. She gave a history of 40 years of alcohol abuse, cirrhosis of the liver, pancreatitis (eventually necessitating a 95% pancreatectomy) and adult-onset diabetes requiring the regular use of insulin. On the morning of her hospitalization, she had accidentally taken too much insulin, which had resulted in the dramatic, mind-altering drop in her blood sugar. (Fishbain & Rotundo, 1988)

Endocrine System

Endocrine glands manufacture hormones that act as powerful chemical stimulants. They are crucial to growth, metabolism, sexual reproduction, and emergency responses. Endocrine disorders frequently cause major mental and emotional changes. Fortunately, most of these conditions are rare. Not so, however, with thyroid disorders. They occur commonly and are prominent on listings of the causes of psychological masquerade.

The thyroid controls the body's rate of metabolism. Excess thyroid hormone produces irritability and anxiety. In some cases, mania and paranoid psychosis may occur. In contrast, too little thyroid hormone causes lethargy and depression and, in severe cases, dementia.

As we saw in the previous case, insulin plays an essential role in glucose metabolism. It is manufactured in the pancreas, a small endocrine gland attached to the duodenum (small intestine). Destructive processes such as inflammation, tumors, and trauma impair the ability of the pancreas to produce and secrete insulin; consequently, blood sugar levels become erratic, being too low at some times and too high at others.

Diabetes mellitus results from failure of the pancreas to produce adequate amounts of insulin. In its most severe form (type I), diabetes develops early in life, necessitating daily, life-saving injections of insulin. Some individuals with type I diabetes have serious difficulty achieving stable blood sugar levels; consequently, despite insulin injections, they may experience wide swings in blood sugar with concomitant psychological changes. If the clinician has no knowledge of an existing diabetic condition, these manifestations are easily misconstrued.

Significant mental and emotional changes also occur in the less severe form of diabetes, type II. On the basis of an extensive investigation, one researcher identified a high incidence of diabetic problems among psychiatric patients (Koranyi, 1979). A clinical account described a couple seemingly on the verge of divorce. They quarreled regularly at nighttime. Marital therapy was tried, but without any improvement in what was a rapidly deteriorating relationship. Eventually, a 5-hour glucose tolerance test was given. It showed that approximately 3 hours after a meal both the husband and wife had significant declines in blood sugar, presumably due to an excessive ("rebound") release of insulin. This "after dinner" hypoglycemia was giving rise to the irritable, anxious, subjective feelings experienced by the quarreling couple. (In Chapter 7, we explore the gamut of psychiatric symptoms associated with endocrine disorders.)

Liver and Kidneys

As the human body consumes energy, it generates waste products that require elimination. Under normal circumstances, this task is ably handled by special pollution-control systems within the body, of which the liver and kidneys are key elements. Both of these organs have tremendous reserve potential; when diseased, however, their limits can be exceeded, leading to the toxic accumulation of waste products. In a polluted environment, the brain fails. If the pollution is slow in developing, the symptoms may be subtle at first, with the person becoming inattentive, apathetic, or withdrawn. As the condition progresses, more serious alterations are likely: loss of the correct sense of time and place, failing memory, and the inability to solve simple problems. If the pollution goes unchecked, the person may experience delusions and hallucinations that are easily mistaken for functional psychosis.

The kidneys can be compromised by infection. They are also susceptible to damage from certain medications and toxic products, such as heavy metals and industrial chemicals. They can also be injured as the target organ of autoimmune reactions, where the body's own immune cells attack by mistake. Regardless of the cause, when the kidneys are severely damaged, serious mental and emotional changes are likely. Persons with end-stage kidney disease are forced to go on renal dialysis. This opens up another avenue for the development of organic mental symptoms due to the metabolic imbalances that can result from maintenance dialysis.

In this chapter we have reviewed aspects of the nervous system that predispose it to the development of organic mental disorders.

Now we are ready to consider the most common clinical traps that lead to errors in distinguishing psychological from organic disorders.

REFERENCES

Alvarez, W. (1966). *Little strokes.* Philadelphia: J. B. Lippincott, 84–85.

Benson, D. F., & Geschwind, N. (1975). Psychiatric conditions associated with focal lesions of the central nervous system. In S. Arieti (Ed.), *American Handbook of Psychiatry;* Vol.4, (2nd ed.; pp. 201–243). New York: Basic Books.

Charaton, F. B., & Brierley, J. B. (1956). Mental disorder associated with primary lung carcinoma. *British Medical Journal, 2,* 765–768.

Dewhurst, K. (1970). Personality disorder in Huntington's disease. *Psychiatrica Clinica, 3,* 221–229.

Fishbain, D., & Rotundo, D. (1988). Frequency of hypoglycemic delirium in a psychiatric emergency service. *Psychosomatics, 29,* 346–348.

Ghadirian, A., Gowthier, S., & Bertrand, S. (1986). Anxiety attacks in a patient with a right temporal lobe meningioma. *Journal of Clinical Psychiatry, 47,* 270–271.

Griffith, J. (1995). Esthesioneuroblastoma: An unusual cause of frontal lobe dysfunction. *West Virginia Medical Journal, 91,* 142–143.

Heilman, K. (1976). Exploring the enigmas of frontal lobe dysfunction. *Geriatrics, 31,* 81–87.

Kluver, H., & Bucy, P. C. (1937). Psychic blindness and other symptoms following bilateral temporal lobectomy in rhesus monkeys. *American Journal of Physiology, 119,* 353–363.

Koranyi, E. (1979). Morbidity and rate of undiagnosed physical illnesses in a psychiatric clinic population. *Archives of General Psychiatry, 36,* 414–419.

Kwentus, J., Hart, R., Calabrese, V., & HeKnati, A. (1986). Mania as a symptom of multiple sclerosis. *Psychosomatics, 27,* 729–731.

MacLean, P. (1958). Contrasting functions of limbic and neocortical systems of the brain and their relevance to psychophysiological aspects of medicine. *American Journal of Medicine, 25,* 611–626.

MacLean, P. (1964). Man and his animal brains. *Modem Medicine, 3,* 95–106.

Omenn, G. (1976). Neurochemistry and behavior in man. *Western Journal of Medicine, 125,* 434–451.

Rhawn, J. (1996). *Neuropsychiatry, neuropsychology, and clinical neuroscience* (2nd ed.). Baltimore: Williams & Wilkins, 300.

Sacks, O. (1998). *The man who mistook his wife for a hat and other clinical tales.* New York: Touchstone, 8–22.

Shulman, R. (1977). Psychogenic illness with physical manifestations and the other side of the coin. *Lancet, 1,* 524–526.

Simeons, A. (1960). *Man's presumptuous brain.* London: Longmans.

Wilson, L. (1976). Viral encephalopathy mimicking functional psychosis. *American Journal of Psychiatry, 133,* 165–170.

Chapter 3

Clinical Traps

Even brute beasts and wandering birds do not fall into the same traps or nets twice. —St. Jerome

Clinicians who consistently avoid a few basic errors greatly improve their chances of correctly identifying psychological masquerade. This chapter covers the four most important clinical traps:

- Mistaking symptoms for their cause
- Getting seduced by the story
- Equating psychosis with schizophrenia (or functional psychosis)
- Relying (unnecessarily) on limited information

MISTAKING SYMPTOMS FOR THEIR CAUSE

Labeling has a magical quality. As clinicians, we sometimes lull ourselves into a false sense of certainty by applying a clinical label, as though by naming the problem, we understood it. One author has termed this proclivity the *Rumpelstiltskin complex*, after the wonderful fairy tale about a lady who, in order to save herself from an evil, ugly little man, had to correctly guess his name—Rumpelstiltskin (Torrey, 1972). At one level, this fairy tale describes the magical power attributed to the act of naming. Name it, understand it, control it!

But labeling a problem prematurely sometimes leads clinicians astray. This is particularly true in the use of certain labels that have come to imply psychological etiology: *anxious, depressed, paranoid, obsessive-compulsive, catatonic*, and *manic*. In actuality, these clinical descriptors signify *nothing* about causation. The symptoms, by themselves, cannot be trusted to differentiate organic from psychological disorders. In short, descriptive labeling is not the same as causative understanding.

Paranoia

Normal psychosocial development requires the reasonable resolution of a series of fundamental life crises. The degree of one's success in resolving one crisis powerfully influences the handling of subsequent crises. According to this perspective, the first major developmental crisis concerns trust versus mistrust (Erikson, 1963). Although this initial crisis will be resolved more favorably by some than by others, it remains somewhat an open question for all of us. Therefore it is not surprising to find moments of irrational suspiciousness experienced by a majority of people. Given half a chance, paranoia emerges, particularly under conditions of increased stress or incomplete information or in the throes of drug intoxication or withdrawal.

The paranoid person ignores contradictory evidence. "Facts"—even the most insignificant and irrelevant—are selectively identified so as to buttress irrational suspicions. Predictably, the person fears what might happen and becomes obsessed with the objects of his or her suspicion. As paranoia intensifies vague suspicions often crystallize into the distinct belief that there is a harmful plot afoot. Sometimes this parallels a growing conviction in the person's own supernatural powers or cosmic importance. At this stage, paranoia is totally absorbing and capable of distorting all contradictory evidence as well as fashioning supporting "evidence" out of irrelevant observations. When the condition reaches psychotic intensity, the person grows extremely cautious. He or she is reluctant to give any information, often speaking, if at all, in a whisper so as not to be overheard. Despite such precautions, the feeling of being in danger persists. This sense of panic sometimes leads to preemptive acts of violence out of the perceived need for self-defense.

Severe paranoia is often equated with schizophrenia. This is a risky assumption.

> A young soldier, 26 years of age, abruptly became apprehensive and suspicious, obsessed with the idea that "the Nationals" were trying to kill him. He exhibited a rapidly fluctuating paranoia. At its height, his suspiciousness was clearly delusional. His thinking was disjointed, and he was disoriented. His body coordination was impaired, and his eyes were reddened.
>
> Over a few hours, the soldier's condition improved. He related that prior to the onset of this frightening, paranoid experience, he had smoked marijuana.

> Two days later, he returned to duty. During a follow-up evaluation, he reported no further episodes of paranoia. (Talbott & Teague, 1969)

The most critical information as to the true nature of this soldier's toxic state was not his paranoid behavior but rather its sudden onset, along with the other symptoms of incoordination, disorientation, and reddening of the eyes. Nothing about the paranoia *per se* was diagnostic of an organic condition.

Consider a second case.

> Officials at a local airport anxiously requested the assistance of the state police when a married schoolteacher in his late forties became combative, screaming about "death by dehydration" and "doctors trying to kill him" with poison pills. The man insisted that he had to make contact with the CIA and the Food and Drug Administration to prevent this crime against himself.
>
> Following his admission to the psychiatric service of a general hospital, he appeared confused and continued to express persecutory delusions. He was unable to name the correct month. Routine laboratory tests showed a severe water and chemical imbalance known as water intoxication. With fluid restriction, his confusion cleared. Although his paranoid delusions persisted for a brief time, they resolved after treatment with antipsychotic medication. (Rosenbaum, Tothman, & Murray, 1979)

Numerous cases of water intoxication associated with dramatic behavioral changes have been reported. In some instances, this strange condition has been traced to the inappropriate production of antidiuretic hormone (ADH), which prevents the proper excretion of water and leads to a "flooding" of the body. But other cases simply result from excessive water drinking. Certain chronic psychiatric patients, particularly those with long-standing schizophrenia, are prone to develop this problem (Illowsky & Kirch, 1988). One review of schizophrenic patients under the age of 53 found water intoxication accounting for 18.5% of hospital deaths (Vieweg et al., 1985).

Clinical recognition of water intoxication depends on being alert to a history of excessive water consumption, unexplained weight gain, and decreased urinary output. When neurological manifestations are present (such as headaches, blurred vision, seizures, or decreasing consciousness), the organic nature of water intoxication should be obvious. As with the man in the airport, however, "psychological" symptoms tend to be misleading.

Paranoid reactions are frequently encountered by the clinician. Despite their "psychological" feel, the causative basis is often biological.

Depression

Depression ranges from "the blues" to suicidal and psychotic melancholia; it has multiple causes. Despite the entrenched clinical notion that depression results from failure to express anger or resentment over personal losses, this is only one of many possible explanations. A variety of organic disorders are heralded by depression prior to the emergence of physical symptoms. Also, medications are a frequent cause of depression as a side effect.

Clinicians should be careful not to overreach for personal loss as an explanation for depression. Few of us go for extended periods without setbacks—financial, social, occupational, romantic, or symbolic. Such losses are not invariably the cause of depression. Individuals who become depressed due to organic illness may also have a notable personal loss that is of no etiological consequence. Personal loss can be a misleading clue in cases of organic conditions presenting as depression.

Regardless of its cause, the defining characteristics of depression are sadness, diminished self-worth, restricted initiative, and reduced capacity for pleasure. Changes in appetite and sleeping habits may occur. For some, food no longer seems desirable and weight loss ensues; for others, depression leads to voracious eating and weight gain. Persons who are depressed may have trouble falling asleep; even when sleep finally comes, it may not last long. Atypically, the opposite problem may appear where excessive sleep seems to provide temporary respite from the unremitting psychic pain of depression.

Usually, depression is accompanied by decreased activity. The person cannot seem to get going; a sense of tiredness pervades his or her life. In its extreme form, psychomotor retardation immobilizes the person, leading to poor self-care. In other cases, however, agitation is prominent. The individual appears anxious and irritable and is easily provoked. Even in agitated depression, however, the more characteristic expressions of depression are never far from the surface. Severe depression is a frequent precursor of suicidal thoughts. As depression deepens, the person may experience mood-consistent delusions such as thoughts of rotting away inside, possession by the devil, or responsibility for all the world's wrongs. But the clinical recognition of depression does not resolve the question of its etiology.

A 29-year-old woman, a college graduate, was seen at a psychiatric clinic for what she described as depression. For several months she had felt "down" to the extent of considering her life an unnecessary burden. She awakened early in the morning, unable to fall back to sleep, and felt lethargic during the day. Even more disturbing, she felt a growing sense of alienation from her children and husband.

Depression ran in the woman's family. Her father had committed suicide, and her mother had been diagnosed with involutional depressive psychosis. The woman herself had been severely depressed on two previous occasions, once shortly after starting on birth control pills and again immediately following the birth of her second child.

With this history of hormone-related depression, her doctor advised her to stop taking the "pill." Over the next several weeks, her depression lifted and her relationship with her family improved.

Six months later the woman discussed contraception with a psychiatrist. He encouraged her to return to her gynecologist for an alternative birth control method. Instead, as a means of economizing, she resumed taking the old birth control pills she had at home. Within a week, severely agitated and depressed, she was admitted to a state mental hospital, where she was diagnosed as having a schizoaffective reaction.

After her release, the woman suffered yet another episode of severe depression, complicated by hallucinations and strong impulses to kill her children. This occurred after she had started taking yet another birth control pill. When she stopped, her symptoms promptly disappeared.

At this point, somewhat belatedly, she was thoroughly instructed about the relationship between her depressive episodes and the taking of oral contraceptives. (Daley, Kane, & Ewing, 1967)

Hormone-related depression is not rare, particularly in women with a family history of mood disturbances (manic or depressive). As in the preceding case, depression can be precipitated by birth control pills or by pregnancy or its termination. In some instances, depression occurs monthly with a woman's menstrual period. Presumably, this premenstrual pattern is related to hormonal changes.

As the next case illustrates, although people with psychological depression sometimes exaggerate minor somatic aches and pains, *persistent* physical complaints should never be assumed to be "psychological" without appropriate medical evaluation.

A 60-year-old lawyer became severely depressed. His initiative declined. After falling asleep at night, he soon awakened. There was an extensive history of depressive episodes; some had been severe enough to require electroconvulsive therapy. With the advent of his current depression, he suffered unexplained persistent diarrhea. It was this troublesome physical symptom that brought him to a physician who, upon reviewing the case, concluded that the diarrhea was a manifestation of his depression.

He was referred to a consulting psychiatrist, who, upon further review, decided to order additional studies. The results confirmed that the patient had ulcerative colitis. He responded favorably to steroid medications and his depression disappeared. (Shulman, 1977)

In certain predisposed persons, mood disturbances, particularly depression, are tied to the seasons. Seasonal affective disorder (SAD) is characterized by winter depression, with increased sleepiness, fatigue, weight gain, and carbohydrate craving. During the spring and summer, there is a reversal of symptoms, which, on occasion, may progress to a manic state (Rosenthal et al., 1984). Exposure to light seems to play a key role in this seasonal mood swing. When *phototherapy* with full-spectrum lighting is administered daily, the symptoms disappear.

Mania

Mania is the polar opposite of depression. It is characterized by inappropriate euphoria with a falsely inflated self-image and a tendency to be flighty, overactive, and unrealistic. The person in its grip is obsessed with his or her own importance and tends to pursue fun and pleasure at any cost. Psychotic thought comes typically in the form of delusional beliefs of omnipotence and omniscience. (Manic-like behavior in the absence of psychotic thought is technically referred to as *hypomania*. The dividing line is often quite vague.) Characteristically, the manic person rarely sleeps and has a diminished appetite. If the episode continues for long, weight loss can result.

The heightened energy level associated with mania does not lead to improved performance. Work usually deteriorates; family relationships are strained. An encounter with a person experiencing full-blown mania is a memorable but sometimes trying experience. It is difficult to get a word into the conversation. It is next to impossible to keep up with the one-sided flow of wild thoughts as the person flits from one topic to another. In modest doses, manic persons can be quite entertaining. Their humor is often infectious, and those in their company may find themselves laughing despite efforts to the contrary. In contrast, at the slightest hint of being ignored or resisted, the manic's nonstop joking can sometimes morph abruptly into belligerence.

Although manic episodes are associated with bipolar disorder (a cyclical mood disorder that runs in families), this is not their only cause. The clinical literature contains many examples of mania arising from medical disorders, including influenza, brain tumors, complex partial seizures, metabolic imbalances, and strokes. It is also triggered by various drugs, such as cocaine, caffeine, antidepressant medications, and steroids.

A 69-year-old retired drawbridge operator without previous psychiatric history abruptly became euphoric. Within 5 weeks, the euphoria evolved into flagrant mania. With his supportive family now exhausted, the man was admitted to a hospital. When interviewed, he belligerently accused the examining physician of plotting against him. He demanded to call his lawyer so that he might bring a suit against the hospital.

The patient's family provided a full description of his inflated self-confidence, hyperactive behavior, and diminished inhibitions. For 8 years, he had suffered from Parkinson's disease. Recently, he had been treated with the medication L-dopa. When the dosage reached 3 grams a day, his parkinsonian tremor and rigidity disappeared. Simultaneously, however, he became increasingly euphoric.

The patient's condition was diagnosed as a drug-induced psychosis caused by L-dopa. With an adjustment in dosage, the symptoms subsided. (Ryback & Schwab, 1971)

An unusually high incidence of mania has been reported in women with endometriosis. Women with this condition have excessive pain during menstruation. Depression—not mania—would be expected, but in a study of 16 consecutive cases of endometriosis, 10 women (62%) met the clinical criteria for bipolar disorder (Lewis et al., 1987).

We tend to associate "strokes" with weakness, slurred speech, and paralysis or difficulty walking, but this can be a misleading stereotype; not all strokes cause such obvious neurological deficits. Strokes, in fact, have presented as manic behavior.

As he was being admitted to a hospital, the patient shouted continuously, proclaiming himself to be both Christ and Krishna. Interspersed in his endless verbal barrage were invitations to the staff to kiss his feet.

This man was 61 years old. Before his admission to the hospital, he had, over the course of a few days, undergone a marked change, becoming wildly euphoric and tirelessly active. He stopped sleeping altogether and he was preoccupied by religious thoughts. He proselytized on the streets, trying to convert others to his new-found belief. At times he was irritable and aggressive toward his aged mother. These changes were completely out of character for him.

In the hospital, he was fully oriented. Testing of language, calculation, and abstraction was normal, but he did have difficulty recalling three objects after 3 minutes. In a drawing he made, he failed to complete the left side. This led to a neurological examination, which established a left visual field deficit. He also had diminished sensory responses to pain, temperature, and vibration.

On the basis of these findings, the man was thought to have suffered a right thalamic stroke, too small to be seen on computed tomography (CT). The manic symptoms responded well to short-term lithium treatment, and although his neurological problems improved, the man was left with residual deficits. (Cummings & Mendez, 1984)

Anxiety

Anxiety is the disturbing sense of being in jeopardy or out of control. It may erupt episodically in the form of attacks or be sustained over long periods of time. Unlike fear, anxiety has no clearly identifiable referent. The anxious person becomes preoccupied with her anxiety, which only serves to aggravate the problem. As dysphoric emotional experiences, anxiety and depression often become fused and may be difficult to distinguish clinically. Physical signs of anxiety include tremulousness, a worried expression, excessive perspiration, and muscle tension, particularly in the muscles of the face, neck, jaw, and paraspinal muscles. Not surprisingly, anxiety is often associated with increased body aches and pains, particularly headache and back discomfort.

Anxiety can manifest behaviorally as restlessness. The person fidgets or paces. Tension-binding habits—such as smoking, drinking, and other drug use—tend to increase. Sexual acting out may provide temporary comfort. Organic conditions that stimulate the sympathetic nervous system are easily mistaken for anxiety disorder. Long before they are diagnosed, certain life-threatening physical diseases manifest as an anxious sense of impending doom.

An unmarried piano teacher, 39 years of age, was nervous much of the time. Fifteen years earlier, he had been accused by one of his pupils of making sexual advances, which led to a court case. Although the teacher was eventually acquitted, the experience represented a severe emotional trauma that left him chronically anxious.

Ten years after the court case, the patient became noticeably more anxious and began to have daily bouts of diarrhea. He was evaluated by two physicians, both of whom concluded he was experiencing aftershocks from his traumatic courtroom experience. During one examination, his blood pressure was elevated.

When the symptoms persisted, the man quite reluctantly agreed to his family's suggestion that he see a third physician. By this time, he had lost 25 pounds and had become virtually homebound. He was tremulously apprehensive and thin, with clammy palms. As part of a full-scale medical workup for persistent diarrhea, radiographic studies of the abdomen and kidneys revealed an abnormal mass over the right kidney. At surgery a pheochromocytoma was removed.

Ten months later, the man had regained his normal weight. He had become outgoing again and his general well-being was vastly improved. (Doust, 1958)

Pheochromocytoma is a rare tumor of the part of the adrenal gland that secretes the body's natural stimulants. The tumor manufactures excessive amounts of catecholamines, the release of which can cause either episodic or continuous feelings of anxiety. The anxiousness is often accompanied by an elevated pulse rate, hypertension, excessive perspiration, severe headache, and diarrhea. Because this tumor is not usually malignant, surgical removal is generally curative.

Coffee, cola, and tea are heavily consumed. These popular drinks contain the stimulant caffeine. Individual sensitivity to caffeine is highly variable, but when a person exceeds his or her threshold, nervousness, irritability, agitation, tremulousness, headaches, palpitations, and sleeplessness are apt to result.

Caffeine is not restricted to popular drinks. It is also an ingredient in chocolate and numerous over-the-counter preparations. Unknowingly, people may become hooked on caffeine. When consumption is stopped or reduced (as may happen on weekends for many persons who consume excessive coffee during the work week), apathy and depression develop (often with headache), only to be relieved when the person consumes caffeine again. This cycle often goes undiagnosed.

> An ambitious, hard-driving lieutenant colonel in the army, 37 years of age, was referred from a military medical clinic to a psychiatric service for his chronic anxiety. As a daily occurrence for almost 2 years, the man had complained of dizziness, tremulousness, anxiety, and difficulty falling asleep. Repeated scores on the Hamilton Anxiety Scale were significantly elevated. Complete medical evaluations had been reported as normal on three occasions.
>
> Treatment with Librium (chlordiazepoxide) for 10 months followed by a 4-month trial of Valium (diazepam) proved ineffective. The man disliked these medications because, he said, they "impair my occupational precision."
>
> Further questioning revealed that the patient was regularly consuming 8 to 14 cups of coffee per day! "My coffee pot is a permanent fixture on my desk," he commented. In addition, prior to going to bed, he habitually drank hot cocoa as a way of relaxing. His soft drink preference was cola, of which he drank three to four bottles a day. His total daily caffeine intake was estimated to be about 1200 mg.

When confronted with his caffeine toxicity (caffeinism), the man at first, exhibited total denial, stating that he was unwilling to alter his caffeine intake even on a trial basis. Shortly afterwards, he reluctantly reconsidered. Within 4 weeks of starting on a caffeine-restricted diet, he was dramatically improved. To prove the causal relationship, his doctor had him resume taking caffeine, whereupon his symptoms promptly returned.

Several months later—back on a caffeine-restricted diet—the man scored much lower on the Hamilton Anxiety Scale, and his improvement came without any decline in his job performance. (Greden, 1974)

People who regularly consume the daily equivalent of 800 mg of caffeine are at risk of developing caffeinism. Table 3.1 lists the caffeine content of some common substances.

Obsession and Compulsion

Being thoughtful and careful, when taken to the extreme, becomes problematic. No doubt vigilance has evolutionary value, but when it crosses the line, the result is psychological and behavioral rigidity. When thoughts become repetitive to the extent that they interfere with a person's life rather than facilitating it, they are said to be obsessive. Compulsions involve actual behavior. When a certain act is performed over and over again without any apparent need, the behavior is said to be compulsive. But obsessive and compulsive patterns have a way of blending together. What the two have in common is a certain non-productive rigidity that, in the extreme, immobilizes a person because it eliminates competitive thoughts and actions. The normal checking to make certain the door has been locked or the coffee maker turned off is not what we are talking about here. *Obsession*

TABLE 3.1 Caffeine Chart

Substance	Caffeine content in milligrams
Coffee	
Brewed	100–150/cup
Instant	85–100/cup
Tea	60–75/cup
Cola	40–60/cup
OTC Drugs	Variable, but often 100 mg/tab

and *compulsion* are terms reserved for extremes: checking the oven 50 times or washing one's hands for hours until they bleed. Normal concerns become elaborated into extensive rituals, mental and physical, that take on lives of their own, gradually eliminating competing interests.

Long thought to arise from unresolved conflicts, obsessive thinking and compulsive behavior, like other "psychological" symptoms, also can have specific organic causes.

> After 2 weeks of obsessing about being infected with AIDS, a 10-year-old boy was taken to a child psychiatric clinic. His obsession was accompanied by the compulsive need to clean his room and wash his hands repetitively. He was given to frequent spitting and evidenced bizarre, twisting movements of his extremities. These symptoms had materialized virtually "overnight." They progressed rapidly, so that after a couple of days the boy was unable to attend school or participate in his usual after-school activities. Eventually, this episode resolved on its own, only to return with the same abruptness 8 months later and again several times over the next 2 years. The symptoms resolved on each occasion. (Swedo et al., 1998)

This boy's condition was determined to be an "autoimmune" disease, secondary to streptococcal infection—most likely an earlier bout of pharyngitis. For unknown reasons, the boy's antibodies to the streptococcal bacteria attacked the basal ganglia of his brain. During each of his obsessive-compulsive episodes, his antibody titers were greatly elevated. As they declined, his symptoms resolved. Interestingly, the boy's mother, a medical technician, reported that her son's brother suffered from a tic disorder that always became worse a few days after a bout of sore throat.

This is not an isolated case. Children with histories of streptococcal infections, compared to those without, are far more likely to exhibit obsessive-compulsive symptoms as well as a variety of movement-related disorders such as tics (Rapoport & Fiske, 1998). In light of these discoveries, the combination of bizarre movements and obsessive-compulsive symptoms seen in conditions such as Tourette's disorder is open to new interpretation.

The equating of "psychological" symptoms with psychological causation is a mistake. Paranoia, depression, mania, anxiety, obsessive-compulsive behavior, and a host of other mental and emotional manifestations can reflect *either* psychological problems or medical disorders. As symptoms, they are indistinguishable regardless of their etiology. It is the overall context in which they appear—clinical history, related symptoms, other risk factors—that raises the red flag for possible organic mental disorder.

BEING SEDUCED BY THE STORY

Various versions of this clinical trap relate to the same basic mistake: accepting the "obvious" clinical explanation without considering all the available facts.

Previously established diagnoses sometimes set the stage for this clinical mistake. A person presents with symptoms similar to those he or she has experienced in the past; therefore, the person must be having the same problem. Open and shut case! Right? Wrong! The clinician should never forget that people frequently have more than one problem at a time. As clinicians we look for a single, all-encompassing explanation, but this is not always available, since psychological and organic problems can exist side by side. There is nothing to prevent a person with a problem in living from being physically ill at the same time. Failure to entertain this possibility is the source of serious clinical mistakes. Recall that in a previously cited study of psychiatric outpatients, researchers discovered that 46% suffered from previously undiagnosed medical illnesses (Hall, Popkin, Devaul, Faillace, & Stickney, 1978).

> A 38-year-old woman with a well-documented history of bipolar disorder complained of fatigue, weight gain, and sensitivity to cold weather. Additionally, she reported that after washing her hair in the mornings, she would find her drain clogged with large amounts of hair.
>
> The woman had been maintained on lithium carbonate for 3 years, with splendid results in controlling her mood swings. It was her psychiatrist's impression that she was showing early breakthrough signs of a depressive episode. (Jefferson, 1979)

This turned out to be an erroneous assumption. Fatigue, weight gain, sensitivity to cold, and hair loss can accompany depression, but they are also expressions of a deficient thyroid gland (hypothyroidism). In this case, hypothyroidism was a side effect of prolonged lithium treatment. Once started on replacement thyroid hormone, the patient' became asymptomatic despite continuing on lithium.

Sometimes we become so taken with "the story" that we fail to register critical observations of a person's physical appearance. Such observations may provide important clues to an unexpected organic disease. When psychological symptoms are found in combination with unexplained physical symptoms, the patient should always be assessed for possible organic disease. Sometimes the physical findings will have no connection, but this cannot be assumed. The clinician's best defense against neglecting physical findings is to develop a systematic approach to looking for them.

Table 3.2 lists some of the more readily observable physical findings that, although not invariably associated with organic disease, should be considered strongly indicative. The listing is not comprehensive, but it does provide a practical starting point.

Reading through the list, you may be slightly overwhelmed by the number of possible observations. Once a routine is established, these observations and others can be quickly and unobtrusively made. Listening carefully to what a patient says is not incompatible with observing how he or she looks. Failure to detect organic mental disorders frequently stems from overlooking the obvious.

A special instance of being seduced by the story occurs with respect to "medical clearance." The clinician should never ignore findings suggestive of an organic problem simply because the person has been examined previously by a physician and "medically cleared." When a person is evaluated, the examination reveals only what is detectable at that particular time. There are periods in the course of physical diseases during which their clinical detection is virtually impossible. Even highly sensitive laboratory tests fail to detect the disease at an early stage. After a person has been medically examined and referred for therapy, enough time may have elapsed for the problem to become manifest. Trust your observational skills. If signs of physical disease are present, do not let a previous medical clearance prevent you from calling for a reevaluation.

Medical clearance should always be viewed as *tentative*, subject to new evidence. Unfortunately, medical evaluations are sometimes performed by incompetent physicians. The medical profession is not unlike other professions with respect to ability. There are competent and incompetent practitioners, and on the surface it may be difficult to distinguish between them. Failure to diagnose a physical disease is not always a function of the invisibility of the disease; it can result from an inadequate examination. Additionally, even the most capable of physicians have bad days. The signs of organic disease may simply be missed, an honest error, which, nevertheless, can be tragic if it is neglected because "the doctor said there was nothing wrong."

The shifting presentation of certain organic diseases—especially organic brain syndromes—creates the distinct possibility of symptoms being absent at the time of an examination. Later, perhaps only

TABLE 3.2 Outward Manifestations of Physical Disease

Symptoms	Disease or condition
Overall appearance	
Dishevelment, gross errors in clothes selection	Various causes of brain syndrome
Movement	
Tremors, jerkiness, twitching, flinging motions, rigidity	Parkinson's disease, Huntington's chorea, tardive dyskinesia, Tourette's syndrome
Disturbances in gait	Intoxications, cerebellar disease, normal-pressure hydrocephalus
Head	
Cuts, abrasions, lumps, dried blood about the ear	Head trauma
Face	
Asymmetries in movement	Stroke
Eyes	
Bulging	Hyperthyroidism; tumors of the orbit behind the ear
Drooping eyelids	Myasthenia gravis (made famous by Aristotle Onassis); selective nerve dysfunction
Difference in pupil size	Brain masses (i.e., brain tumor, hematoma, abcess)
Widely dilated	Numerous drugs, particularly hallucinogens, stimulants, and anticholinergics
Markedly constricted	Opiate drugs (heroin, morphine)
Nonalignment of eyes (not parallel)	Dysfunction in cranial nerves innervating the eye muscles
Neck	
Protruding lumps	Thyroid enlargement, aneurysm of major arteries of the neck, cancerous growths

TABLE 3.2 *(continued)*

Symptoms	Disease or condition
Skin	
Color changes, pallor "yellowing" (jaundice)	Anemia, shock diseases of the liver and gallbladder, cancer of the pancreas, acute anemia
Blue lips	Inadequate oxygenation as seen in certain heart and lung diseases
"Butterfly" rash (nose and face area)	Autoimmune diseases
Black-and-blue marks	Trauma, blood clotting deficiencies
Lines of discoloration	Needle tracks from drug mainlining
Thickening	Hypothyroidism
Excessive perspiration	Certain drugs, hypoglycemia, and hypermetabolic conditions such as hyperthyroidism
Hair	
Extremely coarse and dry	Hypothyroidism
Extremely fine and silky	Hyperthyroidism

after a very brief period, the symptoms may return and be readily observable.

A 26-year-old teacher complained of spells during which she became confused and anxious. At her initial medical evaluation, it was discovered that the woman was in the middle of a divorce and had been disowned by her family for living with a man they felt was "beneath" her. She was referred for supportive therapy.

After her condition failed to show any improvement, a more thorough medical evaluation demonstrated that she was having difficulty doing simple calculations. She also had trouble expressing herself, and her vision was impaired. Further studies led to a diagnosis of stroke, from which the woman fully recovered. (Weissberg, 1979)

What appeared to be a reaction to a stressful life was in fact an organic disorder stemming from circulatory blockage to the brain. The correct diagnosis was made after the woman had been "medically cleared." The moral is this: Look—and trust what you see. Even if the client has been cleared medically but you see or hear something suspicious, a repeat evaluation is indicated.

EQUATING PSYCHOSIS WITH SCHIZOPHRENIA OR AFFECTIVE PSYCHOSIS

Equating psychotic behavior with schizophrenia is an all too common clinical error. Although schizophrenia is perhaps the best known of psychotic disorders, it is by no means the only one. Even when you consider bipolar disorder in combination with schizophrenia, most psychoses arise from other causes. In fact, any case of psychotic behavior should be considered organic until proven otherwise.

If any of the core manifestations of *brain syndrome* (discussed in Chapter 4) are present, the diagnosis of schizophrenia, at least initially, must be questioned. This is not to say that such symptoms are never part of the clinical picture of schizophrenia. Sometimes confusion, disorientation, and recent memory deficits occur; but if this is the case, it is usually temporary, more a reflection of the patient's chaotic inattentiveness and distractibility. If symptoms of brain syndrome persist, further consideration of an underlying medical disorder is warranted.

There is another point to keep in mind. Although brain syndrome is frequently encountered in cases of organic psychosis, exceptions are common. Absence of these symptoms should not be construed as unquestionable proof of schizophrenia or bipolar disorder.

A 31-year-old fifth-year medical student claimed he could read other people's minds and could hear his own thoughts spoken aloud. He believed he was the son of a professor of psychiatry who he thought to be disguised as the Duke of Gloucester. When in public, the patient experienced the embarrassing compulsion to look at men "below the waist." This was of great concern to him for he feared that people thought he was homosexual. The young man's symptoms appeared over a 4-month period and then intensified shortly after his wife gave birth to a second child.

During a mental status examination, the patient saw the face of a dead relative smiling at him, and he expressed the fear that he was being hypnotized against his will. He was, however, fully oriented and capable of coherent problem solving. There was no previous history of mental disorder. (Bell, 1965)

This patient could easily have been misdiagnosed as schizophrenic, but further investigation documented an extensive use of amphetamines. His diagnosis was organic psychosis caused by chronic stimulant abuse.

In summary, psychosis with brain syndrome should be considered organic until disproved. Psychosis without brain syndrome may also be organic and should not be labeled schizophrenia without a complete evaluation. Although none are 100% reliable, there are several other points of differentiation between psychotic conditions arising out of medical illnesses and drug intoxications and those associated with schizophrenia and bipolar disorder.

Persons experiencing schizophrenic symptoms for the first time, are characteristically in their late teens or early twenties. An initial psychotic episode in a person over the age of thirty is most likely not schizophrenia. Serious mistakes in clinical assessment arise out of failure to consider this basic guideline.

Hallucinations are a hallmark of psychosis. These distorted sensory experiences can involve any of the primary senses: sight, sound, touch, smell, or taste. Visual hallucinations are particularly characteristic of organic psychoses and less so of schizophrenia and bipolar disorder. All forms of hallucination are seen in organic mental disorders. In fact, contrary to popular belief, hallucinations—other than the hearing of voices—are more indicative of organic psychoses than of schizophrenia.

Another differentiating feature is *adaptive style* (Golden et al., 1967). In schizophrenic psychosis, things that are familiar to most of us are perceived as unfamiliar. For example, the person might misidentify an old and trusted friend as a spy or an agent of the FBI. In contrast, organic psychosis is more likely to manifest the opposite tendency: mistaking the unfamiliar for the familiar. This might lead to mistaking a total stranger for a friend or relative. It is as though a sense of control is maintained in functional psychosis by attributing special—even bizarre—meaning to common things, whereas in organic psychosis control is retained by translating (erroneously) the unknown or unrecognized into the known or familiar. Illusions—distorted perceptions—represent special instances of making the unfamiliar familiar. They are common in organic psychosis and rare in schizophrenia.

Characteristically, the ability to get outside of oneself and to view one's experience objectively is disrupted in functional psychoses, but the waxing and waning of consciousness seen in organic psychosis produces moments of self-awareness (Taylor, Maurer, & Tinklinberg, 1970). As a sudden and often fleeting insight, the person may express great concern over his mental condition: "Something terrible is wrong with me. This is not like me." Rarely will this happen in schizophrenic or bipolar psychosis.

Certain behaviors erroneously have become equated with schizophrenia. Take catatonia, for example. Muscle rigidity with bizarre posturing, negativism, and mutism is associated with numerous medical conditions.(Galenberg, 1976). A partial listing of organic problems causing catatonia includes:

Viral encephalitis (limbic system)
Brain tumors (frontal lobe and third ventricle)
Petit mal epilepsy
Head injuries
Wernicke's encephalopathy
Syphilitic brain disease
Narcolepsy
Diabetic ketoacidosis
Hypercalcemia
Pellagra
Acute intermittent porphyria
Drug intoxications
Paraneoplastic encephalopathy

Catatonia can even be caused by certain psychiatric medications, particularly the higher-potency neuroleptic drugs such as haloperidol. This is not surprising. For years, catatonic-like rigidity in laboratory animals was one of the important screening criteria used by pharmaceutical manufacturers to identify substances with neuroleptic potential.

Catatonia presents a dramatic clinical picture. The person appears frozen in space, reminiscent of the ray-gun effect portrayed in old science fiction movies. Such fixed posture may be maintained for hours. Characteristically, the person is mute. There is extreme muscle tension, particularly about the face and in the arms and legs. Heart rate and blood pressure are elevated and these may be excessive perspiration and fever. During periods when the person is not frozen in a rigid posture, his or her walking may be stiff or labored. If the person speaks at all, his or her words may be sluggish and barely audible. Peculiar grimacing occurs intermittently. Despite the withdrawn appearance of catatonia, an underlying sense of hostility and obstinacy ("negativism") is often present and may break through in a violent outburst, followed by a resumption of rigid posture.

The presence of catatonic behavior signals a serious disruption, but it says nothing *per se* about its cause. It does not automatically imply schizophrenia.

> A graduate chemistry student awoke with ringing in his ears. Within 30 minutes, after an episode of nausea and vomiting, he became confused. His wife alarmed, rushed him to a hospital emergency room. By the time he was examined, he was belligerent, uncooperative, and violent at times. Gradually, the clinical picture changed to one of incoherence and fearfulness. Upon admission, the patient was described as mute and drowsy.
>
> Over the next few hours, the patient was observed by three different staff psychiatrists. Each of them described a fluctuating clinical picture, cycling approximately every 20 minutes, from extreme, agitated excitement to stuporous catatonia with mutism. They all agreed on a provisional diagnosis of schizophrenic reaction, catatonic type.
>
> The patient received a modest dose of a neuroleptic drug and promptly fell asleep. Twelve hours later he awoke fully coherent, cooperative, and speaking normally.
>
> He reported being in excellent health until 3 days prior to admission, when he began working with a chemical—difluoronitroacetyl fluoride—in a poorly ventilated chemistry laboratory. After first experiencing numbness in his fingers, he awoke on the day of admission with the symptoms that led to his hospitalization.
>
> The patient was discharged with a revised diagnosis of acute organic brain syndrome secondary to organic fluoride poisoning. At a follow-up visit a year later, no residual symptoms or further episodes of catatonic behavior were reported. (Schwab & Barrow, 1964)

With respect to delusional thinking, the clinician should not assume that organic delusions are devoid of specific, "dynamic" content. Organic delusions can be highly specific (Cummings, 1988; Ramachandran & Blakeslee, 1998). Specific delusional themes that may be found in organic psychoses include the following:

- A loved one has been replaced by a clone-like imposter (Capgras' syndrome)
- Unseen and unwelcome guests are living in the person's house (phantom boarder syndrome)
- The person is episodically transformed into a wolf (lycanthropy or werewolfism)

- A lover is unfaithful (Othello syndrome)
- The person is infested with bugs (parasitosis)
- A mysterious persecutor constantly changes forms (Fregoli syndrome)
- The person is secretly loved by a celebrity (De Clerambault syndrome or erotomania)

A final point relates to so-called *Schneiderian first-rank symptoms.* Although these are often discussed as specific to schizophrenia, this is not the case. Hearing one's thoughts broadcast aloud, feeling that thoughts are being inserted involuntarily into one's mind, or sensing one's feelings or actions emanating from an outside force—such delusions also occur in psychotic states associated with medical disorders. With respect to etiology, they have little differentiating value.

RELYING (UNNECESSARILY) ON LIMITED INFORMATION

The task of evaluating psychiatric symptoms often depends on one source: the person coming for help. In such cases clinicians must proceed as best they can. But any experienced clinician will tell you that the absence of secondary information is often the reason for erroneous diagnoses. Supplemental information can be invaluable, especially in cases where the presenting patient is intoxicated, confused, incoherent, or comatose. Failure to utilize secondary sources when they are available is a serious clinical error. The true nature of a puzzling case may become readily apparent when supplementary information is obtained from other persons or clinical records. Such information often clarifies aspects of the case unknown to the patient or beyond recall due to his or her condition. It also protects the clinician against the patient's own blind spots. A person who does not want to face his or her problem may suppress the facts or minimize the symptoms. Getting another perspective from someone who knows the person often makes obvious what was missed during an interview.

Nowhere is this principle more applicable than in the evaluation of a patient in the throes of a brain syndrome. The changing clinical picture that goes with this condition confuses the best of clinicians. It is quite possible for a disturbed patient to hold it together for the duration of a brief interview. Input from a relative or friend describing multiple episodes over the preceding month during which the patient got lost, will go a long way toward preventing an erroneous and embarrassing clinical conclusion.

Secondary information (often in the form of a previous clinical or hospital record) is especially critical in cases of alcohol and drug abuse. Substance abusers are notorious for minimizing their problems. Their families may be falling apart, their jobs slipping away, and their physical health failing; but they will still deny any problems with drinking or drugging. Because substance abusers are at high risk for a variety of serious medical conditions, secondary information can be lifesaving.

> A 23-year-old man with a history of severe alcoholism was seen in an emergency room for "drunkenness." He was groggy and his speech was slurred. Intermittently, he nodded off to sleep. He was accompanied by his wife, who had assumed he was probably drinking again. On closer questioning, however, she concluded that her husband's alcohol consumption over the past 24 hours had actually been quite small. She also related how on the preceding day her husband, while intoxicated, had fallen down the stairs at home and lay unconscious for several minutes.
>
> This additional history from the wife prompted further neurological testing, which pointed to a subdural hematoma. After the clot on this man's brain was evacuated by surgery, he recovered fully. (Cadoret & King, 1974)

This chapter has dealt with four clinical traps—mistaking symptoms for their causes, being seduced by the story, equating psychosis with schizophrenia, and relying (unnecessarily) on limited information. Avoidance of these faulty clinical assumptions is essential to the clinical recognition of psychological masquerade.

REFERENCES

Bell, D. S. (1965). Comparison of amphetamine psychosis and schizophrenia. *British Journal of Psychiatry, 3*, 701–707.

Cadoret, R., & King, L. (1974). *Psychiatry and primary care*. St. Louis: C. V. Mosby, 201.

Cummings, J. L. (1988). Organic psychosis. *Psychosomatics, 29*, 16–26.

Cummings, J., & Mendez, M. (1984). Secondary mania with focal cerebrovascular lesions. *American Journal of Psychiatry, 141*, 1084–1087.

Daley, R., Kane, F., & Ewing, J. (1967). Psychosis associated with the use of sequential oral contraceptive. *Lancet, 2*, 444–445.

Doust, B. (1958). Anxiety as a manifestation of pheochromocytoma. *Archives of Internal Medicine, 102*, 811–815.

Erikson, E. (1963). *Childhood and society.* New York: Norton.

Galenberg, A. J. (1976). The catatonic syndrome. *Lancet, 1,* 1339–1341.

Golden, J., Liston, E., Rimer, D., Rose, A., Sogher, D., & Solomon, D. (1967). Toxic and functional psychoses. *Annals of Internal Medicine, 66,* 989–1007.

Greden, J. (1974). Anxiety or caffeinism: a diagnostic dilemma. *American Journal of Psychiatry, 131,* 1089–1092.

Hall, R., Popkin, M., Devaul, R., Faillace, L, & Stickney, S. (1978). Physical illness presenting as psychiatric disease. *Archives of General Psychiatry, 35,* 1315–1320.

Illowsky, B., & Kirch, D. (1988). Polydipsia and hyponatremia in psychiatric patients. *American Journal of Psychiatry, 145,* 675–683.

Jefferson, J. (1979). Lithium carbonate-induced hypothyroidism, its many faces. *Journal of the American Medical Association, 242,* 271–272.

Lewis, D., Comite, F., Mallouh, C., Zadunaisky, L., Hutchinson-Williams, K., Cherksey, B., & Yeager, C. (1987) Bipolar mood disorder and endometriosis: preliminary findings. *American Journal of Psychiatry, 144,* 1588–1591.

Ramachandran, V. S., & Blakeslee, S. (1998). *Phantoms in the brain.* New York: William Morrow, 158–173.

Rapoport, J., & Fiske, A. (1998). The new biology of obsessive-compulsive disorder: implications for evolutionary psychology. *Perspectives in Biology and Medicine, 41,* 159–175.

Rosenbaum, J., Tothman, J., & Murray, C. (1979). Psychosis and water intoxication. *Journal of Clinical Psychiatry, 40,* 287–291.

Rosenthal, N. E., Sack, D. A., Gillin J. C., Lewy, A., Goodwin, F., Davenport, Y., Mueller, P., Newsome, D., & Wehr, T. (1984). Seasonal affective disorder: a description of the syndrome and preliminary findings with light therapy. *Archives of General Psychiatry, 41,* 72–80.

Ryback, R., & Schwab, R. (1971). Manic response to levodopa therapy, report of a case. *New England Journal of Medicine, 285,* 788–789.

Schwab, J., & Barrow, M. (1964). A reaction to organic fluorides simulating classical catatonia. *American Journal of Psychiatry, 120,* 1196–1197.

Shulman, R. (1977). Psychogenic illness with physical manifestations and the other side of the coin. *Lancet, 1,* 524–526.

Swedo, S., Leonard, H., & Garvey, M. (1998) Pediatric autoimmune neuropsychiatric disorders associated with streptococcal infections: clinical description of the first 50 cases. *American Journal of Psychiatry, 155,* 264–271.

Talbott, J., & Teague, J. (1969). Marijuana psychosis. *Journal of the American Medical Association, 210*, 299–302.

Taylor, R., Maurer, J., & Tinklinberg, J. (1970). Management of "bad trips" in an evolving drug scene. *Journal of the American Medical Association, 213*, 422–425.

Torrey, E. F. (1972). *The mind game: witchdoctors and psychiatrists.* New York: Emerson.

Vieweg, W., David, J., Rowe, W., Wampler, G., Burns, W., & Spradlin, W. (1985). Death from self-induced water intoxication among patients with schizophrenic disorders. *Journal of Nervous and Mental Disease, 173*, 161–165.

Weissberg, M. (1979). Emergency room medical clearance: an educational problem. *American Journal of Psychiatry, 136*, 787–790.

Chapter 4

A First Step: Recognition of Brain Syndrome

The harbingers are come. See, see their mark. —George Herbert

From the outset, this point needs emphasis: brain syndrome is *not* a specific medical disease. It is a constellation of symptoms indicative of global brain dysfunction. Among the various causes are drug toxicity, tumors, infections, degenerative brain diseases, hypertension, endocrine disorders, and nutritional deficiencies.

The detection of brain syndrome is a key element in the search for psychological masquerade. Once such a syndrome is identified, a medical evaluation is indicated to determine the precise cause. It is the underlying disorder that must be treated, not the symptomatic manifestations of brain syndrome. Although certain psychological reactions (particularly depression in the elderly) can resemble brain syndrome, this is relatively rare. In fact, brain syndrome is so closely associated with brain failure that when it is observed as a part of a psychiatric presentation, organicity must be presumed.

Brain syndrome is a surprisingly common condition. One of every five patients admitted to a mental hospital exhibits these symptoms, and the prevalence increases with age. Among elderly persons living in the community, 10 to 20% suffer from brain syndrome; in mental hospital settings, the rate rises to 50% (Seizer & Sherwin, 1978).

Certain causes of brain syndrome are fully reversible, making its recognition essential. In one study, family physicians failed to recognize brain syndrome in more than 80% of moderate to severe cases (Williamson et al., 1964). It is a mistake to look for brain syndrome only among the elderly. The rise of drug and alcohol use among the young, along with the emergence of AIDS dementia, has created a substantial reservoir of potential brain syndrome cases.

Unfortunately for the clinician, the term *brain syndrome* is part of a confusing terminology. *Dementia, delirium, acute* and *chronic organic brain syndrome, toxic psychosis, senility, presenility*—all these terms, while incorporating aspects of brain syndrome, threaten to obscure its clinical utility in semantic chaos. If you look in the *Diagnostic and Statistical Manual of Mental Disorders* of the American Psychiatric Association, fourth edition (DSM-IV), you will not find *brain syndrome* listed. The editors have chosen, instead, the terms *delirium* and *dementia. Brain syndrome*, as used in this book, captures elements of both delirium and dementia. DSM-IV not withstanding, brain syndrome remains a viable clinical concept.

DSM-IV goes one step further by eliminating *organic mental disorders.* The stated rationale is to avoid the implication that certain mental disorders are organic while others are not (Spitzer, 1992). In this book, I hold to the long-standing tradition of differentiating psychological reactions to various problems in living from organic mental disorders caused by specific brain-body breakdowns. They are not the same, and they require entirely different treatment approaches. It is essential that they be clinically differentiated. The main purpose of this book is to outline a clinical approach to making this important distinction.

As for brain syndrome, we will use the following definition: *brain syndrome is a clinical presentation commonly associated with generalized brain failure (resulting from a variety of medical disorders) and characterized by core cognitive deficits.* The material that follows will clarify the details. This characterization of brain syndrome encompasses much of what is covered in DSM-IV as "Delirium, Dementia, and Amnestic and Other Cognitive Disorders," providing—one hopes—a more "user friendly" scheme for organizing clinical observations. While appealing conceptually, DSM-IV presents an artificial set of diagnostic boxes that in the real world of clinical assessment blur together.

The symptoms of brain syndrome are greatly influenced by *rate of onset.* If the compromise in brain functioning happens rapidly, the clinical manifestations are dramatic, global, and severely disruptive. On the other hand, if the underlying problem develops slowly, a much more subtle clinical picture emerges, one that may not be recognized for some time. But regardless of onset, all variations of brain syndrome involve the same basic set of cognitive deficits occurring in various combinations: disorientation, recent memory impairment, diminished reasoning, and sensory indiscrimination.

Scattered throughout this chapter, the reader will find selections from a moving account of a 49-year-old academic researcher who suffered brain syndrome secondary to Parkinson's disease. This was before there was any effective treatment. The selections are taken from an article written by the man's daughter entitled, "Death of a Mind: A Study in Disintegration" (Anonymous, 1950).

> I first remember my father as a well-built, active man with a wide range of interests. His work required both intellectual and practical ability, and those who could judge his achievement spoke highly of it. I was more impressed at the time by the happy enthusiasm with which he would turn from weightier matters to entertain his small daughter. . . . Over the period that we worked together, sometime in the early 1930s, I became gradually aware that the fine edge of his intellect was becoming dulled. He was less clear in discussion and less quick to make a jump from a new piece of evidence to its possible significance. . . . He tended also to become portentous and solemn about his subject, as though one small corner of knowledge nearly filled his world, and the wider horizons were narrowing in. (Anonymous, 1950)

COGNITIVE DEFICITS

In this book, I exclude schizophrenia and bipolar disorder from organic mental disorders. This is done despite the accumulation of considerable evidence pointing to a biogenetic basis for these conditions. But there is a good reason for doing this with respect to the search for psychological masquerade. These "functional" psychoses, whatever their etiology turns out to be, typically, differ in their presentations from organic psychoses arising from specific medical disorders. Many of the observational clues indicative of organicity—as in brain syndrome—are often absent. It is crucial that organic mental disorders not be mistakenly labeled schizophrenia or bipolar disorder, as this will impede the search for the causative medical disorder. The detection of many psychological masquerades depends on the clinical ability to distinguish between these two kinds of psychoses.

Before considering brain syndrome in detail, it is important to take up the subject of *inattention*. The ability to concentrate on the subject at hand is a prerequisite for normal cognitive functioning. Many medical conditions *and* psychological reactions severely compromise this ability, making it impossible for the person to maintain his or her attention for any sustained period. The result is a rapidly shifting of focus from one thing to another. Nothing seems to hold the person's interest for long. Thinking, listening, observing—none of these can be done very effectively in the absence of the ability to attend. Being easily distracted makes concentration impossible. Clinically, the inattentive person's face expresses his or her difficulty in focusing. His or her eyes may make sudden shifts. Restlessness is often extreme. The ability to stay on subject is lost.

A simple test known as *digit-span retention* can be utilized to quantify inattention. The person is asked to listen to a five-digit number and then to repeat it immediately. Five random digits, such as 9-4-1-6-3, are presented, allowing approximately 1 second between each number. Most adults perform this test without a mistake; if not, the test should be repeated, using a different set of digits. Failure on two attempts is strongly suggestive of clinically significant inattention.

Clinical assessment for brain syndrome becomes problematic in the inattentive person. This is because attending is an essential requisite for orientation, recent memory, basic reasoning, and sensory discrimination. The presence of severe inattention makes impossible the accurate appraisal of the cognitive deficits of brain syndrome. False positives are the rule. This is why, if possible, reevaluation at another time when the person is more attentive is indicated.

Disorientation

Orientation is the positioning of oneself with respect to time, space, and person. A disruption in orientation is often an early sign of brain syndrome. Most people have no trouble identifying the correct month and year, and whether it is days or nights. The inability to do so is evidence of disorientation.

Disorientation to place is not knowing where you are: home, workplace, hospital, clinic, or jail. It can be assessed by simply questioning a person about where they are, but the most reliable approach takes into account the person's actions. Does he or she have a history of wandering away from home and being unable to find the way back? Or, if the person is being observed as a patient, does he or she become lost on the way on the ward or go into the wrong room to sleep?

It has been said that, unlike disorientation to time and place, disorientation to person is rarely encountered in brain syndrome. But it depends on the meaning. If disorientation to person implies failure to recognize oneself, then it is rare in brain syndrome. But if it is defined as the failure to recognize people who should be familiar—relatives, friends, family physician, long-term therapist—it is a common manifestation, although not as commonplace as disorientation to time and place.

Orientation is a critical anchor for human experience. When a person becomes truly disoriented, brain disturbance is the most likely explanation.

Recent Memory Impairment

Memory works in three phases, starting with registering (attending) an experience, then recording it (recent memory), and finally, storing the information permanently for future retrieval (remote or long-term memory). Recent memory is operative in the recall of an experience 5 to 10 minutes after it has occurred. As previously discussed, if a person is sufficiently inattentive, there is no possibility of recent memory formation. But even when recent memory fails, old memories are still accessible because they were laid down earlier. Recent memory deficit is a hallmark of brain syndrome, whereas remote memory may or may not be compromised.

The easiest way to test for recent memory is to list three unrelated items (key, stone, book) and to tell the person that you will ask him or her to repeat them in a few minutes. Five minutes later the person should be able to recall all three items (not necessarily in the order presented). (The examiner should avoid using associated words, such as *horse* and *carriage*, since it is easier to recall associated items.)

Failure to recall three items after five minutes on two separate occasions suggests a recent memory deficit. In addition to testing, the clinician should be alert to a history of forgetfulness: missed appointments, repetition of stories or questions, leaving the stove on repeatedly, or other recurring oversights. This kind of "absent-mindedness" often reflects a problem with recent memory.

> In 1935, after a period of absence, I looked forward with special pleasure to my homecoming, but when we met I knew with immediate certainty that I had lost the companion of my earlier years. . . . To me it was as though a light had gone out, but no one else seemed to notice anything amiss. . . . We paused to consider a problem which had thwarted us, and I hit on a solution and outlined the idea. My father could not grasp the principle of it until I gave a demonstration. . . . I was profoundly shocked. . . . His ability was still well within normal limits; but I knew what it had been, and the difference was startling. . . . He tried to carry on with his work, but he did not make any headway and became more and more depressed about it. His character remained essentially the same except that he could no longer endure unorthodox

views . . . if he chanced to overhear one of the eager iconoclastic arguments of youth, he became disturbed and petulant and it seemed as though his mental organization had become less secure even at its deeper levels. (Anonymous, 1950)

Diminished Reasoning

A person's capacity for solving even simple problems is compromised in brain syndrome. Friends, fellow workers, and relatives may point out ridiculous mistakes that are completely out of character. Making the correct change, keeping a golf score, or filling the gas tank may become mystifying. Common sense becomes impaired. When asked what to do if accidentally locked out of the house or if stranded without a ride, the person may become exasperated and embarrassed, unable to come up with any reasonable answer.

Problems in performing simple calculations represents a special kind of diminished reasoning:

- What remains if you subtract 7 from 22?
- How many eggs would you have if you had one-third of a dozen?
- If you wish to divide six books so that twice the number of books are on one shelf as on the other, how many books should you place on each shelf?

Brain syndrome leaves a person unable to solve simple mathematical problems. But a word of caution. The clinician should understand that memory and reasoning are *relative* qualities. There is no standard against which to measure them. Within the "normal range," tremendous variation exists. For the particularly gifted, despite the presence of brain syndrome, the tasks of recalling three items after 5 minutes or doing simple math calculations may present no problem. Prior to the brain syndrome, however, the same individual might have been able to recall 10 items after 5 minutes and to solve complicated "brain teasers." So, whereas failure on these simple screening questions is strongly suggestive of brain syndrome, success cannot always be construed as conclusive evidence against. For this reason, the clinician should obtain information from relatives and friends about the patient's prior level of functioning as a context in which to interpret present performance. Regardless of a person's performance on screening tests, a history of deteriorating cognitive skills at home or work is significant.

Sensory Indiscrimination

During day-to-day living, we are exposed to massive amounts of sensory input from the external world as well as from within. The brain must sort out this information, assigning priorities and construing its meaning. Of all the sensory input we receive, only a relatively small amount is actively considered; otherwise, we would surely fall victim to sensory overload. Our world of meaning would disintegrate into noise and confusion. Diminished capacity for sensory discrimination characterizes brain syndrome. Selectivity fails. The sensory overload leads to confusion.

Illusion is one of the clinical manifestations of sensory indiscrimination. An illusion is the mistaking of something for what it is not. For example, the individual may view dimly lit curtains across the room being gently moved by the wind and mistake them for a person. A street sound may be misinterpreted as the voice of a friend. This kind of perceptual distortion can involve sight, sound, touch, taste, or smell; most often, however, illusions are visual or auditory. Of great importance to the clinician is the fact that illusions rarely occur in psychological reactions. Their presence strongly implies organicity.

Hallucination is a second form of sensory indiscrimination. In contrast to illusions, hallucinations have no external referent; rather, they are internal stimuli projected onto the external world. The person may hear a voice when no one is speaking or see things—a face, spiders on the wall, snakes on the floor, a hooded demon—in the absence of any external object. As with illusions, hallucinations occur in all sensory modes, but visual hallucinations are particularly common in brain syndrome. While they can be extremely terrifying, in some cases the hallucinated experience is pleasurable. One clinician reported a half-hour observation of a person with brain syndrome intently (and apparently with great pleasure) "watching" a football game between two teams of miniature elephants (Lishman, 1997).

Although not as common as visual hallucinations, other kinds of hallucinations occur with brain syndrome. Tactile hallucinations (especially prevalent in cocaine withdrawal) may take the form of tiny creatures crawling over the skin. Olfactory hallucinations are often experienced in the initial phase of temporal lobe epilepsy. Typically, the person smells an awful odor, variously described as "rotten eggs," "burning rubber," or "old cheese."

Auditory hallucinations—a classic symptom of schizophrenia—are also experienced as a part of brain syndrome. Often, the "voices" are threatening or derogatory (Farber, 1959). Since auditory hallucinations are common in schizophrenia, they are a problematic indicator of psychological masquerade. The following rule can be used: Any hallucination—other than auditory—should be assumed, at least tentatively, to reflect an underlying medical problem. Auditory hallucinations—in the absence of other indications of "organicity"— are more likely manifestations of schizophrenia or affective mental disorder. Certain cases of chronic alcohol or drug abuse constitute the most common exceptions to this rule. They may be associated with "hallucinosis," the isolated hearing of voices in an otherwise clear sensorium. The voices are often threatening in nature.

> If my father glanced at a dark shape, which was rather like a black cat, he did not instinctively look again to make sure what it was; he simply saw a cat. His mind fitted the sensory impression to the first rough approximation that suggested itself, and accepted it without further question, however unlikely it might be in the context. . . . My father discussed the problem with me in some detail, as he was naturally disturbed to find that he kept on seeing things that were not there. (Anonymous, 1950)

BRAIN SYNDROME IN CONTEXT

We have considered the four cognitive deficits present in varying combinations and varying degrees in brain syndrome. Now we need to fill in the details by looking at the most typical clinical presentations. There are two main versions: rapid-onset brain syndrome (ROBS) and slow-onset brain syndrome (SOBS). Scattered along a continuum are variations resembling one more than the other but usually incorporating aspects of each.

Rapid-Onset Brain Syndrome

> A request for an "emergency psychiatric consultation" was received a few days after the hospital admission of a 35-year-old man for treatment of pneumonia. The consultation request was accompanied by a brief note describing the patient as "schizophrenic with hallucinations and delusions."
>
> When examined, the man was extremely agitated. In his bed, he fidgeted with the bed coverings and at times waved his arms wildly. He appeared frightened and was highly distractible, leaving him unable to attend to any task for more than a few moments. Although he gave his name correctly, he seemed unaware that he was in a hospital being treated for an illness. When pressed on this matter, he said he was in a bakery. Later, he changed his mind, saying it was a bank.

He gave the year as 1964, rather than 1971 and was unable to identify the month or day of the week. At times he appeared to be "seeing"
things. He expressed the belief that there was an angel standing beside
his bed, caring for him, but he wondered if it was there to harm rather
than to protect him. (Sakles & Ballis, 1978)

This man did not have schizophrenia. Although his severe inattention makes the other findings of his mental status somewhat questionable, there can be little doubt that he was suffering from brain
syndrome secondary to his pneumonia. His lung infection was severe
enough to prevent enough oxygen from reaching his brain. Brain failure and organic psychosis were the result. As the pneumonia came
under control in response to antibiotic treatment, the man's mental
symptoms cleared.

The most common causes of ROBS, otherwise known as "delirium," are drug and alcohol intoxications and withdrawals. But many
acute medical diseases, either through direct impairment of the brain
or compromise of its support system, give rise to ROBS.

Typically, ROBS manifests itself as a sudden and dramatic change.
Overall, the person appears confused, disoriented, and highly dis-
tractible. If his or her attention can be captured long enough to test
for recent memory, it will prove deficient. Similarly, he or she will
have major difficulty with simple calculations and problem solving.
He or she will have insomnia or reversal of the sleep cycle so that
what little sleep he or she gets comes during daylight hours.

Sensory distortions, although often prominent, can be quite subtle.
This is particularly true of persons in the grip of paranoia, afraid that
others will harm them. In such persons the only hint of a hallucinatory
experience may be a slight turn of the head, as though they were trying to hear better, or a shift of the eyes. In other cases, more obvious
manifestations may include the person suddenly shouting back to an
empty room or picking at "things" in the air.

Restlessness is one of the earliest indicators of impending ROBS. It
manifests itself in various ways, including being easily startled, pacing
the floor, continually fumbling with clothes or bed covers, and repeti-
tively searching for things. The clinical appearance of restlessness is
accentuated by tremulousness—the fine, quivering movement of the
muscles—also common in cases of ROBS (Wolff & Curran, 1935)

The term *shifting level of consciousness* describes a fundamental
aspect of ROBS. At one moment the person appears grossly confused, disoriented, and completely illogical; at the next, he or she is
calm, rational, and in control. During these so-called *lucid intervals*
(which may last for minutes to hours), the deficits of brain syndrome,

if detectable at all, are much less noticeable. But the improvement is only temporary. Soon the brain syndrome, like the passing eye of a hurricane, returns in full force. One researcher described an encounter with a patient in the hospital who was recovering from back surgery (Lipowski, 1967). The man, a minister, greeted him by shouting that he had lost his genitals in a car accident. The next moment he was screaming about a dog biting his penis, before segueing into a description of tropical flowers he "saw" in the room. After several minutes of disconnected rambling, the man turned to the researcher and said: "Am I sick? I seem to be hallucinating!" When told this was true, he seemed relieved, but after falling silent for a few moments, he started shouting again. "Look, look, there's this dog again, biting me," he said. "Take the dog away." This is a vivid example of shifting level of consciousness, which to some degree characterizes most cases of ROBS.

ROBS is influenced by environmental factors. It predictably worsens at night ("sundowner" syndrome). Being left alone in a room, particularly one without windows, can also exacerbate the symptoms. Surgical patients who convalesce in an intensive care unit develop ROBS with some degree of regularity, thought in part as a result of relative sensory deprivation.

> The suggestion that he should then go for a trip abroad put me in a difficult position. He felt convinced that it would do him good, and his medical advisors encouraged this belief. . . . We left England at the end of the year. Our destination was an isolated resort in mountainous country about fifteen miles from the nearest small town. . . . It was soon evident, however, that unfamiliar faces and a foreign language were putting too heavy a strain on his fading faculties. . . . Now, listening every day to a background of foreign conversation which, even when fit, he could not easily have followed, he was bewildered. . . . His mind accepted the nearest English equivalent to the sounds he heard, and the task of keeping in touch with reality against such odds became impossible. Hearing what he thought was English spoken, he addressed other hotel residents in his own language, to be met by uncomprehending stares. He naturally came to feel that they were hostile to him, and he began gradually to make order out of his mental chaos by systematizing, in a delusional way, what he heard and saw. (Anonymous, 1950)

Although they involve similar cognitive deficits, there are two different presentations of ROBS. One is characterized by *increased* activity, where the person appears agitated and frenetic. By contrast, the other involves *diminished* activity, with apathy, withdrawal, and drowsiness. Since the person is less disruptive, this second presenta-tion often goes unnoticed. Regardless of which version is manifest, ROBS must be considered a medical emergency requiring immediate evaluation. Unfortunately, it is often mistaken for schizophrenia.

Slow-Onset Brain Syndrome

Slow-onset brain syndrome (SOBS) is more insidious in appearance. Unlike the rapidly emerging clinical picture of ROBS, it is marked by a slow, progressive deterioration in orientation and recent memory combined with a decline in common judgment and problem-solving skills. Given this gradual onset, the person with SOBS has more time to adapt. He or she begins to avoid certain tasks, particularly those that require remembering and problem solving. Social engagements are put off for fear of embarrassment. Eventually, however, the deficits become so great that the person is no longer able to hide the problem. Judgment fails. The person becomes irresponsible and accident-prone. His or her difficulty understanding abstract or sym-bolic meaning is obvious. Jokes are no longer understood; simple proverbs become perplexing. The person interprets things literally. The saying, "The grass is always greener on the other side" may strike the person with SOBS as a commentary on different kinds of grass or various shades of green. The idea that things we do not have often appear more attractive than things we do have is lost. A similar difficulty is observed when the person is asked to identify a common-ality. For example, given a list of five colors, the person may be unable to understand that blue, red, pink, purple, and green are simi-lar in that they are all colors. (The ability to abstract is also compro-mised in cases of ROBS, but this deficit is usually overshadowed by prominent behavioral changes. A similar deficit is also part of schizo-phrenia, but there is often a bizarre twist not typically found in SOBS.)

Of course, the sketch I have given of SOBS is a composite; not all cases include a full complement of cognitive deficits. A host of med-ical disorders cause SOBS; some being permanent alterations, as is the case with Alzheimer's disease. Others, however—as we shall later discuss, give rise to potentially reversible forms of SOBS.

Let me encourage the reader to pause for a moment and imagine the experience of SOBS. What would be your personal response to failing memory, disorientation, and breakdown in reasoning, all of which were dependable aspects of your life heretofore? At first you might try to deny what was occurring; but with time, in the face of accumulating evidence, denial becomes impossible. Your self-confidence would diminish as the disturbing if not terrifying threat of losing control sinks in. You sense that something is dreadfully wrong, but you do not understand what it is. Even though you can no longer keep the truth from yourself, you try to hide it from others, hoping it will magically go away. You guard against putting yourself on display. Social events are avoided, including perhaps the weekly poker game you have enjoyed for years.

Your checking account turns up overdrawn—not once but repeatedly. You lose track of important engagements. Even at home, conversation with family and friends becomes stressful. You are afraid of making a fool of yourself. Gradually, you say less and less, fading off into thinking about other things. When someone directs a question your way, you are forced to make up a response that, more often than not, provokes looks of bewilderment. As time goes on, you find yourself in situations that appear unfamiliar. You are uncertain of what people are talking about. The questions they ask of you make no sense. Old and familiar objects fleetingly appear foreign. Sometimes they seem to come alive, but when you refocus, the animation disappears. You find it difficult to sleep. Restlessly, you toss and turn in bed, fearful sometimes of what might happen if you should fall asleep. Your vitality deserts you. You cease to find humor in stories others find hilarious. You feel hopelessly bewildered and frightened, unavoidably aware of your failing condition.

> At the request of her family physician, a 78-year-old woman was seen in her home by a public health nurse. Until recently, when her middle-aged daughter had required hospitalization for high blood pressure, the woman had lived with her. The nurse found the house messy and the woman unkempt. Throughout the conversation, the woman insisted that her daughter had just stepped out briefly for a walk. She persisted in this story despite being told repeatedly of her daughter's hospitalization. When queried about the date, she was off by 2 years.
>
> Three days later, the police escorted the woman to an emergency room, having found her wandering some distance from her home in her night clothes, "looking for my daughter."
>
> On examination, she was unable to recall more than one of three objects after 5 minutes, and she failed to recognize the name of the current president. She insisted on referring to the physician as "father," commenting that she had not been to church enough lately. When asked the meaning of common proverbs, she said they were "silly." In response to "a stitch in time saves nine," she replied that her eyes were "too weak to sew."
>
> She was diagnosed with senile dementia. (Horvath, 1979)

Dramatic changes in personality often occur with SOBS. In certain cases, this may be the first manifestation. These changes fall into four patterns. First, the person may show an exaggeration of personality traits. A previously compulsive person becomes rigid and obstinate; a passive-dependent individual, demanding and infantile. A mildly nervous and anxious person may show obsessive concerns over small matters. In short, these people become caricatures of themselves.

In some cases of SOBS this change in personality takes the form of emotional outbursts, referred to as *emotional lability*. Given the slightest provocation, the person may laugh hysterically or, as is more often the case, cry uncontrollably. Such emotional outbursts have a stereotypical quality. Associated facial expressions are the same each time, as is the volume and rhythm of the sounds. Typically, the reaction quickly subsides, only to return later at another inappropriate moment. Pathological laughter and crying of this nature has been described in association with brain tumors, Parkinson's disease, amyotrophic lateral sclerosis, Wilson's disease, multiple sclerosis, and stroke (Dark et al., 1996).

A second type of personality change involves a manic-like picture with hyperactivity, social indiscretions, inappropriate bravado, and euphoria, which, when resisted by others often elicits angry and sometimes violent agitation. This pattern is often mistaken for the manic phase of bipolar disorder.

A somewhat opposite, third type of personality change is also seen where the person's appears apathetic, withdrawn, and depressed. These cases of SOBS are misinterpreted as psychological depressive reactions.

The fourth type is characterized by growing suspiciousness if not frank paranoia. Irrational jealousy may be a major element of the person's paranoid thinking.

When personality changes precede or overshadow the cognitive deficits of SOBS, the risk of psychological masquerade is great.

> He spent the days chasing non-existent spies in other people's bedrooms; while I chased after, explaining to the agitated guests and taking what steps I could to deal with the emergency . . . the situation forced me to constrain him. . . . In that moment of despair and disillusion the full force of his love for me was fumed to bitter hatred. . . . When the crisis came we were alone in an upstairs gallery, and he fumed on me with murder in his eyes. . . . For a moment the issue hung in the balance . . . but when my glance met his, he could not bring himself to do it. He relaxed at last with a gesture of sad acquiescence and let himself be quietly led away. (Anonymous, 1950)

Table 4.1 provides a summary of the similarities and differences of ROBS and SOBS.

TABLE 4.1 Brain Syndrome

ROBS	SOBS
Rapid, dramatic onset	Slow, subtle onset
Shifting level of consciousness	Downward progression
Usually reversible	Sometimes reversible

Core deficits
(One or more)
Disorientation
Recent memory impariment
Diminished reasoning
Sensory Indiscrimination

(Behavioral changes)	(Personality changes)
Examples	*Examples*
Acute drug intoxications	Hypothyroid psychosis
Encephalitis	Pernicious anemia
Drug withdrawal reactions	Alzheimer's disease

THE QUESTION OF REVERSIBILITY

Although SOBS can reflect irreversible brain deterioration, there are cases that, if properly diagnosed and treated, are partially or totally reversible. A review of two studies of "progressive intellectual deterioration" found that approximately one out of every four patients had "an underlying disease potentially reversible by medical or surgical therapy" (Freeman, 1967). A later study puts the figure even higher. Of 222 cases of brain syndrome, 35 to 40% were deemed treatable (Wells, 1978). All too frequently, persons with SOBS are dismissed as "crocks" or "senile" for whom nothing can be done. SOBS should never be presumed to be irreversible without a thorough medical evaluation.

A 67-year-old retired farm worker, in good physical and mental health, lost interest in life. Activities that previously had given him considerable pleasure no longer did so. He was increasingly distant and forgetful. One evening he failed to return from his usual walk. A search of the surrounding area found him covered with mud, soaking wet, and extremely confused. It was assumed he had either deliberately or accidentally fallen into the nearby river. After a night's sleep, he seemed recovered.

But the incident left his family quite concerned. Finally, they insisted that he be medically evaluated. "Generalized rhonchi" were heard in his chest. On the assumption that he had inhaled water when he had fallen into the river, he was admitted to a hospital.

During his hospitalization, he appeared depressed. Although fully oriented, he answered questions slowly and with difficulty. Cognitively, he was thought to be slow. The cause turned out to be vitamin B_{12} deficiency (pernicious anemia). Treatment with B_{12} injections was immediately started. Within a few weeks, the man was greatly improved, his mental alertness and spontaneity having returned. There were no more episodes of confusion. Later, it was discovered that his brother had also suffered from pernicious anemia. (Strachen & Henderson, 1965)

The Amnestic Syndrome (Amnesia)

The amnestic syndrome is a narrow version of brain syndrome. The major deficit is a severe loss of recent memory (Benson, 1978). While the person has no difficulty attending to the present situation and solving simple problems, a striking disturbance becomes apparent when he or she is tested for *retention of new information.* The ability to recall even one or two objects after 5 to 10 minutes is lost. The person is simply unable to hold onto recent experience. New information stubbornly resist being recorded as memory. Learning becomes virtually impossible.

Directly related to this severe memory deficit is disorientation to time and place, reflecting the close tie between orientation and the continuing assimilation of new information. Persons with the amnestic syndrome lose their way and, experientially, are continually "meeting" new people whom they have previously met and forgotten only a few minutes prior. While the person with amnesia may be fully capable of immediately recalling five digits and of retrieving distant memories, somewhere between old and immediate experience, he or she has a devastating memory void. As a means of coping with the inability to recall new information, the person resorts to confabulating as a way of filling in the troubling memory gaps. These made-up fanciful tales can be mistaken for psychotic delusions by the unsuspecting clinician.

The amnestic syndrome can develop secondary to trauma, stroke, oxygen deprivation, or thiamine (vitamin B_1) deficiency, most often caused by chronic alcoholism. This alcohol-related amnesia is called

Korsakoff's syndrome, after the Russian physician who first described it in the late 1800s.

> After several months of particularly heavy drinking, a 50-year-old man with long-standing alcoholism was hospitalized. He showed signs of personal and nutritional neglect and talked to himself much of the time. Additionally, he was found to be "completely disoriented," contending that he had "been brought to the hospital after an injury to his leg at the shipyard." In actuality, this event had occurred 10 years earlier.
>
> The day after he was transferred from one hospital building to another, he estimated that one week had passed since his departure. Although he had no memory for the details of his initial hospital setting, recollections of his distant past remained vivid. He was able to recall the exact address of the boarding house where he had lived years before his hospitalization.
>
> The man steadfastly refused to believe that there was any problem with his memory. As a cover up, he often made equivocal statements during conversations, as though he were hoping that they would be accepted as consistent and logical. Sometimes he would fall into blatant fabrications and would back down only when confronted with obvious contradictions. Presented with three pictures and then asked to recall them, he would consistently recall only the last one. (Lidz, 1942)

In summary, brain syndrome is a symptom complex involving one or more of four cognitive deficits: disorientation, recent memory impairment, diminished reasoning, and sensory indiscrimination. The recognition of these cognitive deficits is of considerable clinical import, since they are highly correlated with brain failure, primary or secondary, that in many instances may be reversible. We have considered two versions of brain syndrome—ROBS and SOBS—as well as the amnestic syndrome, an unusual variation, characterized by striking deficits in recent memory and orientation. Although ROBS and SOBS have been portrayed as separate clinical presentations, such clear demarcation is often not valid in the day-to-day world of clinical practice. Persons with SOBS are prone to the superimposition of ROBS as a result of infection, medication side effects, sensory deprivation, drug and alcohol intoxications, and nonspecific stress. In turn, ROBS may be the first manifestation of a slower-evolving case of SOBS. The clinicians intent on ferreting out psychological masquerade must familiarize themselves with these two clinical versions of brain syndrome and their variations. They are often mistaken for psychiatric disturbances.

I once gave a 2-hour lecture on brain syndrome and its significance in helping to differentiate between psychological and organic disorders. At the conclusion, a student raised his hand and said, "I don't get it." He went on to say that all the "psych" patients he had observed acted confused and "out of it". When I pushed him to give examples, he reeled off instances of delusional thought: a man who believed he was king and a woman who felt she was pregnant from watching television. "They don't know what's going on. They all have brain syndrome," he concluded. Clearly, for this one student, I had not made my point. He was still equating "crazy" thinking with brain syndrome. Before concluding this chapter, let me state it a final time:

Persons with classic psychiatric disorders, are typically not disoriented. If they are minimally attentive, they will be found to have intact memories and to be capable of solving simple problems. Other than auditory hallucinations (seen in schizophrenia and affective disorders), they do not exhibit signs of gross sensory indiscrimination. Core cognitive functioning remains relatively intact, in contrast to what happens routinely in persons suffering from brain syndrome.

When brain syndrome is present, brain disease is the most likely explanation. Even when schizophrenic persons express extremely bizarre thoughts, they do not manifest the characteristic cognitive deficits of brain syndrome if you can command their attention. In short, while certain cases of brain disease do not cause brain syndrome, most instances of brain syndrome represent brain failure due to an underlying medical disorder.

The core brain syndrome deficits are summarized in Table 4.2.

In the next chapter, we consider additional clues to organic mental disorder. They, along with the manifestions of brain syndrome, provide the most important clinical clues to psychological masquerade.

> Once we got back to England he was admitted to a mental hospital without delay. He had long since given up the struggle of trying to relate his ideas to reality and had retired into a private world of unimpeded action. When last I saw him he had been put in charge of running the war after Dunkirk and was well pleased with the results. (Anonymous, 1950)

TABLE 4.2 Brain Syndrome Deficits

Disorientation
Time: inability to identify the *month, year, or general time of day (day or nighttime)*
Place: inability to identify one's *present location*
Person: inability to recognize *persons* who should be *quite familiar*

Recent memory impairment
Failure to recall *three items* after *5 minutes* on *two* occasions

Diminished reasoning
Inability to solve simple problems:
- What remains when you subtract 7 from 22?
- How many eggs would you have if you had one-third of a dozen?
- If you wish to divide six books so that twice the number of books are on one shelf as on the other, how many books should you place on each shelf?
- What would you do if you locked your keys in the car?

Sensory indiscrimination
The presence of *illusions* or *hallucinations* (other than isolated auditory hallucinations)

REFERENCES

American Psychiatric Association (1994). *Diagnostic and statistical manual of mental disorders (4th ed. revised)*. Washington, D.C.: American Psychiatric Association.

Anonymous. (1950). Death of a mind: a study in disintegration. *Lancet, 1*, 1012–1015.

Benson, F. (1978). Amnesia. *Southern Medical Journal, 71*, 1221–1228.

Dark, F., McGrath, J., & Ron, M. (1996). Pathological laughing and crying. *New Zealand Journal of Psychiatry, 30*, 472–479.

Farber, L. (1959). Acute brain syndrome. *Diseases of the Nervous System, 20*, 296–299.

Freeman, F. (1967). Evaluation of patients with progressive intellectual deterioration. *Archives of Neurology, 33*, 658–659.

Horvath, T. (1979). Organic brain syndromes. In A. Freeman, R. Sack, & P. Berger (Eds.). *Psychiatry for the primary care physician* (pp. 215-245). Baltimore: Williams & Wilkins.

Lidz, T. (1942). The amnestic syndrome. *Archives of Neurology and Psychiatry, 47*, 588–605.

Lipowski, Z. J. (1967), Delirium, clouding of consciousness and confusion. *Journal of Nervous and Mental Disease, 145*, 227–255.

Lishman, W. (1997) *Organic psychiatry* (3rd ed.). London: Blackwell Scientific Publications.

Sakles, G. & Ballis, G. (1978). Acute brain syndromes. In G. Balis (Ed.). *Clinical Psychopathology* (pp. 65–86). Boston: Butterworth Publishers, Inc.

Seizer, B. & Sherwin, I. (1978). Organic brain syndromes: an empirical study and critical review. *American Journal of Psychiatry, 135*, 13–21.

Spitzer, R., First, M., Williams, J. et al. (1992). Now is the time to retire the term "organic mental disorders." *American Journal of Psychiatry, 149*, 240–244.

Strachen, R. W., & Henderson, J.G. (1965). Psychiatric syndrome due to avitaminosis B-12 with normal bone marrow. *Quarterly Journal of Medicine, 34*, 303–317.

Wells, C. (1978). Chronic brain disease: an overview. *American Journal of Psychiatry, 135*, 1–12.

Williamson, J., Stokoe, I., Gray, S., Fisher, M., Smith, A., McGhee, A., & Stephenson, E. (1964). Old people at home: Their unreported needs. *Lancet, 1*, 1117–1120.

Wolff, H. G. & Curran, D. (1935). Nature of delirium and allied states. *Archives of Neurology and Psychiatry, 33*, 1175–1215.

Chapter 5

More Clues to Psychological Masquerade

Some circumstantial evidence is very strong, as when you find a trout in the milk. —Henry David Thoreau

There are two kinds of clues to psychological masquerade. The first are *alerting* clues. The more that turn up, the greater the possibility of masquerade. *Presumptive* clues provide even more compelling evidence. Until proven otherwise, *any* presumptive clue found in association with psychiatric symptoms indicates a causative organic disorder. As previously discussed, brain syndrome is one important presumptive clue to psychological masquerade, but there are several others.

ALERTING CLUES

No single alerting clue, by itself, makes a strong case for psychological masquerade; but as these clues accumulate, so should the clinician's suspicion. They are important caution flags and should not be overlooked.

No History of Similar Symptoms

Of all the alerting clues, the most compelling is the initial occurrence of significant psychological symptoms. One of the best predictors of the future is the past; therefore, if a person has never before reacted to the stresses and strains of life with psychiatric symptoms, their initial manifestation signals the strong possibility of an alternative explanation. Time after time, masquerading cases included in this book are characterized by *no previous psychiatric history.*

> A 54-year-old woman with no previous history of mental illness had a "delirious" episode lasting almost 24 hours. Although her confusion cleared, she was severely depressed and dependent. After 10 months without any improvement, she was admitted to a hospital. She was diagnosed as having severe depression and was treated with electroshock therapy. During the course of her treatment, however, she developed obvious neurological deficits, including weakness in her left arm and leg. At surgery an inoperable brain tumor was found, infiltrating the right frontal, temporal, and parietal areas of her brain. (Waggoner & Bagohi, 1954)

Extra scrutiny should be given to what appear to be first-episode symptoms of classic mental disorders. Take, for example, schizophrenia. This diagnosis too often is loosely applied to any person exhibiting delusions or hallucinations. Clinicians are well advised to question the diagnosis when symptoms occur for the first time after the age of 30. In most cases, schizophrenia manifests itself in the late teens or early twenties.

The emergence of *new symptoms* in a person *with a psychiatric history* should also be suspect. For example, previous episodes of bizarre behavior may have nothing to do with the later emergence of paranoid confusion. In short, the initial occurrence of any psychiatric symptom should always raise the suspicion of psychological masquerade.

No Readily Identifiable Cause

Typically, psychological reactions are associated with stress or conflict. Organic mental disorders, in contrast, often develop abruptly, "out of the blue," without any obvious psychosocial precipitant.

> The concerned friends of a 31-year-old computer sciences student brought him to an emergency room after he had been acting strangely for 2 days. They reported that, without any warning, he had started hearing voices and had become increasingly withdrawn. For the most part, he avoided any conversation; when he did talk, his comments were incomplete and inappropriate.
>
> The week before, without explanation, he dropped his studies and quit his job as a taxi driver. He also complained of a headache, for which he sought treatment from several physicians without relief.

Described as a loner, he had no history of mental disorder. No precipitating event for his sudden change of behavior could be identified.

On evaluation, although fully oriented, he had difficulty following simple instructions, appearing not to comprehend many of the questions. The examining psychiatrist said that he had "loosening of associations." His memory was "difficult to test."

The young man was admitted to a psychiatric unit with the diagnosis of "acute schizophreniform psychosis." (Carlson, 1977)

The abrupt onset of strange behavior (especially in combination with poor cognitive functioning and an unexplained headache) should have raised the possibility of psychological masquerade. Within 24 hours, the patient developed fever and a stiff neck. An emergency angiogram (a contrast study of the brain) showed a large subdural hematoma. Emergency surgery was performed with excellent results. The man experienced no residual symptoms. (The hematoma had been caused by a "leaking" artery known as an *aneurysmal malformation*, a rare congenital anatomical defect.)

Although psychiatric symptoms in the absence of significant stress should always raise the possibility of organic mental disorder, the reverse is not true. This is an important point. The existence of problems in living, even when severe, is not proof that psychiatric symptoms are psychological in nature. As illustrated by numerous examples throughout this book, the most plausible psychological explanations are often found in conjunction with organic mental disorder.

Age 55 or Older

Older persons are high risk for psychological masquerade. Organic mental disorders account for roughly half of initial psychiatric admissions involving persons age 55 or older. Several factors are at work. First, the margins of safety for the various support systems of the body decline with age; consequently, maintenance of an optimal physiological environment, on which brain functioning depends, becomes less dependable. Second, with age, the brain becomes more sensitive to medication side effects. Finally, the incidence of medical conditions capable of causing psychological masquerade increases with age.

I do not mean to say that psychological reactions are absent from older life. It is just that the chances of psychological masquerade dramatically increase with age and deserve special vigilance from the clinician. Although age 55 may be somewhat arbitrary in defining old age, the point is that as a person gets older, the risk of psychological masquerade increases.

Coexistence of Chronic Disease

Persons with chronic diseases tend to take more than their share of medications, which can cause adverse effects easily mistaken for psychiatric symptoms. Also, long-standing chronic diseases frequently lead to physiological decline and secondary brain failure. Of course, the degree of risk depends on the specific type of disease. Consider the following case.

> After the death of her husband, a 56-year-old woman became extremely agitated. Two days later, when she insisted that her brother was her dead husband returned to life, her relatives took her to a hospital. The day before her admission, she had defecated in a trash can, thinking she was in her bathroom.
>
> The woman, having been "cleared medically," was thought to be suffering from a severe "acute grief reaction." She was admitted to the psychiatric inpatient service. On mental status examination, she was able to recall only one of three items after 5 minutes. The sclerae of her eyes were yellowish. (Weissberg, 1979)

This woman had a known history of chronic liver disease secondary to alcoholism. Her liver disease put her at risk for organic mental disorder. Subsequent laboratory studies confirmed that she had contracted viral hepatitis. The infection had compromised her already debilitated liver, leading to hepatic failure and her florid "grief" symptoms. A history of alcoholism and chronic liver disease were important alerting clues to the true nature of her problem.

Use of Drugs

Psychoactive chemicals cause an array of experiences, ranging from the highly pleasurable to the most frightening and bizarre. Drug reactions are the number one cause of organic mental disorder. Furthermore, with those drugs that are addictive, an interruption in supply leads to withdrawal, with anxiety, agitation, confusion, and even psychosis. While dramatic cases of full-blown, delirious withdrawal are easily recognized, other drug reactions can be far more subtle in their presentation.

In addition to toxic effects, excessive use of drugs (including alcohol) predisposes a person to a myriad of medical problems as well as accidents, particularly those related to driving.

The clinician should keep in mind that prescription and over-the-counter medications are also drugs. They account for their share of organic mental disorders. Persons taking over-the-counter drugs sometimes do not consider them medications. They may unknowingly mislead the clinician by denying the use of medications even though they are taking self-prescribed preparations, some of which have powerful "mind-bending" effects.

In the field of psychiatry, the same medications that are prescribed for psychiatric conditions can cause their own brand of "psychiatric symptoms" via side effects.

> For over 2 months, he had slept infrequently. Sometimes he would work two consecutive shifts, one for pay, the other for free. He threw himself feverishly into whatever he was doing, as illustrated by the way he pursued his interest in bowling. On one occasion he had bowled 50 games, uninterrupted! If he didn't score a strike with the first ball, he became impatient and would reset the pins without bowling a second ball.
>
> Seeing their son's excessive spending and unbridled activity, the parents of this 23-year-old man became concerned. Finally, when he disrobed in front of his mother and tried to climb into a small washbasin, he was taken to a hospital. He was oriented and without obvious delusions. There was no memory impairment or hallucinations. He denied using medications or drugs.
>
> The discovery that this young man had recently experienced a severe, acne-like rash on his face prompted a request for a blood bromide level. The answer came back: "bromide toxicity." Within 1 week, the man had returned to his normal self. On questioning, he admitted the daily use of an over-the-counter bromide preparation as a sedative. (Sayed, 1976)

The clinician should inquire routinely about drugs and medications. If there is any question about this aspect of the history, a secondary source should be used if at all possible. Persons who abuse drugs and alcohol are unreliable reporters, and many older people simply do not keep up with all the medications they take.

There is another aspect of drugs to consider. While many persons get into difficulty abusing drugs, others have problems because they do not take medications they need. For some persons, medications are essential. If they are not taken with regularity, the person becomes seriously ill—as in the case of diabetes, severe hypertension, heart failure, asthma, hypothyroidism, and many other conditions. Despite the risks involved, for one reason or another, patients often stop taking their medications. Psychological masquerade is one of the potential outcomes.

> She was a 36-year-old Mexican woman, married for 10 years and described by her husband as a stable housewife. She had had no history of psychiatric problems until she required hospitalization following a week of sleepless agitation and psychotic behavior. She had grown increasingly suspicious of cars and people. She believed the agents of the Immigration and Naturalization Service were stalking her.
>
> In the hospital, she expressed the belief that someone was impersonating her sister in order to arrange her own murder. She appeared depressed. Her face was expressionless; her movements slow. She was fully oriented and had no problem with recent memory.
>
> Further history revealed that hypothyroidism had been diagnosed 9 years earlier. At the time, she was started on a daily thyroid supplement, but two months prior to her hospitalization, she had stopped taking it. Her hypothyroid condition was confirmed by laboratory tests. Within 11 days of restarting thyroid hormone, the woman was back to normal. (Santiago, Stoker, Beigel, Yost, & Spencer, 1987)

This case is an example of Capgras' syndrome, a delusional condition in which the afflicted person believes that a loved one has been replaced by an identical double. This syndrome can be stress-related, but it has also been described in a number of organic disorders.

The role of drugs and medications in organic mental disorders is so extensive that I have devoted a later chapter exclusively to this subject.

PRESUMPTIVE CLUES

Presumptive clues provide even more compelling evidence for organicity. When such clues are found in association with psychiatric symptoms, an organic mental disorder must be assumed until proven otherwise.

Head Injury

Head injury, depending on its severity, carries the risk of neurological complications. Most cases produce symptoms readily recognized as neurological and thus do not tend to masquerade. A notable exception occurs in alcoholics, where the symptoms of head injury may be mistaken for drunkenness. The inebriated person may sustain a traumatic head injury while passing out, but then, upon arousing, be unable to recall the incident or adequately describe his or her symptoms. He or she runs the risk of being written off as "just another drunk." This can be a fatal oversight.

In emergency settings, clinicians should be alert to any sign of recent head trauma. This would include facial lacerations, broken teeth, dried blood around the ear, or an unexplained lump on the head. In some cases of head injury, symptoms are slow to develop and may be restricted to changes in personality. Automobile accidents frequently cause head injury without leaving any external evidence. The person involved may not recall having lost consciousness. Direct questions, such as "Have you been in a recent automobile accident or otherwise injured?" may bring to light instances of head injury that otherwise might go unacknowledged.

Change in Headache Pattern

A recent *change* in headache pattern should be thoroughly evaluated. Headache is a relatively common experience among adults. Typically, there is a well-established pattern of onset and distribution as well as a predictable relationship to certain stresses in the person's life. Predictably, the headache is relieved when the stress subsides and, often, in the interim, is controlled with over-the-counter pain medication. When a person complains of a *different kind of headache*, the clinician should pay close attention.

Headache can be a symptom of serious brain disease, particularly infections, brain tumors, and subdural hematomas. One researcher estimates that approximately 60% of persons with brain tumors experience headaches. Headache is the *initial* manifestation in one out of every five cases! The percentage for subdural hematoma is even higher. Additionally, as we shall discuss in Chapter 7, the headache classically associated with brain tumors that cause raised intracranial pressure has a characteristic pattern.

In addition to asking about a change in headache pattern, the clinician should also be sensitive to nonverbal clues. Once again, this is especially important in dealing with intoxicated persons and with persons who are confused, drowsy, or psychotic. The person may intermittently pull at his ear or hold his head in his hands. These gestures may be the only clues to headache.

The following case illustrates how easily headache can be neglected when it is overshadowed by psychiatric symptoms.

Agitated and threatening violence, a young man in his early twenties was evaluated in an emergency room. His wife reported that the previous day he had started complaining of a severe headache for which he was seen by his family physician and treated with a "pain shot." But his headache persisted. Later, at home, the man started screaming and attacked his wife and children. The fire department was summoned, and the man was taken to the hospital.

Although appearing in good physical health, he was incoherent. Without provocation, he would scream threateningly at people around him. He was treated with an antipsychotic medication and admitted to the psychiatric unit as a case of functional psychosis (schizophrenia).

Over the next 24 hours, he became stuporous and developed fever and a stiff neck. He was found to have meningoencephalitis, an infection of the brain and its coverings. Fortunately, aggressive antibiotic therapy proved curative. (Sandler, 1975)

Visual Disturbances

Any unexplained, abrupt change in vision should be presumed to stem from a neurological problem. Eye movement is the product of complex muscle coordination, requiring input from several different nerves. The three cranial nerves that control eye movement extend for varying lengths from their points of origin in the brain to their connections with the muscles of the eyes. Consequently, they are susceptible to encroachment by expanding brain masses or injury from certain degenerative diseases. When these nerves are compromised, the fine movement of the eyes is disrupted. To the observer, the eyes may appear out of line or crossed while the affected person complains of double vision.

The visual pathways between the retina and the occipital cortex (and surrounding associative areas) are subject to interruption. In some cases, the visual disturbance may be so subtle that the person fails to notice. Nevertheless, the person is left with a "hole" in his or her sight that may only become apparent after a series of unexplained accidents, such as bumping into doorways or scraping the car when driving into narrow parking spaces. These accidents reflect the person's inability to detect objects in certain parts of the visual fields.

For unknown reasons, the "patchy" manifestations of multiple sclerosis often include transitory visual changes. The person may be blinded for a short time or see flashes of light or "whiteness." Years later these visual changes are recognized as the initial manifestation of multiple sclerosis.

Speech Deficits

Speech deficits fall into two main categories. The first involves mechanical problems. Difficulty articulating words is called *dysarthria*. The most common cause is drug or alcohol intoxication. The person's speech is slurred and "thick," sometimes to the extent of being undecipherable. Dysarthric speech can be mistaken for psychotic language. The point to remember is that the speech of persons with traditional psychotic disorders, although strange in its content, is mechanically intact. It is not dysarthric.

In contrast to dysarthria, *aphasia* is the loss of word comprehension and proper word usage. In one form—known as "nonfluent" aphasia—in addition to the difficulty in finding the right word, the natural flow and rhythm of speech is lost. The person's speech is limited mainly to verbs and nouns. Nonfluent aphasia most often results from a stroke that leaves the person with some restriction of movement on one side of the body (usually the right side). As a result, it is readily identifiable as a neurological disorder and seldom is mistaken for psychiatric illness.

The story with "fluent" aphasia is different. In this condition, the person has no difficulty articulating words. His or her speech is smooth and naturally rhythmic. But he or she has great trouble coming up with the correct words and arranging them so that they communicate the desired meaning. When closely analyzed, the person's speech communicates little substantive content; rather, it is filled with incorrect, inappropriate, or even made-up words. The person talks around the word that cannot be mobilized. For example, in trying to say "key," the person might substitute "what you unlock the door with"; or, in referring to a spoon, he or she may call it "a handle with a little cup on it."

Word substitution is sometimes used, so that *hammer* stands for *nail*, or *fork* for *knife*. Sometimes word substitutions are made on the basis of similar sounds. *Spoot* might be used for *spoon* or *heart* for *hard*. Other times, the substitutions seem almost random, as in one patient who referred to his thumb as an "Argentinean rifle" (Geschwind, 1971). Prepositions and other connecting words are especially troublesome for persons with aphasia. This leads to difficult grammatical transitions. Surprisingly, persons with fluent aphasia sometimes seem unaware that anything is wrong.

One of the most confusing variations of fluent aphasia involves the prominent use of artificial words known as *neologisms*. These fabricated words sound bizarre and can be mistaken for psychotic speech. The difference is that, while the psychotic person periodically uses strange words, there is usually no difficulty with normal descriptive language. For the aphasic, the routine use of language is problematic.

The most common form of fluent aphasia is called *anomia*, the inability to name common objects. Anomia may occur alone or in combination with other forms of aphasia. It is important to recognize because it is a symptom found in a number of neurological disorders. In an article entitled, "Ironman," Dr. Bruce Dobkin, a Los Angeles neurologist and writer, recounts an exchange between himself and an athlete who had become aphasic following a cerebral hemorrhage. Upon finishing an 8-mile run, the 40-year-old man developed a severe headache. Although he tried to work the next day, the pain was incapacitating. Afterwards, he recounted the details for Dr. Dobkin.

PATIENT: I got home and back into bed. My wife called again when it was dark, and told me to call the blotcher.

DOCTOR: Blotcher?

PATIENT: Ah, you know, the one like you. I mean, the. . . .

DOCTOR: Doctor?

PATIENT: Yeah, that's it.

Later on, the same patient, speaking of his physical limitations, commented: "I guess I have some laminations (Dobkin, 1988).

When a person with aphasia is unable to say what he means, he becomes understandably frustrated, often raising his voice in a failed effort to be understood. Add to this agitation a smattering of neologisms plus a few awkward expressions and you have a challenging problem of masquerade.

Differentiation of aphasia from psychiatric symptoms depends on careful listening. One researcher has said: "The acute onset of abnormal speech in a middle-aged person is . . . almost invariably diagnostic of a fluent (receptive) aphasia" (Geschwind, 1971). Evidence of slurred or garbled speech or indications of difficulty communicating simple facts or naming common objects should be considered a neurological problem.

This next case history illustrates the last three presumptive clues we have considered.

A middle-aged man required heavy fishnet restraints to control his violent, explosive behavior. As he was being admitted to the hospital, he was observed snarling, showing his teeth, and lashing out at bystanders. Earlier in the day, he had attacked his wife with a butcher knife. When the police arrived at his home, the man was incoherent; his speech was badly garbled.

Over the previous several months, he had undergone a personality change and had complained of blurred vision and severe headaches.

A neurological workup identified a large right frontal lobe tumor extending into the temporal area of the brain. After surgical removal of the tumor, the man's symptoms, including the bizarre behavioral changes, disappeared. He resumed his work as a night watchman. (Mark & Ervin, 1970)

Abnormal Body Movements

Many clinicians fail to appreciate the close connection between abnormal body movements and organic mental disorders. Consider ordinary walking. This basic human skill is disturbed in many cases of psychological masquerade. Unsteadiness, for example, is an important clue to drug and alcohol intoxication. When manifest by gross staggering, the clinical detection is easy; but when the person compensates by walking with a wider-based gait and moving slowly and more deliberately, clinical recognition is more difficult.

Syphilis of the brain, pernicious anemia (vitamin B_{12} deficiency) alcoholism, multiple sclerosis, and a host of other medical disorders manifest as "psychological" symptoms and disturbances in walking. Normal-pressure hydrocephalus—a condition usually commencing in midlife—causes depression, declining mental ability, loss of bladder control, and a peculiar gait aberration. The person has great difficulty initiating each step, with the feet seemingly stuck to the floor; hence the term *magnetic gait.*

Every clinician should develop a sense of what constitutes normal walking—how the arms swing, how far apart the feet are, the rhythm of normal striding—so that abnormalities are readily identified. The observation of a person walking should be a part of any psychological assessment. In the interview situation, this is easily and unobtrusively accomplished by watching a person enter and leave the office.

There are other abnormal movements that signal psychological masquerade. Persons with Parkinson's disease experience depression and emotional lability along with a characteristic tremor of the hands, sometimes described as "pill-rolling" movements. These patients also have trouble initiating walking without losing their balance. Huntington's disease causes poor impulse control and eventually violence and psychosis. A hallmark finding is spastic jerking and twitching of various muscles, particularly in the extremities and trunk. In Wilson's disease (a disorder of copper metabolism), tremor, spasms, and dysarthria may accompany mania, depression, or schizoaffective psychosis.

The combination of psychological symptoms and abnormal movements is not as surprising as it may first seem. Brain areas active in motor coordination and those active in emotional elaboration both contain high concentrations of the same neurotransmitter, dopamine. It is presumed that disturbances in this brain chemical produce both abnormal movements and psychiatric symptoms. Clinicians cannot afford to overlook tremors, twitches, and difficulty walking. These abnormalities of movement are often important clues to organic mental disorder.

Sustained Deviations in Vital Signs

The term *vital signs* refers to heart rate, blood pressure, respiratory rate, and temperature. These four measures reflect the physiological integrity of the body. Normally, they remain within relatively narrow ranges. With physical stress or anxiety, temporary deviations may occur. As a general rule, when one or more of these vital signs remains abnormal for an extended period, an organic disorder should be suspected.

In some cases, particularly those involving drugs, a change in vital signs can be the only tipoff to psychological masquerade. Vital sign determinations are not highly technical measurements, and their use as screening measures does not necessarily require medical expertise. I am not suggesting that nonmedical professionals assume primary responsibility for measuring vital signs, but they should understand their significance.

In Table 5.1, normal-range values are listed that can be used to evaluate for deviations in vital sign values. If found on repeated measures, values outside these ranges should be considered pathological and a possible indication of organic mental disorder.

> Following 2 days of confusion, disorientation, and obsessive preoccupation with what he believed to be a transistor radio buried in his head, a young man was admitted to an emergency ward.

TABLE 5.1 Vital Sign Values for Critical Assessment Screening

Heart rate:	50–100/minute
Blood pressure:	90–160 (systolic)
	50–95 (diastolic)
Respirations:	6–20/minute
Temperature (oral):	96°F (35.6°C)–100°F (37.8°C)

He was "delirious"; his memory for recent events, grossly impaired. Vital signs were abnormal: blood pressure, 140/100; pulse, 120; and rectal temperature, 100.2°F. Additionally, his pupils were widely dilated and failed to contract in response to light.

Despite these findings, the initial clinical impression was "psychotic excitement." Intramuscular haloperidol was given without beneficial effect.

Three hours later, the young man's family brought in an empty pill bottle that had contained amitriptyline (Elavil). This discovery, combined with the man's clinical appearance and abnormal vital signs, led to a revised diagnosis of anticholinergic psychosis. He received physostigmine and within 45 minutes, the delirium cleared, only to return a few hours later when the short-acting drug had worn off. Repeated treatments, however, produced complete resolution. (Grancher & Baldessarini, 1975)

Initially, this man's abnormal vital signs were the most important clue to the cause of his delirious psychosis. (A word of caution about vital signs: These measures are sometimes hastily taken and recorded. When a significant deviation is discovered, the first thing to do is to repeat the measurement. This simple rule can save considerable time and energy.)

Changes in Consciousness

The term "consciousness" refers to a person's state of alertness and general awareness. There are three alterations that should always be viewed as evidence of an underlying organic condition: persistent drowsiness, lapses, and loss of consciousness.

A person suffering from excessive drowsiness often drops off to sleep in the daytime; sometimes during the course of a conversation. This behavior quickly becomes problematic at work or school. Typically, the problem is made worse by even small amounts of alcohol or tranquilizers.

A lapse in consciousness is a momentary break in awareness. Subsequently, the person may have no memory of such lapses. These "blank" episodes resemble the symptom of thought blocking seen in schizophrenia. For no apparent reason, the person stops talking, only to resume, after a brief pause, as though nothing had happened. More often than not, true lapses indicate seizure activity arising deep in the brain.

The family physician of a 26-year-old man sent him to the hospital with the brief notation that he was "psychotic and needed hospitalization."

While at work, the man thought he smelled acetylene gas. Concerned about a possible explosion, he crawled out on the roof of his shop to look for a possible cause. What he "found" was unexpected. He said he saw "tanks of gas" leaking their contents into the air conditioning system. He called the local police and fire departments, but when they arrived, they found nothing. The man was referred to his physician and then to the hospital.

There was no history of mental illness or drug use. On mental status examination, the man appeared normal. He was oriented and without delusions or hallucinations. Further questioning, however, revealed a history of short lapses in consciousness, one of which had resulted in an automobile accident. (Lawall, 1976)

This man was having seizures, subsequently confirmed by an electroencephalogram showing "random sharp spikes" over the left temporal lobe area. His diagnosis was temporal lobe epilepsy.

Any unexplained loss of consciousness, including fainting, should receive a neurological evaluation. One would think this a rather automatic response, but as the next case illustrates, this is not true.

While on business in another country, an atomic physicist became paranoid, sensing that people were plotting to steal atomic secrets from him. After being sent home, he was diagnosed as "schizophrenic" and hospitalized for psychiatric treatment.

Several months after his release, he passed out from what appeared to be a seizure. His psychiatrist, still firmly convinced that the man was having a schizophrenic break, dismissed the possibility of an organic mental disorder. It was only when the man complained of a severe, unrelenting headache that he was referred for neurological studies. He was found to have a highly malignant brain tumor invading the temporal lobe. (Geschwind, 1975)

SPECIAL CLINICAL TESTING

We have considered five alerting clues and eight presumptive clues (including brain syndrome) that are clinical keys to unmasking psychological masquerade. There will be situations, however, where the evidence is equivocal or only suggestive, leaving the clinician undecided. In such instances, the following three special tests may provide helpful information. These three tests are simple in design and can be administered in a brief period, ordinarily less than 10 minutes for all three. If any of the three are positive, the clinician should consider this presumptive evidence of an organic mental problem. These are "quick and dirty" tests and should not substitute for more sophisticated neuropsychological testing when indicated.

Write-a-Sentence Test

Despite the appearance of simplicity, the task of writing a sentence requires highly complex brain-eye-muscle interaction. The Write-a-Sentence Test is a particularly sensitive indicator of global brain dysfunction and typically shows improvement paralleling a person's recovery from delirium (Chidru & Geschwind 1972).

The test is administered with the following instructions: Write the sentence I read to you as neatly and legibly as you can. "Men and women have equal rights but different needs."

This sentence should be read twice, slowly, to ensure that the person registers it adequately. Ideally, the person should write on lined paper; if there is a preferred language, the sentence should be given in that language. When the person completes the sentence or at the end of 2 minutes, whichever comes first, the sentence should be reviewed for the following: incompleteness, clumsily formed letters, duplication of writing strokes (particularly in letters such as "m" or "w"), improper alignment of letters, with displacement either upward or downward from the line, spelling errors, use of nonexistent words (neologisms), and word repetitions. Detailed, microscopic analysis is not appropriate with this test. Look for obvious, repetitive errors as a basis for calling the test positive.

Draw-a-Clock Test

This test measures a person's ability to handle spatial relationships, write numbers in sequence, and tell time (see Figure 5.1). The task is not dependent on verbal skills and therefore is subject to little cultural distortion. Although a simple exercise for most adults of normal intelligence, the Draw-a-Clock Test often proves problematic for persons with certain brain disorders.

The test is administered by providing the person with a pencil and a previously printed circle approximately 3 inches in diameter. (It is a good idea to have a supply of these printed circles available in the clinic setting.) The subject is instructed to enter the appropriate numbers as they appear on the face of a clock and to draw the hands so that they indicate the time, 10 minutes past 10 o'clock.

When the subject has completed the task or at the end of 2 minutes, whichever comes first, the construction should be reviewed with

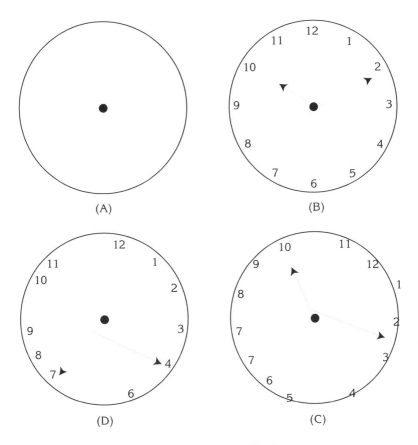

FIGURE 5.1 Draw-a-Clock test.
A: Printed circle with dot in center. B: Adequate reproduction.
C: Displacement and rotation of numbers; repetition of a number
(7). D: Crowding; displacement of hands; deletion of a number
(5); incorrect time.

the following in mind. Persons with brain disease, particularly when it involves certain associative areas, may displace the numbers on the clock so that they fall outside the circle or gravitate toward the center. Crowding, repeating, or deleting of the numbers may also occur, as well as rotation of the numbers so that 12 no longer appears at the top. Sometimes the person will draw the hands of the clock displaced from the center of the circle to the periphery or will simply depict the wrong time. (Robbins & Stern, 1976).

If a person is unable to complete the test without obvious errors, especially on repeated attempts, this is presumptive evidence of organic disorder. Further evaluation is indicated.

Copy-a-Three-Dimensional-Figure Test

This is a test of spatial appreciation. As with the Draw-A-Clock Test, acceptable performance depends on the integrity of various associative areas of the brain. Since these areas are extensive in size and relatively silent with respect to motor movement and sensory perception, this simple constructional test screens for organic dysfunction that might otherwise go undetected.

The test is administered by giving the person a previously printed, three-dimensional figure, such as a cube. He or she is instructed to copy the figure in the space below the printed version. When the person has completed the task or at the end of 2 minutes, whichever comes first, the construction is reviewed (see Figure 5.2). Attention should be directed at whether or not the person has reproduced the three-dimensional effect. Perfection is not the issue. Only if the reproduced figure is completely flat and two-dimensional in appearance should the test be considered positive.

In the preceding two chapters we discussed the most important clinical clues to psychological masquerade. Alerting clues serve as red flags, and the more there are, the greater the case for organicity. Presumptive clues up the ante still more. Any presumptive clue found in combination with psychiatric symptoms necessitates a medical evaluation. In many cases, these will prove to be reflections of an underlying, causative medical condition. Being constantly on the lookout for both kinds of clues is the best strategy for detecting psychological masquerade.

In the next chapter, we will take up a practical approach to integrating the search for psychological masquerade into the basic clinical interview.

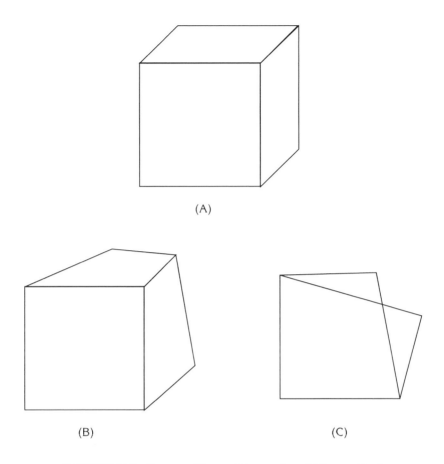

FIGURE 5.2 Copy-a-Three-Dimensional-Figure Test.
A: Printed cube that client copies. B: Adequate reproduction. C: Inadequate reproduction.

REFERENCES

Carlson, R. (1977). Frontal lobe lesions masquerading as psychiatric disturbances. *Canadian Psychiatric Association Journal, 22*, 315–318.

Chidru, F. & Geschwind, N. (1972). Writing disturbances in acute confusional states. *Neuropsychologica, 10*, 343–353.

Dobkin, B. (1988, September 4). The ironman. *The New York Times Magazine.* 40–41.

Geschwind, N. (1971). Current concepts: aphasia. *New England Journal of Medicine, 284*, 654–657.

Geschwind, N. (1975). In F. Benson, D. Blumer (Eds.), *Psychiatric aspects of neurological disease.* New York: Grune and Stratton. (Chapter 7).

Grancher, R. & Baldessarini, R. (1975). Physostigmine. *Archives of General Psychiarty, 32*, 375–380.

Lawall, J. (1976). Psychiatric presentations of seizure disorders. *American Journal of Psychiatry, 133*, 321–323.

Mark, V. & Ervin, F. (1970). *Violence in the brain* (pp. 58–59). New York: Harper & Row.

Robbins, E. & Stern, M. (1976). Assessment of psychiatric emergencies. In R. Glick , A. Meyerson, E. Robbins, & J. Talbott, (Eds.) *Psychiatric emergencies* (pp. 9–48). New York, Grune & Stratton.

Sandler, N. (1975). A case of meningitis admitted as schizophrenia. *Journal of the Kentucky Medical Association, 73*, 25–26.

Santiago, J., Stoker, D., Beigel, A., Yost, D., & Spencer, P. (1987). Capgras' syndrome in a myxedema patient. *Hospital and Community Psychiatry, 38*, 199–201.

Sayed, J. (1976). Mania and bromism: a case report and a look at the future, *American Journal of Psychiatry, 133*, 228–229.

Waggoner, R. & Bagohi, B. (1954). Initial masking of organic brain changes by psychic symptoms. *American Journal of Psychiatry, 110*, 904–910.

Weissberg, M. (1979). Emergency room medical clearance: an educational problem. *American Journal of Psychiatry, 136*, 787–790.

Chapter 6

Looking for Psychological Masquerade in the Clinical Setting

Practice and thought might gradually forge many an art. —Virgil

At this juncture, the reader may feel "stuffed" with clues, so this is a good place to pause, take a breath, and consider how to put this information to work. It is not as overwhelming as it might first appear.

Table 6.1 provides a complete checklist. Resist the temptation to treat these items as a special list. Although that might initially seem easier, in the long run, it is more intrusive than working the questions into the interview naturally. With practice, looking for clues to psychological masquerade becomes second nature and requires surprisingly little extra interview time.

Where various questions fit into the interview is the subject of Figure 6.1. In the clinical setting, the person's *age* (and sometimes *vital signs*) may be given on the admission form or the patient record. Typically, the first part of an interview addresses the person's chief complaint and related stressors. This is also a convenient time to inquire about any *previous history of similar symptoms*.

Throughout the interview, the clinician should be on the lookout for *changes in consciousness, abnormal body movements, speech deficits, and evidence of brain syndrome*. Remaining items can be considered as they naturally come up or at transition points. For example, questions about *head injury, change in headache, and visual disturbances* can be bunched together and introduced as "a few questions about your general health." If any items remain unaddressed, they can be taken up as "wrap-up" inquiries at the end of

TABLE 6.1 Clues to Psychological Masquerade

Alerting clues
  1. No history of similar symptoms
  2. No readily identifiable cause
  3. Age 55 or older
  4. Coexistence of chronic disease
  5. Use of drugs

Presumptive clues
  6. Brain syndrome (one or more core deficits)
  → Disorientation
  → Recent memory impairment
  → Diminished reasoning
  → Sensory indiscrimination
  7. Head injury
  8. Change in headache pattern
  9. Visual disturbances
  10. Speech deficits
  11. Abnormal body movements
  12. Sustained deviations in vital signs
  13. Changes in consciousness
  14. Special tests
  → Write a Sentence
  → Draw a Clock
  → Copy a Three-Dimensional Figure

the interview. Similarly, the *special construction tests* can be administered after the interviewer has had a chance to determine their appropriateness.

HYPOTHETICAL CASES

By way of review, consider the following hypothetical case. You are about to see a new patient. This is your first meeting. The receptionist announces that Mr. B has arrived. You meet him in the waiting area and, after introducing yourself, escort him back to your office. The information sheet says he is a 45-year-old automobile salesman.

By this time—even though the formal interview has not started—you should have made several pertinent observations. You have had an opportunity to observe the man's general appearance and dress

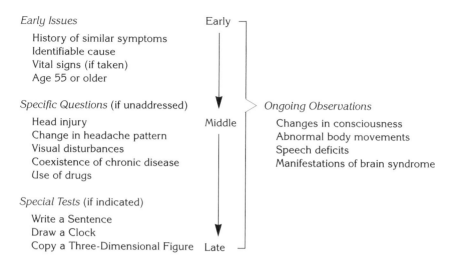

Early Issues

    History of similar symptoms
    Identifiable cause
    Vital signs (if taken)
    Age 55 or older

Specific Questions (if unaddressed)

    Head injury
    Change in headache pattern
    Visual disturbances
    Coexistence of chronic disease
    Use of drugs

Special Tests (if indicated)

    Write a Sentence
    Draw a Clock
    Copy a Three-Dimensional Figure

Early — Middle — Late

Ongoing Observations

    Changes in consciousness
    Abnormal body movements
    Speech deficits
    Manifestations of brain syndrome

FIGURE 6.1 Course of the interview.

as well as the way he walks. Is there anything unusual? Does he have difficulty walking? Positive answers suggest neurological deficits. Before you ask your first question, the search for psychological masquerade has begun.

You begin the interview by asking: "What brings you here?" As the person tells his story, he mentions feeling depressed. The interview might then proceed as follows:

INTERVIEWER: Have you ever been depressed like this before?

PATIENT: Well, I've felt blue at times, a little down . . . you know how it is, things don't always go the way you want, but never like this. I avoid my friends. Nothing means much anymore. Things around the house that need to be done are piling up. I don't want to do anything. Everything seems so hopeless sometimes.

(Of course, the question of self-destructive thoughts and intentions would take priority. For this discussion, we will assume that no serious suicide risk is detected.)

You have established that the man has no prior history of the kind of depression he now is experiencing. As the interview progresses, you continuously observe for shifts in consciousness, abnormal body movements, and speech deficits. These symptoms often appear *episodically* and may be overlooked unless you are actively watching for them. This does not require so much a sustained focus as it does a heightened suspicion; watching "out of the corner of one's eye," so to speak.

From the beginning of the interview, you are unobtrusively collecting information pertinent to the possibility of psychological masquerade. As the patient proceeds with his story, essential pieces of information may be volunteered. You note them as you go, thereby avoiding the need for redundant questions.

Our hypothetical patient elaborates on his depression, describing how nothing seems to be going right. Sales are down. His car has been in the shop twice in the previous 3 weeks. One of his kids has recently had a "brush with the law," and to top it off, the patient has been having "a bitch of a headache" for the past 2 days! While describing situational events, he has mentioned an unexpected symptom—headache. It's essential to explore this complaint.

INTERVIEWER: About this headache you've been having, describe it for me.
PATIENT: Oh, it's the kind I always get, right in the back of my neck. If I take three aspirin early enough, I can usually knock it out. If not, it can go on for most of the day. I've had headaches like this off and on for 30 years. My doctor has never found anything wrong. I think it's just stress.
INTERVIEWER: Is there anything different about your headache this time?
PATIENT: No, it's the same. Every damn time, just like clockwork, when I get loaded down with worries, it's headache time!

Through this brief exchange, you confirm that your patient has a headache with which he has become quite familiar over the years. There has been no change—the stressors that typically cause it are present; thus, it does not constitute presumptive evidence of an organic mental disorder.

By midway in the interview, you start looking for natural transition points to make specific inquiries.

INTERVIEWER: Mr. B, I want to ask you a few questions about your general health. Have you recently had a head injury?
PATIENT: No.
INTERVIEWER: Has your vision changed? Have you had trouble with your eyesight? Blurred or double vision?
PATIENT: No, I haven't had anything like that.
INTERVIEWER: What about medical problems?
PATIENT: My doctor says I have a touch of bronchitis. I know I

INTERVIEWER: smoke too much.

INTERVIEWER: Do you take medications, either prescribed or those you get for yourself at the drug store?

PATIENT: No, I'm not much for taking medications.

INTERVIEWER: No medications for your lung problems? Nothing?

PATIENT: Well, I use aspirin every once in a while, and sometimes I take TUMS for heartburn, but I don't use either one of them very often.

INTERVIEWER: How about alcohol or other drugs? How much do you use?

PATIENT: I have a cocktail every evening and sometimes a beer or two on weekends. I don't use drugs.

INTERVIEWER: Has a doctor ever told you something was wrong with your heart, your blood pressure, or the way you breathe?

PATIENT: No. Even with all my smoking, every time my doctor checks me, he says everything is pretty good.

This short series of questions takes only a few minutes to cover. From the answers given by our hypothetical patient, the only item remotely suggestive of psychological masquerade is the possibility of chronic lung disease. This and the fact that the man has never before been seriously depressed are two alerting clues.

No presumptive evidence has turned up. You have been watchful for signs of brain syndrome. There are none. The man is obviously aware of the time and where he is. The way he goes about telling his story shows he is alert. At one point you test his recent memory by giving him three objects to remember. After 5 minutes, he recalls them all. Throughout the interview you have looked for changes in consciousness and have seen nothing even remotely suspicious.

If his vital signs are noted in the chart, you might check to confirm they are normal. If during the interview you have heard anything that makes you suspicious of the man's denial of drug and alcohol use, you may want to pursue further questioning; or, better still, if his spouse is waiting outside, you may want to pose the question to her.

No further clues are detected. You are left with a middle-aged man whose life situation is compatible with depression, something he has never before experienced. He has mild bronchitis for which he takes no medication. Organic mental disorder is an unlikely possibility. Even so, if you are still concerned about the possibility of psychological masquerade, you might administer the three special construction tests. Let us assume that this is done and our hypothetical patient completes them, quickly and without error.

You conclude that the man's depressed mood is a psychological reaction, realizing that presumptive evidence for an organic mental disorder may still turn up later. The process of looking for psychological masquerade is never finished. An ongoing vigil is required. These misleading conditions have a way of popping up at the most unexpected times.

Consider a second hypothetical case. A woman, age 45, accompanied by her husband, is brought for psychological evaluation. The intake form lists "nervousness" as her chief complaint. The woman's husband immediately takes over the interview, relating how his wife has been hospitalized on two previous occasions for manic behavior. In each instance, she had been agitated, sleepless, and talking nonstop. As the husband talks, the woman appears anxious. You interrupt him politely, saying you would like to hear from his wife. But even with this prompting, the woman seems hesitant to talk. Finally, when she does, she has difficulty giving a coherent story. As you attempt to clarify the problem, she becomes frustrated and begins to cry. Her husband interrupts, insisting she be hospitalized immediately since she "obviously is having another manic attack." When you ask him to describe how this episode started, he appears perplexed, admitting it was quite different from her other attacks. "It came on so suddenly," he says. "Out of the blue, yesterday, she starts talking crazy. No going without sleep, no spending the limit on credit cards."

By this time, you have observed the patient for possible changes in consciousness and any abnormal body movements. There are none. The woman is oriented. There is no evidence that she is experiencing hallucinations or illusions. When you check her recent memory, she recalls three items but has to point to the third item, a book, appearing to have difficulty coming up with the right word. You ask her specifically about recent head injury, changes in headache, visual problems, chronic disease, and drug/alcohol use. Before she can answer, her husband breaks in and answers for her. Other than for infrequent drinking on weekends, she has had none of these.

You cannot quite put your finger on it, but something does not add up. You decide to administer the three special tests. The woman has no trouble reproducing the stated time on a printed clock face or copying the three-dimensional figure. She does, however, have difficulty writing the sentence you have given her. She leaves out a word and gives a strange spelling to a second word. As you are discussing this with her, you realize that she is having trouble understanding what you are saying. You check this out by having her name a few common objects in your office. She is unable to identify several of them.

This woman has a speech deficit, probably aphasic in nature. You now have presumptive evidence for an organic mental disorder. You tell the patient and her husband that her problem likely is something other than a manic episode. She needs further evaluation, which you can arrange for her the same afternoon.

In a case where presumptive evidence for psychological masquerade is uncovered, the clinician should not communicate his suspicion prematurely. Instead, the person should be told of the need for further assessment, and an appropriate referral should be arranged as soon as possible. Follow-up is important, first, to ensure that the evaluation actually takes place and, second, to ascertain invaluable educational feedback concerning the ultimate outcome.

SELF-TEST

Before proceeding to the next chapter, let us see how well you have absorbed the major clues to psychological masquerade. On the following pages are six case histories. Read them and identify any evidence for a diagnosis of organic mental disease; then turn the page and review the discussion that follows.

CASE HISTORY #1: SENDING A MESSAGE

A 25-year-old college student was escorted to the emergency room of a city hospital. The friend who accompanied him related how the man's wife, arriving at home after work, had found him acting strangely, stumbling about the apartment, alternately laughing and crying.

When examined, the patient mumbled incoherently and would not respond to direct questions. Periodically, he bent down close to the floor, as though he were trying to pick things up. Over the course of several hours, his condition fluctuated from passive withdrawal to combative agitation. His pupils were widely dilated.

Later, when the man's wife arrived at the hospital, she insisted that her husband had never before acted this way. He was not a drinker and did not use drugs. Upon further questioning, she acknowledged that she and her husband had been having serious marital problems over the past several weeks (Greiner, 1964).

DISCUSSION OF CASE HISTORY #1

Initially, the patient was diagnosed as having an acute schizophrenic reaction. But there was not much to support this diagnosis. The sudden onset of *staggering incoherence* along with *visual hallucinations* and an *alternating level of consciousness* provide compelling evidence for an organic mental disorder. This is a classic picture of rapid-onset brain syndrome. *Dilated pupils* suggest drug intoxication. Unfortunately, the patient's vital signs were not reported; most likely, there would have been striking elevations in pulse, blood pressure, and temperature.

Belatedly, the man's wife revealed a letter written by her husband the previous day. It was addressed to his parents and included the statement: "Whatever happens is not my wife's fault." She was instructed to go home and search for signs of drugs or medications that might have been ingested. At the bottom of a wastebasket she found a bottle containing a few remaining Sominex® (diphenhydramine) tablets. Based on this new information, the clinical diagnosis was changed to acute anticholinergic poisoning.

Within 24 hours the man fully recovered.

Condition: organic mental disorder secondary to drug ingestion ("anticholinergic psychosis").

CASE HISTORY #2: THROWING IN THE TOWEL

A 33-year-old woman, without any history of significant mental or physical illness, was referred to a psychiatrist for depression. She complained of loss of interest in her work and in her friends. She also described a painful obsession with her husband's possible infidelity— a concern that had some basis. This issue had led to many arguments and had grown more intense over the preceding few months.

She complained of feeling trapped in her role as a housewife. She was drinking more but apparently not to excess. She denied any other drug use. There was no evidence of disturbances in memory or orientation, and she was above average in intelligence. She denied any change in headache pattern. There were no deficits in speech, vision, or walking and no history of head injury or unexplained shifts in consciousness (Taylor, 1980).

DISCUSSION OF CASE HISTORY #2

The *emergence of psychiatric symptoms for the first time* in a 33-year-old woman raises the suspicion of an organic mental disorder, but this was not supported by other findings.

With the patient's permission, information from a close friend was obtained. It substantiated the woman's account of her problem. There was no evidence for alcoholism or heavy drug use. The woman's suspicions regarding her husband were realistic.

She entered psychotherapy and continued for 12 months. After a painful reappraisal of her marriage (in the absence of her husband, who would not consider couples therapy), she decided to seek a divorce. Subsequently, she trained in real estate and secured a license. Her depression resolved. After 2 years of living alone, she married a man whom she had dated for a year. She continued her real estate career with considerable success.

Condition: Psychological reaction secondary to marital conflict.

CASE HISTORY #3: OUT OF CONTROL

A 25-year-old man, out of control, was admitted to a hospital psychiatric service 1 week after Army summer camp. He was hearing voices and seeing things not visible to others. His wife described him as elated one moment and depressed the next. When he was unable to resume work, his family sought psychiatric help.

On observation, he smiled inappropriately and was unable to describe coherently what he was experiencing. He repeated himself. His behavior gradually grew unmanageable, and seclusion was required. He removed his clothes and assumed a series of bizarre postures, some of which were highly sexualized. After receiving an antipsychotic medication (chlorpromazine), he became calmer and his behavior seemed, for a time at least, less bizarre.

Further questioning of his family established that this behavior was quite uncharacteristic. Although the young man was described as "fuzzy" on occasion, his family portrayed him as generally predictable, stable, and hard-working. There was no history of mental illness.

A thorough mental status examination documented visual and auditory hallucinations with paranoid delusional thought and an agitated, anxious demeanor. Periodically, the young man appeared confused, and he was highly unpredictable. (Penn et al., 1972).

DISCUSSION OF CASE HISTORY #3

The admission diagnosis was acute schizophrenic reaction. This was changed to catatonic schizophrenia based on the episodes of fixed posturing, alternating with wild and violent outbursts. But on the third hospital day, the patient spiked a fever. Despite electroconvulsive treatments, he became progressively more violent. His condition deteriorated, and on the ninth hospital day, he died, presumably as the result of a "malignant" catatonic reaction.

At autopsy, however, definitive evidence of *viral encephalitis* was discovered. There had been a summer outbreak in the army camp area. Just prior to leaving, the patient had suffered a sudden episode of abdominal pain with body stiffness and a brief loss of consciousness. Medical evaluation at a nearby community hospital failed to turn up any basis for this attack. A follow-up visit was recommended but not pursued.

The *sudden onset* of uncharacteristic bizarre behavior with *no previous history*, combined with *visual hallucinations* and *confusion*, strongly indicated organicity. *Fever* on the third hospital day (information the reader did not have) provided additional presumptive evidence of psychological masquerade.

Condition: Organic mental disorder secondary to viral encephalitis.

CASE HISTORY #4: IT COULD NEVER HAPPEN TO ME

A married man, age 34, a plumber by occupation, was evaluated for bizarre personality changes. Throughout the interview, he sucked a red lollipop and described in a slow monotone how anxious and physically ill he felt. (At one point, he pulled out a bottle of methadone and started to drink it!) He told how, at age 29 he had first smoked heroin, and then, after the breakup of his first marriage, quickly progressed to intravenous drug use. He continued for the next 5 years (with the exception of 1 year of self-imposed abstinence).

Later in the interview, he expressed (incorrectly) the belief that someone was "watering down" his methadone and selling it for a profit. He also recounted seeing bugs in his bed at night and hearing a stranger's voice. On mental status examination, given five objects to recall, he remembered only three after 5 minutes.

For the preceding 8 months, the man had had a chronic sore throat and had lost approximately 45 pounds. (Thomas & Szabadi, 1987)

DISCUSSION OF CASE HISTORY #4

There are several clues to this psychological masquerade. A man in his middle thirties, with *no previous psychiatric history*, has an unexplained personality change. He complains of a *chronic sore throat with significant weight loss*. He has both *visual and auditory hallucinations*; on mental status examination, he can remember *only three of five objects*.

A medical evaluation added several important physical findings. White patches of discoloration were found in the man's throat, and he was coughing up thick green (obviously infected) sputum. There was a rash covering his arms and chest.

With a history of intravenous drug use (and its attendant risks from needle sharing), these physical findings pointed to the possibility of *acquired immunodeficiency*. Laboratory testing confirmed a depressed white blood cell count and the presence of antibodies to the HIV virus. Computed tomography scan demonstrated brain atrophy and dilated ventricles.

The patient was treated with an antifungal agent, along with methadone, chlorpromazine, and diazepam. At times he was confused, particularly at night. On one occasion he lost his way on the ward and could not find his own room. He was transferred to a local infectious disease hospital, but—within a few days—he left against medical advice. At home he became increasingly paranoid, threatening his mother and resisting all medical help out of a belief that his doctors were imposters. After being returned to the hospital against his will, he rapidly deteriorated from septicemia (blood infection) and died. An autopsy confirmed *Pneumocystis carinii infection* as the immediate cause of death.

(As we will discuss further on, many persons with AIDS eventually develop brain disease and the risk of psychological masquerade.)

Condition: Organic mental disorder secondary to brain infection from HIV or an opportunistic agent.

CASE HISTORY #5: HEAVY METAL

A 30-year-old woman grew apathetic and socially withdrawn. Her housework became an impossible burden; she just did not have enough energy. She let herself go, and her personal appearance suffered. She sat for hours with her eyes closed in front of the television set. Her appetite was poor, and she had trouble sleeping. At night she often paced about the house for hours.

Eight years earlier, she had been treated for a "hysterical reaction." Her recovery was excellent. She had no further problems until the onset of her present symptoms. There was no history of substance abuse or serious medical illness. Her only medication was an oral contraceptive.

She was readmitted to a psychiatric hospital. Unkempt and often drooling on herself, she walked with a stiff posture. Her facial expression was fixed. She walked slowly, in stooped fashion, and avoided eye contact with others. Questions asked of her were seldom answered. Her attempts at communication were limited to infrequent mumbling about hell and the voice of the devil. Her memory, however, was intact and she was fully oriented. Aside from a mild tremor in both hands, she had no other neurological abnormalities. (Chung, Suseela, & Borge, 1986).

DISCUSSION OF CASE HISTORY #5

This woman was diagnosed as having a "functional psychosis," and treated, first, with chlorpromazine and then with haloperidol. There was no improvement. In fact, on the fourth day of treatment, her symptoms escalated. Her delusional thought became more florid. Periodically, without provocation, she screamed. At times restraints were necessary. Her hand tremors worsened until she could no longer hold her own cup and required assistance to eat. A neurologist was consulted. He said she was having parkinsonian side effects to haloperidol. Her medication was stopped.

When still she failed to improve, a full-scale neurological evaluation was undertaken, which uncovered the true diagnosis. She had a major elevation in her urinary excretion of copper; on split-lamp eye examination, a Kaiser-Fleischer ring was found in her cornea. The diagnosis was Wilson's disease, a genetic condition that causes a destructive depositing of copper in body and brain tissue.

After being started on penicillamine (a drug that binds copper and facilitates its excretion from the body), her psychiatric symptoms showed a prompt and dramatic improvement, as did her hand tremors. She was discharged on her medication and a low-copper diet.

In this case the major clinical clues to psychological masquerade were her *abnormal body movements*. The rigid posture and stooped walking in a 30-year-old woman, combined with hand tremors, were significant neurological findings that should not have been overshadowed by her psychiatric symptoms. To anyone who was paying attention, they signaled the strong possibility of an organic mental disorder.

After 4 months, the woman was able to return to work. One year later, her husband said that she was in the best shape, both emotionally and physically, she had been in since they were married.

Condition: Organic mental disorder secondary to Wilson's disease.

CASE HISTORY #6: LOVE DELUSION

Almost overnight, a 15-year-old Indian girl's personality showed a dramatic change. She went from being a well-adjusted, capable student to a dependent, fearful recluse. Her personal hygiene suffered; she urinated and defecated on the floor. Her schoolwork showed a steep decline. Simultaneously, she started to hear "voices" calling her name.

Three months passed before her parents took her to a hospital. She was admitted to the psychiatric unit, where she was described as staring blankly into space and pacing aimlessly up and down the halls. At times she would smile or laugh loudly for no apparent reason. She often mumbled to herself, but on closer examination did not appear particularly disorganized. She was clearly delusional. Her delusional thoughts centered on a mysterious lover.

Eventually, as a result of her refusal to eat or drink, tube feeding was required. Treatment with an antipsychotic medication for almost a month produced no improvement. (Ang, Ko, & Tan, 1995)

DISCUSSION OF CASE #6

Additional laboratory studies showed a low serum calcium. Follow-up skull x-rays revealed bilateral calcifications in the basal ganglia area of the brain. A diagnosis of *idiopathic hypoparathyroidism* was made.

The psychiatric medications were stopped and calcium was started, leading to a gradual resolution of the patient's psychosis and personality changes. Later, she went on to have similar episodes. On each occasion, the symptoms reflected a significant calcium imbalance, despite ongoing treatment. Treatment entailed reestablishing a proper calcium balance.

Hypoparathyroidism is a disorder of the parathyroid glands: small, pea-sized structures residing in close proximity to the thyroid gland. Their main job is to regulate calcium metabolism. The most common cause of hypoparathyroidism is iatrogenic, an unintended consequence of thyroidectomy. (The parathyroid glands are small enough to be overlooked and removed surgically by mistake.) The cause of *idiopathic* hypoparathyroidism is unknown. Typically, the sufferer experiences tetany (involuntary muscle contractions), early-age cataracts, calcium deposits in the skin and brain, and sometimes unexplained seizures. As this case well illustrates, psychiatric symptoms may be the initial manifestation of this disorder.

A *first-time episode* of psychosis in a 15-year old girl should be presumed organic until proven otherwise. Similarly, an *abrupt change in personality* and a *dramatic decline in school performance*, while sometimes resulting from psychological trauma, are more likely manifestations of a medical disorder. No significant interpersonal problems were reported in this case.

Condition: Organic mental disorder secondary to hypocalcemia (hypoparathyroidism).

REFERENCES

Ang, A., Ko, S., & Tan, C. (1995). Calcium, magnesium, and psychotic symptoms in a girl with idiopathic hypoparathyroidism. *Psychosomatic Medicine, 57,* 299–302.

Chung, Y., Suseela, R., & Borge, C. (1986). Psychosis in Wilson's disease. *Psychosomatics, 27,* 65–66.

Greiner, T. (1964). A case of "psychosis" from drugs. *Texas State Journal of Medicine, 60,* 659–660.

Penn, H., Racy, J., Lapham, L., Mandel, M., & Sandt, J. (1972). Catatonic behavior, viral encephalopathy and death. *Archives of General Psychiatry, 27,* 758–761.

Taylor, R. (1980). Extracted from private clinical files.

Thomas, C., & Szabadi, E. (1987). Paranoid psychosis as the first presentation of a fulminating lethal case of AIDS. *British Journal of Psychiatry, 151,* 693–695.

---------------------------------- *Chapter 7* ----------------------------------

Four Masqueraders

And after all, what is a lie? 'Tis but the truth in masquerade.
—Lord Byron

Fortunately, many of the disorders with the greatest propensity for masquerading are uncommon. Not so, however, with the four masqueraders we are about to consider: brain tumors, epilepsy, endocrine disorders, and AIDS.

In their most subtle guises, these masqueradering medical conditions fool even the most astute clinical observer. More commonly, however, they exhibit certain telltale clues of organic disease. An active search for them is the clinician's best defense against being fooled.

BRAIN TUMORS

Brain tumors do not have to be malignant to prove fatal. Roughly one out of five brain tumors are benign meningiomas—tumors of the outer coverings of the brain (Waggoner, 1967). If discovered early enough, these tumors can be removed, but with delay in diagnosis, they may enlarge to where curative surgery becomes impossible without causing gross destruction of surrounding brain tissue. In these tragic cases, the question of whether or not the tumor is malignant becomes immaterial.

Brain tumors are either primary or secondary. Primary tumors arise from brain tissue itself while secondary tumors spread to the brain via "seeding" from other parts of the body. The emergence of unexplained mental symptoms in persons with past histories of cancer raises the possibility of a *secondary* brain tumor. This is particularly true of breast and lung cancers.

Symptoms from brain tumors are produced primarily in one of two ways. First, depending on the exact location, the expanding tumor may destroy brain tissue by invading, displacing, or compressing it within the closed space of the skull. In some instances, nerve tracts in the oncoming path of the tumor may be falsely stimulated. For example, if a tumor is located in the visual area of the brain, partial loss of vision or, more rarely, visual hallucinations may arise.

The second cause of symptoms is increased pressure in the fluid surrounding the brain (cerebrospinal fluid). Tumor growth in certain areas leads to a significant rise in intracranial pressure. Typically, this causes headache, vomiting, and blurred vision. (Although these three symptoms are considered classic manifestations of brain tumor, they are not always present. Of the three, headache is the most consistent.)

Although only one out of 1,000 headache sufferers has a brain tumor, approximately 60% of persons with brain tumors experience *headache* (Kaufman, 1990; Rushton, & Rooke, 1962). In 20% of cases, headache is the initial symptom (Gilroy & Meyer, 1973). The headache associated with brain tumor is highly variable in severity, but with increasing intracranial pressure, a recognizable pattern emerges. The pain is described as "pressure" or "throbbing" and is made worse by coughing, sneezing, straining, or exertion. Usually, the headache is most severe upon awakening. Sometimes it even awakens the person from sleep. Typically, the headache persists for several hours and then gradually diminishes, only to recur the following day. Over time, the headache tends to persist longer each day until it becomes continuous. Of course, other headache patterns should not be ignored, *particularly* when they are of recent onset and are experienced by the person as unlike previous headaches.

Another symptom highly suggestive of brain tumor is *seizure* (in the absence of an established history of epilepsy). Seizures may be *focal* (localized) or *generalized*. If they are focal, the clinical picture reflects the area of tumor growth. Accordingly, the person may have abrupt episodes of involuntary movement, shifts in consciousness, or perceptual distortions. In contrast, generalized seizures cause a sudden loss of consciousness with total body collapse, followed by spastic jerking of the arms and legs. The reader may be surprised to find (as shown by several cases in this book) that seizures are sometimes judged to be of minor consequence compared to the person's "psychological" symptomatology. This is a serious mistake, as is the writing off of seizure-like behavior as "hysterical" by anyone but a specialist in neurological diseases.

Excessive drowsiness is yet another symptom of brain tumor. It may be the cause of puzzling declines in school or job performance. With this drowsiness goes a reduced tolerance for alcohol and tranquilizing medication. Even small amounts may greatly accentuate the person's drowsiness.

Finally, elements of *brain syndrome* are present in a high proportion of persons with brain tumor. In one study of 326 cases, 77% of the patients had some cognitive deficit: 50% appeared confused and 39% were disoriented. Brain syndrome is particularly likely to occur when there is increased intracranial pressure.

Brain tumors located in areas involved with motor movement or sensory perception are readily recognized as neurological problems. With the possible exception of conversion reactions, these tumors are seldom mistaken for psychological reactions. Tumors of the frontal lobes are another matter.

Frontal Lobe Tumors

The frontal lobes include an area of the brain that is relatively "silent." This is not to say that nothing of neurological consequence is transacted there; it is, after all, that portion of the brain most involved in abstract thinking, judgment, and modulation of impulses. It is silent only in the sense that dysfunction is not reflected in obvious neurological problems such as paralysis or sensory anesthesia. The "prefontal cortex," anterior to the motor cortex, is the frontal lobe area most likely to be involved in psychological masquerades.

During the clinical course of frontal lobe tumors, 70% of patients have psychiatric symptoms (Soniat, 1951). One researcher, reporting on 56 cases, found that 46% of the patients initially received a psychiatric diagnosis. These mistaken diagnoses included depression (5 cases), presenile dementia (6 cases), schizophrenia (5 cases), anxiety state (2 cases), and inadequate personality (1 case) (Kanakaratnam & Direkze, 1976).

Two distinctive psychiatric syndromes have been described in frontal tumors. The more common one is characterized by depression, apathy, indifference, emotional flatness, reduced spontaneity, and sometimes diminished intellectual ability. These cases closely resemble psychological depression.

> A retirement-age government clerk was referred to a local emergency room by his physician with a note recommending that the man be admitted to the psychiatric service for treatment of severe depression.

A more extensive history revealed that for more than 3 years the man had complained of drowsiness. Additionally, for the past preceding months, he had experienced severe headaches and brief periods of memory loss and confusion. Allegedly, these symptoms had played a major role in his recent failure to obtain a job promotion.

In the emergency room, the man was irritable and uncooperative. A cursory neurological examination failed to turn up any abnormalities; but based on the history of confusion and memory loss, a brain scan was done. It showed a "space-occupying lesion."

At surgery, a right frontal lobe tumor (astrocytoma) was removed. The man recovered without complications. He was described later by his wife as being "his old self" again. (Carlson, 1977)

The second clinical syndrome seen with frontal lobe tumors is somewhat the opposite of the first. The person becomes euphoric and light-hearted. Often this devil-may-care, don't-give-a-damn attitude leads to antisocial or outright criminal behavior. Social and sexual inhibitions disappear, and the person's personal hygiene suffers. This pattern resembles the mania seen in bipolar disorder. In some instances the euphoria evolves into silly, childish behavior with a notable decline in good judgment.

The following case illustrates this "manic" presentation of a frontal lobe tumor.

After a brief observation period during which he was agitated, talking rapidly in nonstop fashion and compulsively naming objects, a 29-year-old veteran was admitted to a Veterans Administration hospital. When he was asked what troubled him, he replied: "Nothing sir, just ignorance; just gross ignorance around here." His response to a question about his occupation was: "I was a carpenter, like Jesus." He alternated between grandiose statements and expressions of persecution. Although he was fully oriented and had no memory deficit, his judgment was poor.

His medical records contained a 6-year history of seizures thought to be alcohol-related. These convulsive episodes were heralded by a peculiar feeling of strangeness, followed by loss of consciousness, collapse to the floor, and jerking of his arms and legs. Despite these seizures, he was sent overseas during World War II and, reportedly, suffered no further episodes over an 11-month period. Upon discharge he received a 50% service-connected disability for "neurosis." The seizures subsequently returned.

Three months prior to his admission, the man was treated in a psychiatric outpatient clinic for intractable anxiety. Gradually, his condition progressed to severe restlessness, agitated elation, and flights of ideas. On a leave of absence from work, he became hostile and belligerent at home. After going several days without sleep, he was unmanageable at home and required hospitalization.

Neurological studies, including an electroencephalogram and pneumoencephalogram, showed a frontal mass, which was confirmed at surgery. A "parasagittal meningioma" was removed from the right frontoparietal area. One month later, the man's mental condition was normal again. (Oppler, 1950)

This was a difficult case. The key was the history of long-standing seizures for which no explanation had been provided other than the possibility that they were related to drinking. In retrospect, the man's 6-year history of seizures reflected his slow-growing meningioma, the most common form of frontal lobe tumor.

The relatively silent nature of the frontal area makes it imperative that the clinician be familiar with those few neurological deficits that are likely to occur. These are best understood in light of the anatomical relationships of the frontal lobes. Along the medial aspects is situated a micturition center, crucial to bladder control. This is a common site for meningiomas and explains the frequent loss of bladder control associated with these tumors. Mental symptoms associated with unexplained incontinence should always be considered organic.

The major nerves and brain tracks involved in smell and sight maintain a close anatomical juxtaposition to the underside of the frontal lobes. For this reason, frontal tumors may produce changes in vision and, more rarely, smell. Connections also exist between the anterior frontal lobes and the motor cortex. When these connections are disrupted, deficits similar to those seen in Parkinson's disease appear: shortening of steps and a progressive loss of balance.

Although the precise mechanism is unknown, frontal lobe tumors can also trigger catatonic-like episodes.

At age 22, a woman began to have peculiar attacks during which she was unable to move or speak. Periodically, while eating, she would suddenly go into a daze, dropping whatever she was holding in her hands. She complained of vague sensations in her head as well as attacks of sleepiness. Her condition was considered "psychological." She was treated briefly by a hypnotist without any change. Within a short time, she began to hear strange voices muttering obscenities. She reported to the police that she was being victimized. Six months later, preoccupied with bodily sensations and constantly hallucinating, she was admitted to a psychiatric hospital. Her report read: "hallucinated in all senses, worried by visions of wild animals and indecent sexual activities."

On the unit she accused doctors and nurses of playing with her brain. She believed her eyes were "being made to work in Morse code." At times she became catatonic. Her diagnosis was schizophrenia.

Twelve years later, still in a psychiatric hospital, she claimed to be a lieutenant in the army as well as a psychologist at Cambridge, Horatio Bottomley's sweetheart, and heiress to the British throne. *After 17 years she was described as being impulsively violent. Her continuing somatic complaints were interpreted as delusional.*

Her doctors were so convinced that her mind was failing that they ignored her complaint of failing vision. "Still wildly deluded—she believes she cannot see her own image in the mirror," read one doctor's note.

After 26 years of institutionalization, a neurological examination revealed that the nerves conducting visual impulses from her eyes had completely deteriorated (optic atrophy). Even then (unbelievably) she was still presumed to be schizophrenic. Only after she started having generalized seizures was she transferred to a research hospital. Studies showed a large intracranial mass identified at surgery as a frontal lobe meningioma. By this time, it was inoperable. The woman died 2 days later, never having regained consciousness. (Hunter, Blackwood, &, Bull, 1968)

This case extended over 43 years! For virtually the entire period—despite such clues as sudden shifts in consciousness, muscle weakness, visual deterioration, attacks of drowsiness, and generalized seizures—the diagnosis of schizophrenia was doggedly maintained. This case illustrates the slow growth of meningiomas and shows how a false diagnosis blinds clinicians to what would otherwise be recognized as evidence of organicity.

Limbic System Tumors

The limbic system consists of a group of interrelated brain structures whose primary concern is individual and species survival. Primitive human drives, with their attendant emotions, arise in this ancient brain (MacLean, 1964). Tumors often manifest as dramatic behavioral-emotional aberrations such as rage attacks or bizarre sexual patterns. Since the limbic system is extremely compact, even small tumors can cause dramatic personality changes as well as disruptions in eating, drinking, and sleeping patterns.

A study of 18 cases of limbic tumor showed that all the patients initially had received an erroneous psychiatric diagnosis: schizophrenia (10 cases), depression (4 cases), severe neurosis (3 cases), and mania (1 case) (Malamud, 1967).

Taken together, tumors of the limbic and frontal areas cause psychological symptoms in 88% of cases (Skuster, Digre, & Corbett, 1992).

The following case illustrates a limbic tumor's capacity for masquerading as psychological sexual dysfunction.

A 36-year-old married man with sexual impotence was referred to a psychiatrist. He had been married for 13 years and had two children. His work history was exemplary, and he did not appear to be under any unusual stress.

Sixteen months prior to seeking treatment, he had noticed a decline in sexual interest. Five months later, he was unable to obtain an erection. He also started having brief episodes of anxiety—"feelings of dread" that persisted for 5 to 6 seconds and then disappeared. These episodes increased in intensity until they became full-fledged panic attacks. Sometimes an attack would be preceded by the "compulsion to stare" and by the conviction that everyone else was going through a similar experience. The man's wife noticed, during these attacks, that her husband's face blanched and that he stopped talking, even in midsentence.

A neurological evaluation identified a limbic tumor, which was removed surgically. The man's recovery was rapid and complete. He had no further episodes of panic, and his sexual interest and ability to perform returned to normal (Johnson, 1965).

Tumors outside the limbic area sometimes cause clinical presentations resembling limbic tumors. This condition is known as *paraneoplastic limbic encephalitis*. It is found most commonly in association with small-cell cancer of the lung but has also been reported in cancers of the breast, stomach, uterus, kidney, colon, thyroid, and testes. The condition does *not* reflect a direct invasion of malignant cells through metastases but rather an inflammatory process that for unknown reasons selectively targets the limbic area. Of 19 patients with this diagnosis, 10 were initially admitted to psychiatric hospitals and treated with psychotropic medications or electroconoulsive therapy. They exhibited a variety of psychiatric symptoms including personality changes, hallucinations, catatonia, and delirium (Skuster, Digre, & Corbett, 1992).

The medial aspects of the temporal lobes merge into the limbic system. Connections between the two areas of the brain are numerous. The temporal lobes have the highest incidence of tumors involving the limbic system directly or indirectly. Temporal lobe tumors may set off seizure activity, producing symptoms resembling temporal lobe epilepsy (complex partial seizures), a disorder taken up in the next section.

A 53-year-old man suffered the onset of "spells" during which he heard the sound of music and became profoundly depressed. After the spells began to occur with increasing frequency, he was committed to a state hospital, where he was diagnosed as having involutional depression.

Over the next 3 months, he grew lethargic and developed notable weakness in his left arm and leg. Eventually, he slipped into a coma and died. At autopsy, a large tumor of the right temporal lobe was found. (Malamud, 1967)

This man had no previous psychiatric history. His "involutional depression" was atypical in that he experienced it as short-lived episodes, and the musical hallucinations were not consistent with a depressed mood. These findings argued against a psychological depressive reaction.

Before proceeding to our next masquerader, perhaps a brief summary of what we have said about brain tumors would be worthwhile. Table 7.1 provides an overview. Any brain tumor can give rise to psychological symptoms, but they are more typical with tumors of the frontal, limbic, and temporal areas. I have emphasized the importance of headache, seizures, excessive drowsiness, and brain syndrome as clues to brain tumors. Slow-growing, benign meningiomas represent approximately 20% of all brain tumors. Their most common location is the frontal area, where they produce two distinctive patterns of mental and emotional changes: apathetic depression and antisocial mania. Encroachment on the "nonsilent" areas of the frontal lobes can lead to important clues, such as urinary incontinence, abnormal movement, deficits in vision and smell, disordered speech, and catatonic-like behavior. Finally, limbic system tumors characteristically cause powerful emotional and behavioral changes.

EPILEPSY

Epilepsy (seizure disorders) involves episodic brain dysfunction that manifests as attacks of motor, sensory, or perceptual disturbances or as altered consciousness. Seizures are aberrant electrical brainstorms. They can result from a variety of causes, including infection, tumors, brain damage, hypertension, hemorrhage, trauma, and drug withdrawal. In a majority of cases, the precise cause cannot be established. Such cases are referred to as *idiopathic epilepsy.*

The clinical manifestations of a seizure depend on its site of origin. The most common form is grand mal epilepsy. These seizures result from *global* brain discharges that involve the entire cerebral cortex, including, most dramatically, the motor area. During an initial aura,

TABLE 7.1 Brain Tumors—Suggestive Findings

General
  Headache
  Seizures
  Drowsiness
  Brain syndrome

Frontal lobes
  Two characteristic clinical patterns:
    Apathetic-depressive
    Antisocial-manic
  Loss of bladder control
  Shortening of walking steps
  Deficits in vision and smell
  Catatonic reactions

Limbic system
  Strong emotional discharges
  Disturbances in instinctual behavior: eating,
    drinking, sex, aggression
  "On-off" shifts in consciousness or perception
  Aphasia (left temporal lobe)

the person may feel strange or even sense that a seizure is coming on. Suddenly, the person cries out and loses consciousness. If standing, he or she likely will collapse and fall to the floor. The muscles of the body undergo a sustained spasm followed by a series of short jerking movements in the arms and legs that usually subside after a few minutes. In addition to the dramatic jerking movements, the person may drool, make biting movements, and lose bladder or bowel control. As the seizure subsides, the person appears flushed. The person remains unconscious throughout this entire sequence and retains no memory of what has transpired except possibly the aura. Since the individual is fully aware during the brief prelude to such an attack, it is often the last thing remembered.

Grand mal seizures are usually followed by a period of residual (postictal) confusion. During this twilight period, the person may act strangely. Occasionally, this phase is drawn out as a period of erratic behavior and incoherent speech, suggestive of schizophrenia. Suspiciousness and unprovoked aggression may also be part of the clinical picture, reflecting the person's fear and uncertainty. A study comparing 30 patients with postictal psychosis and 25 patients suffering from chronic psychosis identified several differentiating factors. The patients with postictal psychosis were far more likely to report "psychological" auras as well as feelings of mystic fusion of the body with the universe and thoughts of impending death. They were much less likely to report auditory hallucinations (Kanemoto, Kawesaki, & Kawai, 1996).

Although grand mal epilepsy can be mistaken for a psychiatric condition, especially immediately following a seizure, this possibility is much greater in cases of *complex partial seizure*, the official designation for what was formerly known as temporal lobe epilepsy or psychomotor seizures. This term was selected to emphasize the combined cognitive and behavioral (complex) aspects while at the same time noting its circumscribed nature (partial). Anatomically, these seizures arise in the limbic system, including its temporal lobe connections. Table 7.2 summarizes the factors suggestive of this disorder.

The temporal lobes are the largest brain area with a propensity for complex partial seizures. This area of the brain plays a pivotal role in perceptual integration. It is here that various kinds of sensory information are synthesized and interpreted; thus, it is not surprising that seizures in this part of the brain result in unusual and distorted perceptions, particularly during the aura phase. A wide range of perceptual aberrations is possible; however, in any given individual, the same distortion is typically repeated each time. The person may have an uncanny sense of familiarity about a first-time experience (déjà vu) or the opposite sensation of strangeness about something old and familiar (jamais vu).

TABLE 7.2 Complex Partial Seizures—Suggestive Findings

Temporal lobe epilepsy
  Unprovoked, episodic behavioral changes
  Trance-like appearance
  On-off shifts in consciousness or perception
  Stereotypical movements of the face and neck

Episodic dyscontrol
  Unprovoked spells of violence associated with an altered state of consiousness
  Precipitation by alcohol or minor tranquilizers

Powerful feelings of fear, loneliness, sadness, or anger can erupt. In other cases, perceptual distortions predominate. Objects seem far away and small—or the opposite, close at hand and gigantic. Sounds become extremely muted or very loud. Strange voices or musical sounds are sometimes heard. The person's body may feel hideously distorted. A sense of abdominal distress may grip the person. Foul smells are particularly common, often described as the smell of "rotting eggs" or "burning rubber." The aura or first phase of a temporal lobe seizure usually lasts only a matter of seconds and is immediately followed by an equally brief second phase during which the person goes blank. Often, this is manifest by a vacant stare. If the person has been talking, his speech may be abruptly interrupted. In other cases the person continues to "speak" but is incoherent and repetitive, making for a confusing clinical picture.

The third stage is the longest. It can persist for several minutes and, in exceptional cases, several hours. The primary manifestation is automaton-like behavior. Movements of the face and neck include lip smacking, teeth grinding, chewing, tongue sucking, and robotic-like turning motions of the neck from side to side. Such movements are the most definitive clinical signs of temporal lobe epilepsy, but they can be quite subtle. In rare cases, prolonged complicated behavior has occurred, such as driving an automobile or performing surgery.

The fourth and final stage is a gradual reentry transition, occurring over several minutes. The automatic activity recedes and consciousness returns. The person feels groggy and, other than the initial aura, has little memory for what has transpired.

More often than not clinicians are given a history of strange "spells" without any first-hand observation. It is the abrupt on-off behavior, uncharacteristic of the person and inappropriate to the situation, that must capture the clinician's attention if he or she is to recognize this unusual form of seizure disorder.

A single man in his early twenties was admitted for the thirtieth time to a psychiatric service. His various admissions, extending over a 5-year period, always involved the same hyperactive, frenzied behavior.

The patient was started on what had become routine treatment for his schizophrenic episodes: an injection of chlorpromazine and seclusion in a side room until the medication took effect. On this particular admission, due to a shortage of beds, the patient was admitted to a different ward. A physician unfamiliar with his case evaluated him.

The patient was observed "muttering, grunting, groaning, or humming" as he rolled and crawled on the floor. At times he made masturbatory movements and had strange expressions on his face, sucking, blowing, and grinning in a peculiar fashion. He scratched and scraped the walls, muttering over and over again: "Hare Krishna, Hare Krishna, Hare Krishna . . ." Within 3 hours, this strange behavior was gone.

As though awakening from a turbulent sleep, the patient rubbed his eyes and calmly asked for a cigarette. The psychiatrist could find no disturbances in thought, mood, or speech. The patient had only the faintest recollection of what had transpired over the past several hours. After he was removed from seclusion, he remained for 5 days on the psychiatric service without any recurrence of symptoms.

A thorough review of his hospital records (twelve volumes) turned up a variety of diagnoses, including acute schizophrenia, chronic undifferentiated schizophrenia, psychotic reaction, obsessive-compulsive personality, and, on his most recent previous admission, "hypomania in the context of chronic schizoaffective illness." The events leading up to each hospitalization were virtually identical. The man suddenly began to experience auditory hallucinations, after which he ran wildly down the street in the nude.

Despite this exhaustive review, the patient was again discharged without detection of his real problem. Ten days later, he was readmitted for similar symptoms and (based on the observations recorded during the previous admission) was moved to a long-term unit for more intensive diagnostic assessment. In a relatively short period, five additional episodes occurred. All attacks were ushered in by a period of withdrawn behavior, during which the patient expressed feelings of hopelessness and became increasingly less coherent. Invariably, the full-blown picture of bizarre behavior appeared within a short time.

Despite several evaluations, no seizure pattern was found on the patient's electroencephalogram (EEG); nevertheless, based on clinical observations, a diagnosis of complex partial seizures was made. Three subsequent seizures were quickly terminated with a rapidly acting antiepileptic agent (diazepam). During a 6-month follow-up period, the patient was successfully controlled on an antiepileptic medication (acetezolamide). (Adebimpe, 1977)

This case illustrates several key features of complex partial seizures. The dramatic contrast in the patient during the episode and afterwards—the on-off effect—should always get the clinician's attention. Acute psychiatric disruptions seldom have the "rerun" quality of seizures. In addition, they rarely ever resolve in the course of a few hours. In the foregoing case, the man went from being wildly psychotic to being normal within a 3-hour period. Even drug-related psychiatric disturbances usually require longer to resolve as the drug clears the system.

The four stages of complex partial seizures are not invariably present. They often blur together. Wide variations in clinical presentation occur. Virtually any of the characteristic symptoms can become the most prominent. Given the extensive connections between the temporal lobes and other parts of the limbic system, a variety of unusual clinical presentations are to be expected. Consider the following case.

> A woman called the police (for the second time in a week) after her neighbor's husband removed his clothes in his backyard and exposed his genitalia to her. The man was taken into custody. An investigation turned up a police report filed 4 months earlier, when the man was found standing motionless by the roadside, naked from the waist down. Under intensive questioning, his wife related that a year earlier, without any explanation, her husband had removed all his clothes in front of his children. He appeared confused, she said.
>
> A psychiatrist evaluated the man and diagnosed him as suffering from exhibitionism.
>
> But when it was discovered that at 17 years of age the man had been knocked unconscious for several minutes by a falling tree, further neurological evaluation was undertaken. An EEG revealed a wave-and-spike pattern over the left temporal area. The diagnosis was changed to temporal lobe epilepsy and the man was started on Dilantin (phenytoin). At follow-up after almost 2 years, he had experienced no further episodes of "exhibitionism." (Hooshmand & Brawley, 1959)

The most important clinical clue in this case was the patient's confused, trance-like states, followed closely by the history of his having lost consciousness for several minutes after receiving a severe blow to the head. Head trauma can cause scarring of brain tissue, with development of seizures years later.

Another form of epilepsy (presumably originating in the limbic system) presents as rage attacks. These episodes of violence last from a few seconds to hours. Often, the attack is completely unprovoked; in other instances, a minor provocation precipitates a vicious assault. The use of alcohol and minor tranquilizers greatly increases the likelihood of these violent seizures. These individuals often have extremely low tolerances for such drugs, so that even minimal usage brings on an attack.

This condition has been termed episodic dyscontrol (Bach-y-Rita, Lion, Climent, & Ervin, 1971). Persons suffering from it often have a history of childhood hyperactivity, arrest records of violence-related crimes, extensive traffic violations, and automobile accidents. The attacks are preceded by a trance-like state or aura, often consisting of visual hallucinations, body numbness, or a heightened awareness of sounds. Once the episode is over, the person complains of drowsiness or a headache and has no memory for what has transpired. The strongest evidence for the epileptic nature of episodic dyscontrol derives from good treatment responses to seizure medication.

In one study, after 2 months of treatment with Dilantin (phenytoin),an antiepileptic medication, 19 of 22 patients with episodic dyscontrol had at least a 75% reduction in the frequency and severity of their attacks (Maletzky, 1973). This is a particularly impressive finding given that these persons had previously received other forms of therapy without significant benefit. (On the other hand, this was not a controlled study.)

Repeated instances of unprovoked, violent outbursts, especially when associated with shifts in consciousness and intensified by alcohol or tranquilizers, suggest the possibility of episodic dyscontrol.

> A 23-year-old unemployed mechanic beat his wife with a metal candlestick, causing multiple lacerations and loss of consciousness. Afterward, the wife recalled how he "went into a blank stare" prior to attacking her.
>
> The same man shot his best friend. Abruptly, for no apparent reason, he grabbed the man's hunting rifle and shot him dead. This happened shortly after the two of them had consumed a couple of cans of beer. He was jailed but released on bond. Shortly afterwards, he hurled his daughter out of the window of a moving automobile. His comment was that she had "talked back" to him.
>
> This man had a history of childhood truancy and hyperactivity. Having quit school in his early teens, he was jailed on numerous occasions for assault and drunken driving. He was evaluated by a psychiatrist who, concluded that he had episodic dyscontrol. (Maletzky, 1973)

Consider a second example.

> A man referred himself for treatment, complaining of anxiety, intrusive thoughts of self-destruction, and, most disturbing of all, spells of violent behavior. He was 25 years old and unmarried. He had completed several years of college, having concentrated on electronics. At the time of referral, he was employed as an electrical technician, a job he found quite stressful. There was no history of psychiatric treatment. He denied using drugs.
>
> Several months before, while at work, he started having intrusive thoughts—vivid suicidal fantasies of himself with his throat slit, bleeding to death. At about the same time, as he drove home from work each day, he crossed a train track, at which point a visual image flashed into his mind of being hit and horribly crushed by an oncoming train.

He denied actual hallucinations or delusions, but his ability to concentrate had suffered considerably; at work, he was having frequent "staring" spells.

Several weeks after first seeking psychological help, he was traveling in a car with members of his family when his brother made a casual comment. Without any warning, the patient became terribly upset, shouting and threatening the others in the car. In a rage, he broke his own glasses. Before the car came to a complete stop, he jumped out, slamming the door on his grandmother's ankle. Other similar unprovoked episodes followed.

When questioned, the patient said he was unaware of what was going on while these incidents were actually happening. He had no memory of them. He described a "funny feeling" or "buzzing in his head" a few minutes before they occurred. After they were over, he felt drained, physically and emotionally. There were no instances of loss of consciousness or incontinence.

On examination he was alert, fully coherent, and oriented. An electroencephalogram EEG was ordered. During hyperventilation (a procedure performed to bring out EEG abnormalities), bursts of 6-second spike-and-wave complexes were detected. Sleep recordings showed 6 and 12 rhythmical sharp waves in the midtemporal areas.

Given the clinical history and EEG abnormalities, treatment was started with carbamazepine (Tegretol®), an antiepileptic medication. Ten months later, the EEG pattern was normal and the patient had experienced no further outbursts or staring spells. He was continued on medication indefinitely. (Stone, McDaniel, Hughes, & Hemman, 1986)

Despite such cases, the reader should understand that the relationship between violence and epilepsy is not well established. This is a controversial topic among neurobehavioral specialists. Violence and epilepsy need to be kept in perspective: the vast majority of persons who are violent do not have seizures; conversely, most persons with epilepsy are not violent.

ENDOCRINE DISORDERS

Hormones exert powerful emotional and behavioral effects. The slightest imbalances produce striking psychological and cognitive changes as well as alterations in physical appearance (Smith, Barrish, Correa, & Williams, 1972). In this section, we focus on three endocrine disorders that occur with considerable frequency: hypoglycemia, hyperthyroidism, and hypothyroidism. They serve as illustrative examples of the masquerading potential of endocrine disorders.

Hypoglycemia (Low Blood Sugar)

The simple sugar glucose is the nervous system's essential nutrient. Whereas other parts of the body readily utilize additional sources of energy, the nervous system relies exclusively on glucose. In order to ensure a continuous supply of "brain" energy, consumed foods are absorbed and stored in a form readily convertible into glucose when the need arises. Through this mechanism, wide fluctuations in blood glucose levels that could cause neurological havoc are avoided.

Low blood sugar (hypoglycemia) has a variety of causes. It develops if dietary intestinal absorption of glucose is deficient, if the pancreas supplies too much insulin, or if the liver—in its role as storage reservoir for glucose (as glycogen)—fails. Reduced blood sugar can also result from human error as when a person with diabetes mellitus takes too much insulin. In fact, insulin overdose is the single most common cause of hypoglycemia. Diabetics are at high risk.

Regardless of the cause, hypoglycemia elicits a powerful emergency response from the sympathetic nervous system. This automatic discharge, while raising blood sugar, produces a host of other changes, including nausea, sweating, tremulousness, increased heart rate and blood pressure, dilation of the pupils, and anxiety. If hypoglycemia persists, the sympathetic reaction eventually subsides, giving rise to more flagrant mental symptoms as a result of the brain's dwindling energy supply. The person can exhibit confusion, bizarre behavior, irrational fear, delusions, hallucinations, and, in the most serious cases, coma. These manifestations of hypoglycemia have misled even the finest clinicians. The emergency treatment is simple and immediately effective, but first the clinician must correctly identify the problem.

Cases of hypoglycemia provide some of the most dramatic recovery stories from hospital emergency rooms. The police bring in a dazed person found wandering the streets. In the absence of a reliable medical history, the clinician encounters an incoherent individual who appears "out of it." As the person is readied for admission to a psychiatric unit, blood is drawn for routine laboratory tests, after which an intravenous solution of glucose is given. This is a standard procedure adopted by most emergency-room physicians out of recognition of the tremendous masquerading potential of hypoglycemia. Within minutes—sometimes even seconds—the "crazy" person becomes sane. Calmly and coherently, the person inquires as to what is happening (since his or her memory for what has transpired is usually defective). He or she volunteers to be a diabetic; recently, the person has had trouble regulating his or her daily insulin. Obviously, given what transpired, he or she took too much.

Hypoglycemia also results from certain tumors that secrete *insulin-like substances*. A review of 91 cases of insulin-producing tumors showed that 40%, initially, had been misdiagnosed, half being mistaken for psychiatric problems (Laurent, Debry, & Floquet, 1971).

> A young man in his early twenties complained of weakness, especially in the morning upon awakening. On one occasion he actually fainted while shaving. Within 3 months, he was having episodes of confusion, after which he was unable to recall what had happened. His personality changed; he became withdrawn and negativistic.
>
> Finally, he was taken to a hospital, where he was thought to be having a schizophrenic break. Despite treatment, he became more unresponsive and withdrawn. One morning he could not be awakened. A stat blood glucose determination was done and found to be one-third of normal. After receiving a 50% glucose solution intravenously, he recovered fully within minutes.
>
> On physical examination, a mass was felt in the man's lower posterior abdomen. At surgery it was determined to be a retroperitoneal fibroma. This benign tumor was secreting an insulin-like substance that, in turn, was causing hypoglycemic episodes.
>
> Eighteen months later, the man reported no further problems. (Silvis, & Simon, 1956)

The next case is an unusual history. I have included it as an illustration of the unusual clinical presentations associated with this baffling disorder. It is an example of a condition known as "reactive hypoglycemia." For reasons not well understood, certain individuals are prone to hypoglycemia, particularly after increased alcohol use, extended periods of not eating, and meals high in sugar contents.

> Driving home from a nearby town, a woman was stopped by the local police. They were investigating a hit-and-run automobile accident and the resulting death of a cyclist. The woman said she recalled passing the scene of the accident, but seeing that help had arrived, she decided not to stop.
>
> She was a social worker by training, the wife of a practicing family physician, and well respected in the community—a "citizen of excellent character." She cooperated fully with the police, submitting to two breath-analyzer tests for alcohol (negative results). The police escorted her home, where they questioned her further. After more than an hour of extensive interrogation, the questioners could find no evidence of the woman's involvement in the fatality, despite her admission of being in the area where the accident occurred. Within a few days, however, the

situation changed, after damage to the woman's car was linked to the scene of the crime.

The woman had no history of psychiatric disease, but close friends and family members described "uncharacteristic behavior" over the preceding 3 years. She had difficulty completing her thoughts and at times was easily irritated. There were episodes of irrational suspiciousness during which she became angry and even threatening. A short time later, she would be her normal self again. It was as though these stormy episodes had never happened.

On occasion, she broke out in cold sweats and appeared tremulous, also complaining of nausea and exhaustion. The people around her thought that these episodes were related to her drinking. Although she admitted to the regular use of alcohol "as a sedative" before going to bed, she firmly denied drinking to excess.

During the days immediately preceding the accident, under considerable stress and preoccupied, she failed to eat properly. In fact, on the day of the accident, she had not eaten anything. When she left for the neighboring town, her family noticed that she was not quite herself, but no one felt she was incapable of driving.

An extensive medical examination was conducted. It included a 5-hour glucose tolerance test that showed profound rebound hypoglycemia (30 mg/100mL) 4 hours after the ingestion of a standard glucose meal. This finding led to a diagnosis of reactive hypoglycemia. The court accepted a plea of guilty, imposed a nominal fine, and disqualified the woman from driving because of her hypoglycemic disorder. (Bovill, 1973)

The clinician should not assume that hypoglycemia always causes dramatic behavioral changes. To the contrary, this condition is capable of producing much more subtle alterations such as irritability, nervousness, and inability to concentrate. In these more subdued guises, hypoglycemia is more likely to be overlooked as a psychological masquerade.

Hypothyroidism (Myxedema)

The thyroid gland is situated in the midline of the neck at the level of the Adam's apple. It comprises two lobes, one on either side of the windpipe, connected by a narrow bridge of tissue. Unless it is abnormally enlarged, the gland cannot be seen. In certain disorders it *is* enlarged, appearing as a prominent bulge in the neck. The major hormones regulating a person's metabolic rate come from the thyroid gland. Excessive amounts cause a "revving up" of the body; too little hormone results in a slowdown.

Hypothyroidism is a state of thyroid deficiency. Women develop it five times more often than men. The condition results from different diseases and, ironically, as a consequence of treatment for an overactive thyroid gland. Too much of the thyroid may be destroyed, leading to hypothyroidism years later. Regardless of the specific cause, hypothyroidism usually has a gradual onset. Physiological processes are depressed. It is as though the body's "pacemaker" had been set too low, so that the processes of life proceed too slowly. The heart rate drops; blood pressure is lowered. The gut becomes sluggish, causing constipation. Because less energy is expended, the person gains weight despite maintaining his or her usual food intake. Body temperature declines, leading to complaints of feeling cold when others are comfortable or even overly warm. The person has the a subjective sense of being slowed down. Fatigue is common. Women frequently experience changes in their menstrual periods. These symptoms often appear sequentially, making it easy to overlook their common origin.

Despite the numerous somatic changes, psychological symptoms can be the most prominent manifestations of hypothyroidism. The person feels "down," even outright depressed. His or her ability to concentrate and solve simple problems is compromised. At this stage, hypothyroidism is easily mistaken for depression.

> A 48-year-old housewife lost her energy. She became easily fatigued, listless, and irritable. Looking for an explanation, she blamed her symptoms on menopause, even though her menstrual periods remained unchanged. Finally, she made an appointment to see her doctor. He concluded she was depressed and started her on a tricyclic antidepressant. Her symptoms failed to improve.
>
> She then sought a second medical opinion. Upon hearing her story and observing certain physical changes (pale skin color and facial puffiness), the consulting doctor decided to evaluate her thyroid. The lab results confirmed hypothyroidism. The woman was started on thyroid hormone. Her symptoms disappeared. (Martin, 1979)

As hypothyroidism deepens, a person's physical appearance undergoes significant changes. The skin becomes dry and thickened, taking on a creamy hue. The hair grows brittle and dry and starts to shed. Facial puffiness develops, especially in the eyelids. The eyebrows thin; the outermost portions may even fall out. The person's voice deepens, becoming husky and raspy to the point that the person's speech becomes difficult to understand.

Psychological changes show a similar intensification and can reach psychotic proportions ("myxedema madness"). Paranoid delusions are common and can lead to "retaliatory" violence. The psychotic symptoms sometimes mask a notable decline in cognitive ability.

Following an outburst of rage during which he destroyed furniture and threatened his family, a middle-aged man was committed to a mental hospital. Eight years earlier, this previously healthy and highly proficient academic administrator complained of fatigue and a peculiar tingling sensation in his arms. At the time, a medical examination failed to turn up any specific problem.

Over the next several years, the man underwent several changes. He became sluggish of movement and his intellectual ability declined. He grew suspicious of people and eventually exhibited angry tantrums, during which he smashed things and on occasion, beat his wife. His outward appearance changed as his skin grew pale, dry, and excessively wrinkled. He gained weight and began to lose his hair.

When finally admitted to a hospital, he spoke in a deep, husky voice and exhibited blatant paranoid delusions. He was diagnosed as a case of severe hypothyroidism, and replacement thyroid hormone treatment was started. Ten weeks later, when he was discharged, he was described as being mentally intact. Within 6 months his weight and appearance had also returned to normal. He resumed his work in academic administration. Given the long delay in diagnosis and treatment, this case had an unusually satisfying outcome. (Olivarius & Roder, 1970)

Unfortunately, the screening tests for thyroid disease often fail to pick up marginal cases, known as "occult" hypothyroidism. In a study of 15 depressive patients (all women) unresponsive to antidepressant medication, researchers discovered that despite normal levels of the two main thyroid hormones (T3 and T4), one-third were hypothyroid based on their metabolic rates and TSH (thyroid stimulating hormone) levels. The women were all overweight. They complained of sluggishness, obsessive thoughts, and slowed thinking. Their depressions responded favorably to thyroid hormone treatment (Gewirtz et al., 1988).

A hearing-impaired, 65-year-old woman was convinced that strangers living in her attic were poisoning her food. Her family described her growing agitation and inability to sleep. She appeared to respond to auditory and visual hallucinations, but when treated with thiothixene (20 mg/day) she failed to improve.

After being hospitalized, she was described as disoriented, confused, and very sad. What little she said often concerned losses she had experienced in her life. Standard thyroid tests, including T3, T4, and free thyroxine, were within normal limits. Her TSH level, however, was markedly elevated. (TSH has an inverse relationship to thyroid functioning.) It was also determined that, 4 years earlier, thyroid hormone had been prescribed for the patient, but she had stopped taking it after a short time for no apparent reason.

Within a week, thyroid hormone treatment produced dramatic changes. The woman's mood improved and her delusional beliefs receded. Her discharge diagnosis was organic brain syndrome secondary to hypothyroidism. (Haggerty, Evans, & Prange, 1986)

One final point. Various lithium preparations (widely prescribed for affective disorders) can induce hypothyroidism, typically after prolonged use. In a study of 116 lithium-treated patients, hypothyroidism was detected in roughly 8%. The average duration of lithium therapy was 3.4 years (Yassa, Saunders, & Camille, 1988). Any person on lithium who begins to experience mental dullness, apathy, depression, sensitivity to cold, or unexplained weight gain should be checked for hypothyroidism. It is an iatrogenic condition easily misinterpreted as psychological depression.

Hyperthyroidism (Thyrotoxicosis or Graves' Disease)

Hyperthyroidism is the opposite of hypothyroidism. The body's metabolic rate is increased so that excessive caloric energy is continuously consumed. It is as though the body were readying itself for a stress or struggle that never materializes. The boiler room is working overtime.

Like hypothyroidism, however, hyperthyroidism occurs more often in women. It tends to develop during puberty and in middle life. Severe stress often precedes its onset. Heart rate, blood pressure, and temperature are elevated. The person is overly sensitive to heat and sweats excessively. There can be a fine tremor in the hands and a bulging appearance to the eyes. The person's skin is flushed and warm, in contrast to the cold, clammy skin of an anxious person. Despite a voracious appetite, weight loss is common. Insomnia is often a problem, which, in part, may be caused by heart palpitations and shortness of breath. Women undergo changes in their menstrual pattern and sometimes stop having a monthly menstrual flow altogether.

Cognitive changes vary from distractibility to paranoid delusions and symptoms of brain syndrome. Affective symptoms include anxiety, irritability, and an emotional fragility characterized by crying or laughing at the slightest provocation. Despite the appearance of nervous energy, the person complains of fatigue. The occurrence of "high-energy" fatigue should suggest the possibility of hyperthyroidism.

Along with hypoglycemia, pheochromocytoma, and hyperadrenalism, an overactive thyroid is one of the most frequent medical conditions misdiagnosed as primary anxiety disorder. (Hall & Hall, 1999).

> For no apparent reason, the wife of a resident physician started to feel extremely anxious. She felt tremulous and had difficulty sleeping. Much of the time she was exhausted. For no apparent reason, she began to sweat excessively.
>
> She discussed these changes with her husband, who interpreted them as signs of the stress of being a resident physician's wife. He started her on a minor tranquilizer for "anxiety." *Her symptoms failed to improve; in fact, she became more agitated and anxious and eventually obsessed with the thought that she was probably losing her mind.*
>
> Like a self-fulfilling prophecy, she was ultimately admitted to a psychiatric hospital. No significant "emotional conflicts" were identified, but she did have an unexplained increase in her heart rate, and she had lost weight. Laboratory studies confirmed hyperthyroidism. She was treated with radioactive iodine, after which her "anxiety" disappeared. (Martin, 1979)

Hyperthyroidism also is associated with manic behavior *without* euphoria. The person may be expansive and grandiose, but the "feeling-good" element of classic mania, is usually missing. (The more difficult distinction is between the agitated, angry version of mania and hyperthyroidism.)

In cases of prolonged hyperthyroidism, the clinical picture may eventually change to one of depression and apathy. It is as though the extended, hypermetabolic state eventually exhausts the body's reserves. This paradoxical presentation of hyperthyroidism has been described frequently in elderly persons and can be mistaken for depression or dementia.

Hyperthyroidism has been associated with a spectrum of psychiatric presentations, including anorexia nervosa, periodic catatonia, and rapid cycling bipolar disorder (Byerley, Black, & Grosser, 1983; Gjessing, 1974). A recent study of 13 untreated cases of hyperthyroidism confirmed this diversity. Of the total, 9 patients presented as major depression; 8 as generalized anxiety disorder; 4 as panic attacks; and 3 as hypomania; while 7 patients met the criteria for *both* major depression and generalized anxiety disorder. This same study reported no instances of psychotic symptoms. While there is no doubt that hyperthyroidism sometimes causes psychosis—schizophreniform and affective—this appears to be a relatively infrequent complication. (Trzepacz, McCue, Klein, Levey, & Greenhouse, 1988).

Being alert to major mood alterations in combination with the characteristic physical symptoms is the key to recognizing hyperthyroid masquerade.

Hormones have powerful effects on the brain as well as the body. When they are out of balance, mental and emotional dysfunction is to be anticipated. One study showed that endocrine disorders (especially thyroid), account for over 20% of psychological masquerades. (Hall, Popkin, DeVaul, Faillace, & Stickney, 1978).

Table 7.3 provides a concise summary of the major symptoms of the endocrine disorders discussed above.

AIDS

AIDS (acquired immunodeficiency syndrome) is the life-threatening disease that results from incapacitation of the body's immune system by the human immunodeficiency virus (HIV). When immunosuppression reaches a critical point, the person becomes susceptible to a host of opportunistic infections as well as cancers such as Kaposi's sarcoma.

HIV infection spreads through intimate sexual contact and blood exchanges, as occurs when needles are exchanged for intravenous drug abuse. In this country, gay men, intravenous drug users, prosti-

TABLE 7.3 Endocrine Disorders—Suggestive Findings

Hypoglycemia
   Episodes of sweating, nervousness, and nausea
   Unusual behavior after long periods without food, relieved by eating
   Unusual behavior a few hours after heavy intake of sugar
   Unusual behavior in a person with diabetes mellitus

Hypothyroidism
   Depression with weight gain, sensitivity to cold, and
      characteristic physical changes
   Previous history of treatment for hyperthyroidism
   Intellectual decline with characteristic physical changes

Hyperthyroidism
   Unexplained anxiety or manic behavior with warm, flushed skin
   Energized fatigue
   In older population, unexplained apathetic depression with
      intellectual decline

tutes, and persons who have intimate sexual contact with people in these groups are at highest risk for AIDS. No one, however, is invulnerable. It is not who you are but rather what you do that determines the risk.

Coming to grips with AIDS (and for others living with the ongoing threat), can generate powerful psychological reactions in the form of anxiety, panic, depression, and grief. Additionally, persons infected with HIV are susceptible to the development of organic mental disorder. It remains unclear exactly what percentage of persons exposed to HIV will come down with full blown AIDS, but for those who do, it is usually years after they have become infected. The initial symptoms include some or all of the following:

- Night sweats
- Unexplained weight loss and fatigue
- Fever
- Unusual infections, particularly of the mouth and respiratory tract
- Purplish skin blotches
- Persistent diarrhea

Initially, it was believed that HIV exclusively infected T-cell helper/inducer lymphocytes, thereby immobilizing the body's immunological defenses against potential pathogens. It is now clear that HIV does not limit itself to the immune system. Brain cells are also susceptible. In addition, many of the opportunistic organisms that attack the body under cover of immunosuppression infect the brain. Add to these potential causes of organic mental disorder the spread of tumors to the brain (particularly lymphomas), and it is clear why a majority of persons with AIDS have neuropsychiatric symptoms (Perry & Jacobson, 1986; Fenton, 1987).

The initial symptoms of AIDS commonly include cognitive and behavioral changes. In some cases such symptoms are the only manifestations (Bradford & Price, 1987). In the early stages they may be limited to poor concentration, mild memory problems, mental slowing, depression, and changes in personality, but brain syndrome is not an uncommon presentation. It can arise from infections of the coverings of the brain (meningitis) by *cryptococcus* or herpes simplex virus; or, from infections of the brain, itself, by syphilis, toxoplasmosis, or tuberculosis. The most common etiology is "subacute encephalitis" caused by HIV.

This condition has been called *AIDS dementia complex* (ADC). The clinical picture includes a mix of cognitive, motor, and affective disturbances. Early studies suggested that more than 50% of AIDS patients eventually develop the complication (Newton, 1995).When cognitive deficits have a rapid onset, delirium results, with confusion, disorientation, delusional thinking, and hallucinations. The more characteristic pattern is a slow, insidious onset over many months. Often, the first sign is difficulty concentrating. The person's thought processes become sluggish (bradyphrenia). What previously were routine matters now become confusing. Memory fails. Emotional responses are blunted until finally there is little reaction to events that earlier would have elicited strong emotions. The person's energy level drops. Apathy and withdrawal from social involvement are the predictable results. Sexual interest declines and may disappear altogether. At this point the person's condition can be mistaken for depression. In fact, depression is a likely part of this clinical picture, but it occurs in the context of a major disruption in cognitive functioning.

Along with these changes, the person loses coordination. Walking becomes slow and unstable. The handling of objects such as utensils in the kitchen is problematic. Involuntary movements, such as tremors, appear. Weight loss is common. In certain patients, this progressive decline will be intermittently punctuated by psychotic symptoms in the form of schizophreniform, paranoid, or manic reactions.

Given the seriousness of AIDS, psychological reactions are to be expected, but organic mental disorders are common. In persons at high risk for AIDS, psychiatric symptoms should suggest HIV infection or any one of its numerous secondary complications, such as lymphoma, cerebral toxoplasmosis, menigitis, and multifocal leukoencephalopathy.

> After 3 months of deepening depression, a homosexual man in his middle thirties was admitted to a hospital for psychiatric treatment. He had no previous psychiatric history.
>
> For some time, he had complained of fatigue and a loss of strength in his arms and legs, and he had lost a noticeable amount of weight. His previous medical history included hepatitis. One month before his admission, he had been treated for a yeast infection of his throat and esophagus.
>
> He had a low-grade fever and swollen lymph glands. Although he appeared emaciated, there were no neurological deficits. During his initial interview, he looked directly ahead with a blank, wide-eyed stare. His speech was slow, as were his body movements. Other than a reflex-like smile that infrequently crossed his face, he was without animation or spontaneity. He did not speak unless questioned and then gave only one- or two-word replies. His recent memory was intact, and there were no hallucinations or delusions. On three occasions, an electroencephalogram (EEG) failed to show any abnormalities. Computed

tomography (CT), however, revealed diffuse cortical atrophy and enlarged ventricles, indicative of serious brain pathology.

The patient remained in the hospital for 7 weeks, eventually becoming mute, profoundly confused, and disoriented. He was finally discharged to a convalescent hospital where (after 4 months) he died of pneumonia secondary to AIDS. (Hoffman, 1984)

Consider a second example of AIDS masquerading as a psychiatric disorder.

Suddenly, a young man in his early twenties became grandiose in his thinking and sleepless. His mind seemed to go nonstop; he would not finish one thought before going off on another. His personality was different. Previously easygoing, he was now easily irritated. He was preoccupied with sex and was given to concocting elaborate and unrealistic schemes. He spent money he did not have and eventually started hearing voices.

His condition became worse until he was finally hospitalized. Clinical observation confirmed the "hypomanic" symptoms; otherwise, he was fully alert, oriented, and capable of abstract problem solving. His physical examination and a battery of laboratory studies, including thyroid tests, were normal, as was his CT scan.

There was no previous psychiatric history and no family history of affective disorder. He admitted to drug use, but said it was restricted to occasional recreational use of cocaine and marijuana. He described himself as bisexual.

The patient improved dramatically on antipsychotic medication, but when the mood stabilizer lithium carbonate was added, he reacted with fever, sweating, and muscular rigidity, consistent with the clinical picture of neuroleptic malignant syndrome. All medications were stopped.

Within a few days, his agitated, psychotic condition reappeared. Various substitute treatments were employed, including amobarbital, lorazepam, and two courses of ECT, all without benefit. He remained hospitalized.

Four months later, tests showed evidence of immunosuppression (T4/T8 cell ratio inversion) not previously present. Within 2 weeks, the patient contracted *pneumocystis carinii* pneumonia along with purplish skin blotches. The pneumonia was successfully treated, but the patient remained physically debilitated, depressed, and cognitively compromised. (Gabel et al., 1986)

A review of 112 AIDS patients followed in a special AIDS clinic showed that over a period of 17 months, 9 patients (roughly 8%) experienced manic symptoms. (Lyketsos et al., 1993).

There is a final point to keep in mind. AIDS patients are exquisitely sensitive to psychotropic medications. (As in the above case, there has been a large number of reported cases of neuroleptic malignant syndrome in AIDS patients.) Overdosage is a common problem in the psychopharmacological management of psychosis, depression, and anxiety. In addition, because of the various infections and cancers that complicate these cases, patients often require treatment with neurotoxic medications. This provides yet another basis for the emergence of organic mental disorder.

The newer multimedication regimens for treating HIV have made what was virtually an incurable condition into a treatable one. This means fewer people dying of AIDS, but at the same time more people being subject on a continuing basis to the possibility of medication side effects, opportunistic infections, and the reemergence of the HIV virus, all of which carry considerable risk for psychological masquerade.

The capacity for masquerading is by no means limited to the medical disorders reviewed in this chapter. Hopefully, the discussions of brain tumors, epilepsy, endocrine disorders, and AIDS—in addition to providing specific information about these four masqueraders—broadens the reader's clinical perspective of psychological masquerade generally.

REFERENCES

Adebimpe, V. (1971). Complex partial seizures simulating schizophrenia. *Journal of the American Medical Association, 237*, 1339–1341.

Bach-y-Rita, G., Lion, J., Climent, C., & Ervin, F. (1971). Episodic dyscontrol: a study of 130 violent patients. *American Journal of Psychiatry, 127*, 49–54.

Bovill, D. (1973). A case of functional hypoglycemia—a medico-legal problem. *British Journal of Psychiatry, 123*, 353–358.

Bradford, N., & Price, R. (1987). The acquired immunodeficiency syndrome dementia complex as the presenting or sole manifestation of human immunodeficiency virus infection. *Archives of Neurology, 44*, 65–69.

Byerley, B., Black, D., & Grosser, B. (1983). Anorexia nervosa with hyperthyroidism: case report. *Journal of Clinical Psychiatry, 44*, 308–309.

Carlson, B. (1977). Frontal lobe lesions masquerading as psychiatric disturbances. *Canadian Psychiatric Association Journal, 22*, 315–318.

Fenton, T. (1987). AIDS-related psychiatric disorder. *British Journal of Psychiatry, 151,* 579–588.

Gabel, R., Barnard, N., Norko, M., & O'Connell, R. (1986). AIDS presenting as mania. *Comprehensive Psychiatry, 27,* 251–254.

Gewirtz, G., Malaspina, D., Hattere;, J., Feureisen, S., Klein, D., & Gorman, J. (1988). Occult thyroid dysfunction in patients with refractory depression. *American Journal of Psychiatry, 145,* 1012–1014.

Gilroy, J. & Meyer, J. (1973). *Medical neurology (3rd Ed.).* New York: Macmillan.

Haggerty, J., Evans, D., & Prange, A. (1986) Organic brain syndrome associated with marginal hypothyroidism. *American Journal of Psychiatry, 143,* 785–786.

Hall, C., & Hall, R. (1999), Anxiety and endocrine disease *Seminars in Clinical Neuropsychology, 4,* 72–83.

Hall, R., Popkin, M., Devaul, R., Faillace, L., & Stickney, S. (1978). Physical illness presenting as psychiatric illness. *Archives of General Psychiatry, 35,* 1315–1320.

Hoffman, R. (1984). Neuropsychiatric complications of AIDS. *Psychosomatics, 25,* 393–400.

Hooshmand, H., & Brawley, B. (1959). Temporal lobe seizures and exhibitionism. *Neurology, 19,* 1119–1124.

Hunter, R., Blackwood, W., & Bull, J. (1968). Three cases of frontal meningiomas presenting psychiatrically. *British Medical Journal, 3,* 9–16.

Johnson, J. (1965). Sexual impotence and the limbic system. *British Journal of Psychiatry, 106,* 300–303.

Kanakaratnam, G., & Direkze, M. (1976). Aspects of primary tumors of the frontal lobe. *British Journal of Clinical Practice, 30,* 220–221.

Kanemoto, K., Kawesaki, J., & Kawai, I. (1996). Postictal psychosis: a comparison with acute interictal and chronic psychosis. *Epilepsia, 37,* 552–556.

Kaufman, D. (1990). *Clinical neurology for psychiatrists* (3rd Ed; pp. 410–428). New York: W. B. Saunders.

Laurent, J., Debry, G., & Floguet, J. (1971). *Hypoglycemic tumors.* Amsterdam: Excerpta Medica.

Lyketsos, C. Henson, A., & Fishman, M. (1993). Manic syndrome early and late in the course of HIV. *American Journal of Psychiatry, 150,* 326–327.

MacLean, P. (1964). Man and his animal brains. *Modern Medicine, 3,* 95–106.

Malamud, N. (1967). Psychiatric disorder with intracranial tumors of the limbic system. *Archives of Neurology, 17,* 113–123.

Maletzky, B. (1973). The episodic dyscontrol syndrome. *Diseases of the Nervous System, 34,* 178–185.

Martin, J. (1979). Physical diseases manifesting as psychiatric disorders. In G. Usden & J. Lewis (Ed.), *Psychiatry in general medical practice.* (pp. 337–351). New York: McGraw-Hill.

Newton, H. (1995). Common neurologic complications of HIV-1 infection and AIDS. *American Family Physician, 51,* 387–398.

Olvarius, B., & Roder, E. (1970). Reversible psychosis and dementia in myxedema. *Acta Psychiatrica Scandinavia, 46,* 1–13.

Oppler, W. (1950). Manic psychosis in a case of parasagittal meningioma. *Archives of Neurology and Psychiatry, 64,* 417–430.

Perry, S., & Jacobson, P. (1986). Neuropsychiatric manifestations of AIDS—spectrum disorders. *Hospital and Community Psychiatry, 37,* 135–142.

Rushton, J., & Rooke, E. (1962). Brain tumor headache. *Headache, 2,* 147.

Silvis, R., & Simon, D. (1956). Marked hypoglycemia associated with nonpancreatic tumors. *New England Journal of Medicine, 254,* 14–17.

Skvster, D., Digre, K., & Corbett, J. (1992). Neurologic conditions presenting as psychiatric disorders. *Psychiatric Clinics of North America, 15,* 311–333.

Smith, C., Garish, J., Correa, J., & Williams, R. (1972). Psychiatric disturbances in endocrinologic disease. *Psychosomatic Medicine, 34,* 69–86.

Soniat, T. (1951). Psychiatric symptoms associated with intracranial neoplasm. *American Journal of Psychiatry, 106,* 19–22.

Stone, J., McDaniel, K., Hughes, J., & Herman, B. (1986). Episodic dyscontrol and paroxysmal EEG abnormalities: successful treatment with carbamazepine. *Biological Psychiatry, 21,* 208–212.

Trzepacz, P., McCue, M., Klein, I., Levey, G., & Greenhouse, J. (1988). A psychiatric and neuropsychological study of patients with untreated Graves' disease. *General Hospital Psychiatry, 10,* 49–55.

Waggoner, R. (1967). Brain syndromes associated with intracranial neoplasm. In A. Freedman, H. Kaplan (Eds.), *Comprehensive textbook of psychiatry* (pp. 786–791). Baltimore: The Williams & Wilkins.

Yassa, R., Saunders, C., & Camille, Y., (1988). Lithium-induced thyroid disorders: a prevalence study. *Journal of Clinical Psychiatry, 49,* 14–16.

Chapter 8

Drug-Induced Organic Mental Disorders

There are some remedies worse than the disease. —Publilius Syrus

Drugs (including medications) are the most common cause of organic mental disorders, thus the need for a special chapter devoted to drug-induced psychological masquerade. Under the designation "drugs," three categories are considered: psychiatric medications, general medications, and street drugs. The discussion is not comprehensive but rather a more selective review of those drugs with a special propensity for causing psychiatric symptoms. From the outset, however, this key point deserves emphasis: With *respect to psychological masquerade*, all *drugs are suspect.*

Despite the war on drugs, we remain a drug-using society. Our drug habit includes the use of alcohol, nicotine, and caffeine as well as street drugs, prescription medications, and over-the-counter preparations. All of these drugs can cause psychological masquerades. Information about personal drug use is not always volunteered. Even when people are assured that the information will be held in strict confidence, they underreport their use of drugs. A study of 225 persons entering a community mental health program found that 13% were covertly using hard drugs (opiates, cocaine, and amphetamines) without their therapists and doctors knowing. (Hall, Popkin, Stickney, & Gardner, 1978).

The failure to disclose drug use is not restricted to deceptions about illicit drugs. Sometimes a person does not consider what is being taken a drug. This is particularly common with over-the-counter medications and alternative medicines. Certain medications are not mentioned because the individual separates physical health concerns from psychological symptoms. For example, medicine taken for high blood pressure may not be mentioned because the person does not think that it is relevant to his or her depression. In other instances, the person may simply be unaware. For example, parents may have no idea that their child suffers from lead intoxication as the result of eating lead-based paint off the apartment walls. Similarly, an employee may unknowingly absorb an industrial or agricultural toxin as he or she goes about his or her work. An illicit drug user may report the use of marijuana, unaware that it has been laced with strychnine or phencylidine (PCP).

In addition to the pervasive and often hidden nature of drugs, clinicians should be sensitive to the untoward effects that drugs (including medications) sometimes exert on one another. One drug may increase or decrease the effect of another drug; or, when taken together, the two drugs may produce an entirely different reaction. As more and more potent drugs come to market, the risk of hazardous *drug-drug interactions* increases. In an era of polypharmacy (particularly among the elderly), drug interactions represent a growing cause of psychological masquerade.

PSYCHIATRIC MEDICATIONS

All psychiatric medications have side effects. Improvement in the target symptoms must not blind the clinician to the emergence of problems related to the medication itself.

Neuroleptics

Neuroleptics, also called antipsychotics or major tranquilizers, are used to treat psychotic symptoms. See Table 8.1. (The newer "atypical" neuroleptics are considered at the end of this section.) Although they are effective therapeutic agents, these medications cause numerous side effects. Parkinsonian symptoms (EPS) are among the most vexing reactions. This is particularly true of higher-potency neuroleptics such as haloperidol and prolixin. These distressing symptoms emerge over several hours to a few days. In its most severe form, a parkinsonian reaction is extremely uncomfortable and frightening. The person's neck twists to one side, as though pulled by an invisible force. Speech is garbled or absent. Due to the fear these *acute dystonic reactions* elicit in the affected person, these drug reactions are sometimes mistaken for hysterical behavior.

TABLE 8.1 Neuroleptics (Selected List)

High potency	Low potency	Atypical (new generation)
haloperidol (Haldol®)	thioridazine (Mellaril®)	olanzapine
fluphenazine (Prolixin®)	mesoridazine (Serentil®)	(Zyprexa®)
thiothixene (Navane®)	chlorpromazine (Thorazine®)	quetiapine
molindone (Moban®)		(Seroquel®)
loxapine (Loxitane®)		

After biting her tongue several times, an agitated, mentally retarded teenager was taken to an emergency room (ER). The cuts were sutured and the girl was sent back to her nursing home. Shortly afterwards, she bit her tongue almost completely through and required 50% surgical removal. An ER physician hastily interpreted this tongue-biting incident as a psychological reaction to the girl's dislike of the nursing home.

Several days later, a psychiatric consultation was requested. A review of the patient's record showed that 4 days earlier she had received prochlorperazine, 10 mg initially and then 5 mg three times a day for nausea and vomiting. The night before she returned to the emergency room, she complained of a painful and enlarged tongue. Although it was obvious that she was biting it, the staff (not understanding that this was caused by the medication) did nothing. (Meyers, 1988)

Especially in older persons, neuroleptics can cause brain syndrome. This risk increases when these medications are given in combination with anticholinergic drugs such as tricyclic antidepressants or antiparkinsonian agents.

A 23-year-old man had been treated for several years at a local mental health agency for psychotic and impulsive behavior. One evening he was brought involuntarily to a hospital, violently agitated and disoriented. His pupils were widely dilated, his pulse was 120 beats per minute, and his temperature was elevated. He appeared to see things that were not present.

Recently, the young man had been on multiple medications, including thioridazine and an antiparkinsonian medication. This combination suggested the possibility of anticholinergic toxicity. Emergency treatment with physostigmine (an anticholinergic "antidote") was started. The patient's psychotic behavior resolved, and his vital signs returned to normal. (Granacher & Baldessarini, 1975)

This case could have been mistaken for an acute flare-up of chronic psychosis. Fortunately, it was correctly identified and treated.

Anticholinergic side effects merit special comment. These troublesome symptoms are associated mainly with tricyclic antidepressants, low-potency neuroleptics (such as thioridazine and chlorpromazine) and antiparkinsonian medications. This latter group of medications plays a prominent role in psychiatry as "antidotes" to the parkinsonian side effects of neuroleptics. "Anticholinergics" are also found in over-the-counter medications. Diphenhydramine (Benadryl®) is the active ingredient in many sleeping preparations as well as in antiallergy and motion sickness medications.

Anticholinergics are additive in their effect. Less florid cases of toxicity cause mild disorientation, apathy, and drowsiness, while more severe reactions lead to delirious psychosis, often involving terrifying visual hallucinations. The person's pupils dilate and are unaffected by bright lights, which normally cause constriction. Due to partial paralysis of the small muscle controlling the thickness of the lens, vision is blurred. The skin flushes, especially about the face, probably as a result of the dilation of small blood vessels. Despite a notable increase in body temperature, the skin remains dry.

The combination of mental confusion, widely dilated pupils, and fever *without* sweating defines anticholinergic drug toxicity. The following rhyme summarizes this clinical picture.

> Mad as a hatter,
> Blind as a stone;
> Red as a lobster,
> Dry as a bone.

(In the nineteenth century, the art of hat making required exposure to highly neurotoxic mercurial compounds; consequently, going "mad" became a recognized occupational hazard of hatters.)

A 17-year-old man was forcibly taken to an emergency room. Delusional and disoriented to time and place, he appeared to be having both visual and auditory hallucinations. Unpredictably, he sometimes became combative. His pulse was 120 beats per minute and his pupils were dilated. His skin was flushed and warm. Despite a rectal temperature of 105°F, his skin was dry.

The following morning, the young man was lucid and calm. He explained that he had bought Asthmador® pipe tobacco at a local tobacco shop, returned home, and used it to brew a tea-like drink. After drinking one cup of this unusual brew, he "freaked out" and started hallucinating, believing that strange bugs were crawling on his body. (Shader & Greenblatt, 1971)

Designed for asthmatics, Asthmador® was a special pipe tobacco containing anticholinergic medication to reduce the irritating effect of pipe smoke. This man's unorthodox and ill-advised use of this product produced a classic case of anticholinergic psychosis.

High-potency neuroleptics, particularly in large doses, sometimes cause bizarre, rigid posturing that resembles catatonia. The person assumes fixed postures for extended periods, usually without speaking or acknowledging others. Even if the person is able to speak, his account of this strange experience may be misinterpreted as "crazy," resulting in treatment with even higher doses of the causative agent.

> Five years earlier, a 44-year-old woman had been hospitalized for severe obsessive-compulsive symptoms. After receiving more than 60 electroconvulsive treatments, she was moderately improved.
>
> Over the next several years, her obsessive-compulsive behavior escalated again until, finally, she was rehospitalized. She was treated with Haldol® (haloperidol), 20 mg daily. After discharge, she continued the medication, but her obsessive-compulsive symptoms returned and she developed a strange, robot-like appearance. She would stand motionless, drooling on herself. Eventually, she lost bowel and bladder control, necessitating the present hospitalization.
>
> When interviewed, she sat rigid and motionless, staring ahead with her mouth open. Her speech was labored and sparse, and she appeared to have difficulty moving her arms and legs. She assumed strange, unmoving postures for long periods. (Gelenberg & Mandel, 1977)

Haldol® was stopped, and the woman was started on amantadine, an antiparkinsonian drug. Within 3 days she was speaking in her normal voice; after a week, she was no longer rigid. Her posturing disappeared and her ability to initiate movements improved. Only her obsessive-compulsive symptoms remained. (Biochemically, she had suffered the opposite of anticholinergic excess—cholinergic toxicity.)

Akathisia, an excruciating feeling of restless agitation, is yet another frequent and bothersome consequence of neuroleptics. Its potential for masquerading is great, and it is the side effect that most often leads individuals to stop taking these medications This agitation leads to endless pacing, one of the few things that provides any relief. It can be mistaken for anxiety, leading to an increase in medication and a vicious cycle. The possibility of akathisia should always be considered when patients on neuroleptics become anxious, fidgety, or agitated.

Akathisia explains many episodes of "loss of control" in persons on neuroleptics. Regrettably, restraints and locked side rooms, are often employed inappropriately. You can imagine the frustration and anger felt by the person who is the target of this kind of clinical mistake.

> An on-call physician was paged for a "stat" order for antipsychotic medication. An earlier admission, an 18-year-old high school senior with previous psychiatric hospitalizations for schizophrenia, was "about to blow." He was described as showing "imminent assaultive potential."
>
> When the physician reached the unit, he found the young man pacing back and forth in front of the nurses' station, shouting that it had been a mistake to sign himself into the hospital. He said he couldn't stand "being cooped up" and "needed out right away."
>
> One week earlier he had received a long-acting, intramuscular neuroleptic (fluphenazine decanoate). Simultaneously, he was started on an antiparkinsonian drug, three times daily. On the day of his hospital admission, he had received another injection of the neuroleptic, but without any parkinsonian antidote. Even though the patient showed no obvious physical signs of parkinsonism (such as rigidity or tremor), the examining physician surmised that he was experiencing akathisia as a drug reaction to fluphenazine. Within half an hour of receiving the antiparkinsonian medication, the patient stopped pacing the floor and became much calmer. He went to bed and, within a short time, fell asleep. (Siris, 1985)

By blocking dopaminergic activity in the anterior pituitary, traditional neuroleptics increase prolactin secretion. This causes various "feminizing" effects (Gelenberg, 1999). Women may, commonly experience breast enlargement (gynecomastia), sometimes with lactation. When this occurs in combination with failure to menstruate, the uninformed female patient may erroneously assume that she is pregnant. Men, as a result of elevated prolactin levels, have difficulty getting an erection and ejaculating. They also may develop enlarged breasts. These effects are especially common in patients treated with lower-potency neuroleptics such as thioridazine (Mellaril®).

When taken for extended periods, traditional neuroleptics impose a significant risk for tardive dyskinesia, especially in older persons. Tardive dyskinesia (delayed abnormal movements) is characterized by purposeless jerking and twitching movements, usually most severe in the muscles of the tongue, face, and extremities. A person with moderate to severe tardive dyskinesia can also exhibit lip smacking, blowing of the cheeks, tongue protrusion and grinding movements of the chin and jaws. Less commonly, writhing of the arms and legs or the torso of the body occur. At a minimum, tardive dyskinesia causes embarrassing disfigurement; in rarer cases, it becomes disabling and even life-threatening.

After tardive dyskinesia appears, continued use of neuroleptics increases the chances of its becoming permanent. Oddly enough, tardive dyskinesia improves temporarily with higher doses of the causative neuroleptic. The best time to observe it is when the patient stops his or her medication or when the dosage is reduced.

The side effects of neuroleptics are so ubiquitous that there is a danger of viewing them as part of the clinical condition itself. This misperception unnecessarily condemns patients to the agony of troublesome side effects and, in the case of tardive dyskinesia, to an irreversible neurological disability. It is essential to distinguish it from the psychiatric disorder itself, so that, if at all possible, treatment can be discontinued or the medication switched to one of the newer atypical medications.

The newer atypical neuroleptics, such as Zyprexa® (olanzapine) and Seroquel® (quetiapine)—the newest generation of antipsychotics—have far fewer troublesome side effects. This is probably their greatest overall advantage. Gone, for the most part, are parkinsonian symptoms, and the risk of tardive dyskinesia is significantly reduced. But the "atypicals" are not free of complications. Significant weight gain occurs, and there may be severe drowsiness. They also are not completely free of the risk of the neurolepic malignant syndrome, the life-threatening reaction that masquerades as catatonia (Hason & Buckley, 1998).

Unfortunately, these newer medications are quite expensive and, will probably remain so for the foreseeable future. The older neuroleptics are going to be around for quite a while.

Antidepressants and Mood Stabilizers

Although psychotherapy retains an important place in treating depression, it has been displaced by antidepressant medications as the treatment of choice. There are three major classes of antidepressants: tricyclics, monoamine oxidase (MAO) inhibitors, and SSRIs (serotonin reuptake inhibitors) (See Table 8.2). On the horizon is a fourth class, known as NRIs (norepinephrine reuptake inhibitors).

The tricyclics are the oldest. These medications have potent anticholinergic actions and cause a variety of adverse effects, including dry mouth, dizziness (particularly upon standing), constipation, blurred vision, and drowsiness. Especially among the elderly, they can produce psychosis and brain syndrome. But the greatest problem

TABLE 8.2 Antidepressants

Tricyclics	MAO-Inhibitors	SSRIs
imipramine (Tofranil®)	isocarboxazide (Marplan®)	fluoxetine
amitriptyline (Elavil®)	pheneizine (Nardil®)	(Prozac®)
doxepin (Sinequan®)	tranylcypromine (Parnate®)	paroxetine
desipramine (Norpramin®)		(Paxil®)
		sertraline
		(Zoloft®)

with the tricyclics is their potential lethality. A relatively small over-dose (1200 to 1500 mg) can set off life-threatening cardiac arrhythmias. In the hands of a severely depressed patient, such medications become a tool for committing suicide.

MAO inhibitors, at least in this country, are infrequently prescribed. The reluctance is based on the risk of hypertensive crisis when certain foods (such as aged cheese, wine, beer, soy sauce, and others) are consumed. Still, they have an important role in the management of atypical depressions and in the treatment of those patients who fail to respond to other classes of antidepressants. They are *never* to be used in combination with the next group of medications, the SSRIs.

Over the past decade, the SSRIs have revolutionized the psychopharmacological approach to depression. They are superior in how well they are tolerated. They do not have significant anticholinergic side effects and they are relatively safe, even when taken in large overdoses; still, they are not without side effects. Some patients experience severe jitteriness (akathisia), easily misconstrued as anxiety. There are also reports of transient choreiform movements and dsytonia in persons treated with paroxetine (Paxil®) (Fox, Ebeid, & Vincenti, 1997). Additionally, sexual interest and sexual performance are sometimes compromised, especially after a patient has taken an SSRI for several months (Sussman, 1999). An "apathy syndrome" has been described, characterized by passivity and loss of motivation. This reaction appears to be dose-dependent and is reversible with a reduction in medication (Marangell, Yudofsky, & Silver, 1999).

In some cases, SSRIs are associated with what appears to be a withdrawal syndrome. After abruptly discontinuing their medication, patients have complained of difficulty concentrating, memory problems, increased emotionality, vertigo, light-headedness, and unsteadiness on their feet (Arya, 1996). Less commonly, "shock-like" sensations and impulsive and aggressive behavior have been reported (Haddad, 1997).

In recent years the practice of combining antidepressants has increased. When tricyclics and SSRIs (most) are used together, there is the possibility of significant elevations in tricyclic blood levels. This results from the SSRIs interfering with the normal breakdown pathway. In persons prone to cyclical mood swings, virtually any antidepressant medication can precipitate manic attacks. The addition of a mood stabilizing medication may be indicated.

So-called mood stabilizers are pharmacological mainstays in the treatment of bipolar disorder (See Table 8.3). In recent years, these agents have also been used as treatment for other problems such as explosive behavior. Lithium is the oldest of the mood stabilizers. This naturally occurring mineral has great efficacy in the treatment of acute manic attacks and is a preventive deterrent against future episodes. Unlike most other psychiatric medications, lithium requires close monitoring. As long as the blood level remains within a narrow therapeutic range, few troublesome effects are seen. When this range is exceeded, however, serious problems can arise.

Generally the first manifestation of lithium toxicity is nausea, vomiting, or diarrhea. The person appears physically sick. Unfortunately, these early warning symptoms are not always present. Instead, the clinician may find an unexplained deterioration in the patient's ability to think clearly, along with slurring of speech and tremulousness. It is essential, in these cases, to recognize the cause since the margin of safety between therapeutic and toxic levels of lithium is relatively small. One important drug interaction involving lithium is the toxicity-enhancing effect of certain diuretics commonly used for treating hypertension. Lithium rises to toxic levels in the relative absence of sodium and potassium, minerals that are depleted by certain diuretics. For this reason, combined treatment (lithium and diuretic) requires close medical monitoring.

Alternatives to lithium include several medications that, in addition to being mood stabilizers, are also antiseizure medications: carbamazepine, valproate, and most recently, gabapentin and lomotrigine. As with lithium, increased blood levels of these agents can cause confusion and aberrant behavior (gabapentin is the exception).

TABLE 8.3 Mood Stabilizers

lithium	(Lithobid®, Lithonate®)
valproate or valproic acid	(Depakote®, Depakene®)
carbamazepine	(Tegretol®)
gabapentin	(Neurontin®)
lamotrigine	(Lamictal®)

Minor Tranquilizers (Anxiolytics)

The most widely prescribed medications in the United States are the benzodiazepines (See Table 8.4). They are used primarily for the treatment of anxiety and insomnia. Although relatively safe (especially when compared to the medications they replaced, the barbiturates), these drugs pose their own problems.

Certain benzodiazepines are long-acting. They (or their active metabolites) remain in the body for extended periods. Thus, if the same dose is taken day after day, there is a gradual buildup. The individual becomes drowsy, slowed down, confused and even depressed. These symptoms are intensified by alcohol.

Rarely, individuals treated with the benzodiazepines experience a "paradoxical" reaction, characterized by agitation, psychosis or even rage. Mike Nichols, the famous theatrical and movie director, is reported to have suffered a "horrific episode" in reaction to Halcion® (triazolam), which was given to him to help him sleep after minor surgery. He became delusional, believing that all his money had been stolen in retribution for his having escaped the Holocaust (Applebome, 1999).

The most serious problem associated with antianxiety agents is their addiction potential. With extended use, these medications "wear out," thereby necessitating higher and higher doses. After prolonged, heavy use, the sudden cessation of the drug precipitates dramatic withdrawal reactions, characterized by agitation, delirium, and psychosis. Withdrawal can also be experienced by individuals who have been treated for panic attacks with high doses of short-acting benzodiazepines such as alprazolam (Xanax®). Attempts to reduce the medication bring on tremulousness and anxiety. Getting the individual off the medication can be a long and slow process. Later in this chapter, we will consider the clinical features of drug withdrawal in greater detail.

TABLE 8.4 Benzodiazepines (Selected List)

diazepam	(Valium®)
chlordiazepoxide	(Librium®)
triazolam	(Halcion®)
alprazolam	(Xanax®)
oxazepam	(Serax®)
lorazepam	(Ativan®)
clonazepam	(Klonopin)

GENERAL MEDICATIONS

Antihypertensives and Cardiac Medications

High blood pressure medications are widely prescribed. Some achieve their antihypertensive outcome by reducing the body's catecholamines. While advantageous in lowering blood pressure, the same action can cause depression. In fact, the first tranquilizer—rauwolfia—was accidentally identified when it was discovered that persons treated with it for hypertension often experienced a calming influence (an effect that with time, unfortunately, evolves into depression). Clonidine (Catapres®) is an example of an antihypertensive agent that works by reducing sympathetic tone. Predictably, patients taking this medication are at risk for becoming depressed.

Diuretics are also commonly used to treat hypertension. Because of their tendency to deplete potassium, prolonged use of certain diuretics causes depression and fatigue. This is a problem some bulimic patients run into after extensive use of diruetics in misguided attempts to keep their weight down.

Propranolol (Inderal®) and a host of other beta-adrenergic blocking drugs are used to treat hypertension, angina pectoris, and migraine. Depression is a troublesome unintended consequence, as is sexual impotence in men. Less frequently, visual hallucinations, catatonia, and brain syndrome result from high doses.

Anti-inflammatory Drugs

Steroids have magical effects on certain diseases, especially those involving chronic inflammation, such as rheumatoid arthritis and ulcerative colitis. Unfortunately, this potent anti-inflammatory action also causes severe physical and mental side effects. Manic behavior may erupt out of the general euphoria experienced by most individuals started on large doses of steroids.

Anabolic steroids are a special class of steroids used for their muscle-building effect. Their use is commonplace in the sports world, particularly in power sports, where brute strength is critical. (Although most of these drugs cannot be obtained legally without a prescription, they are readily available on a thriving black market.) "Stacking" is a practice involving several steroids used sequentially to achieve an optimal result. This pattern of use reduces the chances that these drugs will be detected through drug testing. There is little doubt that anabolic steroids increase muscle strength. Athletes who use them, while well aware of the strength-enhancing effect, usually, are far less knowledgeable about the risks involved. Long-term use of anabolic steroids can cause liver and heart damage and can precipitate striking changes in mood and thought (Pope & Katz, 1987).

Two Harvard researchers interviewed 41 body builders and football players who had taken anabolic steroids. Of these 13 reported manic-like symptoms, including hyperactivity, inflated self-esteem, and reckless behavior. One of them bought a $17,000 sports car. It was only when he stopped taking the drug that he realized he could not make the payments and was forced to sell the car. A year later, during a second manic episode, he impulsively made a similar purchase. A second athlete, while on anabolic steroids, became convinced of his own invincibility. To prove the point, he arranged for one of his friends to videotape him driving a car into a tree at 40 miles per hour! (Discover, 1988). In this same study, five athletes reported psychotic episodes. One experienced auditory hallucinations for 5 weeks; another developed paranoid delusions about his friends stealing from him. When he stopped taking the steroid, the psychotic symptoms disappeared.

Serious depression has been reported in persons coming off anabolic steroids. A 23-year-old body builder who had taken four different kinds of steroids, told his doctor that he could not stop because of the depression and fatigue he would experience without them. Sure enough, one week after giving up his steroids, he became so depressed that he resumed taking them (Los Angeles Times, 1988).

Miscellaneous Medications

"Stimulant" medications are prescribed for asthma and other chronic respiratory diseases, such as bronchitis; despite their questionable effectiveness, they continue to be used as diet pills. Similar preparations are sold over the counter. These stimulant drugs have some of the same effects as cocaine and methamphetamine. They can cause restlessness, irritability, insomnia and, with prolonged use, paranoia. (We consider stimulants at greater length in the section on street drugs.)

Phenytoin (Dilantin®) is an effective anticonvulsant. Its efficacy depends on maintenance of an optimal blood level; if this is exceeded, the result can be incoordination, mental dullness, and hallucinations. In addition, by interfering with the intestinal absorption of folic acid, phenytoin can produce brain syndrome.

The discovery of levodopa for the treatment of Parkinson's disease was a major breakthrough. A sizable percentage of patients respond well, but psychiatric symptoms are a common complication. In a group of 88 patients treated with levodopa, half experienced psychiatric symptoms over a year's time. Paranoid delusions occurred in 9% of the patients, and 3% exhibited brain syndrome (Klawans, Moskovitz, Navsieda, & Weiner, 1979). Levodopa treatment is also sometimes complicated by a strange "on-off" effect, where parkinsonian symptoms reoccur momentarily.

Since the introduction of levodopa, a large number of so-called dopamine agonists have come to market. Bromocriptine (Parlodel®) is an ergot derivative (as is lysergic acid diethylamide, or LSD) with potent dopamine-like effects. Bromocriptine is used to prevent lactation in mothers who have just given birth and to restore normal menses in 89 to 90% of women with hyperprolactinemia. The problem is that the drug has been known to cause delusions, visual hallucinations, hypersexuality, and manic behavior.

Cimetidine (Tagamet®) and ranitidine (Zantac®) are histamine (H_2 receptor) antagonists that reduce gastric acidity. These drugs have been welcome additions to the medical management of ulcers and esophageal reflux pain, but—in older persons particularly—they can cause depression, confusion, and visual hallucinations. There are also reports of impotence and loss of sexual interest.

The clinician should be alert to the adverse effects associated with two popular pain medications. Propoxyphene (Darvon®) is prescribed for headache and other minor pains. Chemically, it is related to the narcotic methadone and has caused addiction and severe withdrawal reactions after prolonged use. Certain people react to small doses with psychosis. A similar reaction has been seen in persons taking pentazocine (Talwin®).

The use of skin patches to deliver drugs *transdermally* is growing rapidly. With respect to the prevention of motion sickness, flat circular disks about the size of quarters are impregnated with scopolamine. This adhesive "patch" is placed behind a person's ear, where it provides sustained release of the drug targeted specifically at the inner ear. Theoretically, this minimizes unwanted side effects; unfortunately, it does not always work out that way.

Upon arriving at a holiday resort, a 77-year-old woman was unable to recall where she was. After a brief hospitalization, her mind cleared, but no cause for her memory lapse could be found.

She was discharged and resumed her vacation. At the end of 2 weeks, she returned home, where she once again became confused. As on the first occasion, she quickly recovered. This time a more detailed history identified the problem. The woman had used a transdermal scopolamine patch to prevent car sickness on her travels to and from the resort. The diagnosis was scopolamine (anticholinergic) delirium. (Rozzini et al., 1988)

Recombinant DNA technology holds out the promise of a new generation of natural drugs. For example, the *interferons* are a class of naturally occurring antiviral agents. Thanks to advances in biotechnology, they now can be produced in large quantities and used in the treatment of AIDS and chronic viral hepatitis. In one study of patients treated with interferon for hepatitis, roughly one out of five developed psychological changes, including irritability, depression, extreme emotional liability, paranoia, and confusion (Renault et al., 1987).

The fight against AIDS is generating a steady stream of new antiviral agents. Efavirenz (Sustiva®) is a recent addition. Some patients, particularly early in treatment, go through an untoward psychiatric reaction. Their cognitive abilities decline. Things seem unreal, and they may begin to hallucinate.

New birth control pills and delivery systems continue to come to market. These preparations involve powerful hormones that, in certain women, cause dramatic mental and emotional changes. Depression is the most common problem, but a wide range of symptoms is possible, including psychosis.

Alternative Medications

Alternative medicine is taking the country by storm. Drug and grocery stores are devoting increasing amounts of shelf space to vitamins, herbs, minerals, and other esoteric substances touted to have health and life-extending benefits. As with traditional medicines, alternative substances have their share of adverse effects.

> A 51-year-old man became overactive and couldn't sleep. His wife said that it was as if his personality had suddenly changed. He was more emotional and grandiose. After 4 months, the man required involuntary hospitalization for what by that time was described as delusions. There was no previous history of mania or depression. After a few weeks of combined treatment with haloperidol and divalproex, his symptoms completely disappeared. The psychosis apparently had been triggered by his taking of DHEA (dehydroepiandrosterone) in an attempt to increase his energy. The symptoms appeared within 2 weeks after he began this self-medication. (Psychiatry Drug Alerts, 1999)

DHEA is an adrenal steroid that is widely available as a dietary supplement. Apart from whatever else it does, it functions as an excitatory proserotonergic neuroregulator in the brain (Markowitz, Carson, & Jackson, 1999).

Derived from the bark of a tree, yohimbine, because of its action as an adrenoreceptor antagonist (alpha$_2$), has been used as a treatment for erectile dysfunction. It is also reported to have aphrodisiac properties. Unfortunately, in susceptible individuals, it can trigger panic attacks and mania (Wong, Smith, & Boon, 1998).

The most widely used herbal antidepressant bears the unlikely name of St. John's wort. Although it has minor MAO-inhibiting activity, this is not thought to account for its demonstrated effectiveness. This action, however, *in combination with an SSRI*, can produce a serotonin syndrome, with resulting delirium. (Recall that MAOIs are never to be given in combination with SSRIs.)

STREET DRUGS

The drug scene is a constantly evolving drama. Today's street favorites regularly give way to tomorrow's newer entries. Many street drugs are readily synthesized in backyard laboratories or even bathtubs. As there are no required quality controls in the illegal production of homemade psychoactive substances, the most recent batch may not be precisely the same as the one before it. There is also widespread adulteration of drugs after they are synthesized. The active drug is mixed with a lower-priced substance—or even completely replaced—to maximize profit margins. The effect on the unknowing user is unpredictable.

Given these confounding aspects of the world of street drugs, the clinician is well advised to supplement patient histories with careful clinical observation. Patients may not know what they have taken or, if even they do, they may not want to divulge this information. Physical manifestations of street drugs often provide the most compelling evidence for a drug-induced mental problem: changes in pupil size, deviations in vital signs, slurred speech, or motor incoordination. Street drugs can be divided roughly into three groups: stimulants ("uppers"), depressants ("downers"), and hallucinogens (See Table 8.5).

"Uppers" (stimulants), such as the amphetamines and cocaine, induce an energized euphoria with heightened activity, rapid speech, and feelings of superiority. Because stimulants trigger the sympathetic nervous system, the person's eyes are widely dilated and pulse

TABLE 8.5 Street Drugs (Selected List)

"Uppers"
    "Speed" (methamphetamine)
    "Bennies" (amphetamine)
    "Coke" or "Crack" (cocaine)

Hallucinogens
    LSD (lysergic acid diethylamide)
    PCP (phencyclidine)
    "Buttons" (psilocybin)

"Downers"
    "Barbs" or "Reds" (barbiturates)
    "Booze" (alcohol)
    "Crank" (heroin)

and blood pressure elevated. From a clinical perspective, an "upper trip" has the appearance of a manic episode, but the physiological changes are usually more prominent. If the drugs have been injected, track marks on the arms and legs may confirm the drug-related nature of the problem.

Prolonged use of stimulants makes a person increasingly suspicious. Eventually, a paranoid psychosis, virtually indistinguishable from paranoid schizophrenia, emerges. The cognitive deficits associated with brain syndrome, are typically *not* present. In fact, an unusual degree of mental clarity is preserved. Also, the physiological changes seen in acute stimulant intoxication are absent. Due to the appetite-suppressing quality of stimulants, extended use causes considerable weight loss. The emergence of paranoid delusions in a person who has been taking medication to lose weight should always suggest the possibility of stimulant psychosis.

> After 2 months of strange behavior, a 20-year-old woman was referred for psychiatric evaluation. She explained how upon first meeting people, she sensed she had met them previously. She was convinced that students at her college were playing tricks on her, such as turning back all the clocks. Her mother, she believed, was planning to poison her. The woman explained these troubling events as manifestations of a great struggle going on inside, involving the Holy Spirit, the Devil, and her own will. Each of these competing forces was expressed in a different language.
>
> During the interview, she appeared anxious. Although obviously delusional, she was fully oriented and coherent. She had no previous

history of psychiatric problems and was in excellent physical health. When questioned, she denied using street drugs, over-the-counter drugs, or prescribed medications. A diagnosis of acute paranoid schizophrenia was made. She was started on trifluoperazine (Stelazine®).

Three weeks later, after her mental aberrations had disappeared, she revealed to her therapist that she had lied. She had been taking "diet pills" for 3 months. Her revised diagnosis was "diet pill (stimulant) psychosis." (Hoffman, 1977)

After stimulant use is discontinued, severe depression sometimes sets in. Unless the clinician is alert to the possibility of post-stimulant depression, he or she runs the risk of engaging in a fruitless search for other precipitating events.

Once considered a relatively safe recreational drug, cocaine is now recognized as a dangerous and highly addictive substance. Because of its high cost, the use of cocaine was limited to the wealthier segments of the population until 1984, when a cheaper and more addicting version known as "crack" was introduced. Since then cocaine use has surged. More recently, methamphetamine appears to be on its way to becoming the stimulant of choice, largely because of the ease with which it can be manufactured.

Stimulant abuse causes a variety of physical symptoms, ranging from the relatively mild discomforts of itching and coughing to life-threatening seizures, strokes, and cardiovascular collapse secondary to heart attack or arrhythmia. The possible psychological masquerades are varied. The initial euphoria can evolve into hyperexcitability similar to that found in manic reactions, or it can take a different direction, resulting in anxiety and even panic attacks. As mentioned, with prolonged use, the person's growing suspiciousness becomes paranoid psychosis. Acute stimulant intoxication can cause brain syndrome, usually of the rapid-onset variety. Hallucinosis often manifests in the form of seeing and feeling bugs crawling on one's body. When a user's supply is disrupted or an attempt is made to get off the drug, depression threatens. Finally, because of stimulant craving, the person acts out sociopathy and criminal behavior as he or she struggles to keep up a habit that threatens to outstrip his or her financial resources.

After several days of hospitalization, a 27-year-old man, agitated and obsessed with his craving, left the hospital against medical advice. He had been admitted for treatment of paranoid psychosis. At the time of his admission, he was notably underweight. He had been on a string of serious cocaine binges that had left him penniless. In fact, he had financed his latest binge by selling his brother's car. His family considered this the last straw and disowned him. (Manschreck, 1988)

Hallucinogens

A number of street drugs are capable of creating perceptual distortions. Despite the name *hallucinogen*, not all of these effects are actually hallucinations. Illusionary phenomena, for example, constitute a major part of the hallucinogenic experience. Hallucinations are only one of several possible perceptual distortions involving vision, taste, touch, smell, and self-awareness (Taylor, Maurer, & Tinklinberg, 1970).

Synesthesia, where one sensory modality is perceived as another, is a common experience under the influence of hallucinogens. Music may sound like the taste of honey or the smell of lemon, or a strawberry may taste like the smell of vanilla or the sound of rain. Obviously, such experiences, when communicated to someone else (particularly a person who is not having the same experience and may not be aware that the speaker has taken a drug), can appear more psychotic than esthetic.

Hallucinogenic experience is affected by factors other than the drug itself. The setting, the prevailing mood, and the relationship with other participants add a potent context. Given the wrong mix, drug reactions can become extremely frightening, filled with panic and paranoia. In other instances, the individual may become immobilized and mute, leading the unsuspecting clinician to a premature impression of catatonic schizophrenia.

Flashbacks plague a small percentage of persons who have taken hallucinogens. The specific cause is unknown. Days, weeks, and sometimes even months or years after, a sudden fragmentary episode reminiscent of the actual drug experience erupts. Usually the flashback lasts no more than a few seconds before disappearing. The frequency is quite variable; but typically, over time, these episodes decrease. Unaware of their origin, an individual may become quite troubled and suspect that he or she is going mad, and the clinician, hearing a flashback described, may mistakenly think of it as a psychotic episode.

Because it is made easily and cheaply, phencyclidine (PCP) is a readily available hallucinogen. The drug is both a potent analgesic and an anesthetic agent that creates a kind of chemical sensory deprivation. Bizarre, "spaced-out" behavior with a predilection for unprovoked violence characterizes PCP bad trips. There may be long periods of a blank, dazed expression and frozen postures. When these patients do move, they are usually unsteady on their feet. There is a tendency not to speak; in fact, responses of any kind are reduced.

The symptoms of rapid-onset brain syndrome ROBS are often present and may include dramatic behavioral swings from catatonia to rage attacks. Unlike many other hallucinogens, PCP does not produce dilated pupils. It does cause, however, a characteristic up-and-down and side-to-side jerkiness of the eyes, known as *nystagmus*.

> The parents of a 14-year-old boy became concerned when he returned home from a friend's house acting peculiar. After talking nonstop for extended periods, he would suddenly stop and rush to another room, only to resume talking nonsense. His parents took him to the emergency room of a nearby hospital. His pupils were widely dilated and he had a low-grade fever with an increased heart rate. His mouth was extremely dry and he had no bowel sounds.
> After an overnight hospital stay, the teenager was his normal self again. He told his parents that he had eaten angel's trumpet seeds. (Holleman, 1998)

Angel's trumpet seeds are an increasingly popular hallucinogen. They are loaded with an anticholinergic alkaloid that causes cognitive deficits and perceptual distortions within minutes of ingestion. (Green, Patterson, & Warner, 1996)

"Downers"

Alcohol is the prototypical downer drug. Downers produce a loosening of inhibitions and an expansive sense of well-being. With large doses, the pleasant sensations give way to depression, decreased awareness, drowsiness, and loss of consciousness. Numerous downers are available, including benzodiazepines, barbiturates, and various opiate narcotics. The action of various downers is additive, probably accounting for a number of unintended, self-inflicted deaths.

Downer abuse is typically denied or minimized. Recognition requires an index of suspicion and careful observation. The intoxicated person may be unsteady and have slurred speech. It is important to keep in mind that downers are not used exclusively by the "drug culture." There is extensive use of these substances throughout the adult population.

Alcohol, the king of downers, is such a pervasive part of the social scene that it is often not even perceived as a drug. It is, in fact, the most extensively used drug in this country. The emotional and behavioral concomitants of chronic alcohol abuse—depression, anxiety, and suspiciousness—are frequently mistaken for psychological problems.

Telltale signs such as absenteeism, automobile accidents, and declining job or school performance are important indicators of alcoholism. Family problems and other personal conflicts often tend to obscure the real problem. They should be viewed as important problems that are *secondary* to alcoholism.

Alcoholics are not immune to other diseases; they have a high incidence of serious organic conditions, including subdural hematomas, hypoglycemia, liver disease, and several forms of cancer. Failure to suspect a serious medical problem masked by drunkenness is an all too common clinical mistake.

Alcohol potentiates many psychoactive drugs, including antidepressants, neuroleptics, minor tranquilizers, and other downers. In combination with these drugs, alcohol causes confusion, sedation, and sometimes death.

DRUG WITHDRAWAL

The body routinely develops a tolerance to downer drugs. With extended use, increasing amounts of the drug are needed to achieve the same effect. This is a defining characteristic of physically addicting substances. The time it takes to develop tolerance varies tremendously from one drug to another. Whereas, with heroin or morphine, tolerance ensues within days or weeks, alcohol tolerance occurs over years. The end result, however, is the same.

Tolerance makes a person susceptible to withdrawal reactions. When the drug is suddenly stopped, the adapted brain is no longer under its suppressing influence. "Overshoot" occurs. Drug withdrawal symptoms—mental and physical—are the result of this excessive neuronal activity.

Drug withdrawal occurs in four phases; but in any given case, various phases may blend together or even fail to appear.

Phase 1: Agitation

In the initial phase of withdrawal, the person looks ill. He or she is tremulous and anxious, on edge, and easily startled by noises or unexpected events. Sleep may be impossible. This triggers drug-seeking behavior. If more drug is obtained and taken, withdrawal may be aborted.

Phase 2: Physiological Changes

Physiological changes dominate the second phase. A hypermetabolic condition is reflected in raised blood pressure, heart rate, and temperature and in excessive sweating. (Similar changes also can indicate an infectious disease such as pneumonia, which is not an uncommon complication in drug-addicted persons.) Pupils are often widely dilated.

Phase 3: Perceptual and Cognitive

Although they usually appear after the earlier phases of withdrawal, perceptual distortions can be the initial manifestation. They usually begin with misperceptions of things in the immediate environment (illusions) and progress to hallucinations. Hallucinated voices are often insulting and accusatory. Visual hallucinations are commonplace. The standard objects of alcohol jokes—pink elephants and little green men—are actually "seen" sometimes by persons in the throes of delirium tremens. As a general rule, the more severe the withdrawal reaction, the more frightening the hallucinations. Snakes and spiders may appear on the walls, the ceiling, or the floor and the person may sense infestation by bugs that no one else can see.

As for cognitive functioning, symptoms of rapid-onset brain syndrome as well as paranoid delusions are commonplace in severe drug withdrawal except in cases of opiate addiction. With opiates, withdrawal is restricted mainly to flu-like symptoms and abdominal cramps and pain. There is little cognitive or perceptual distortion.

Phase 4: Seizures

Seizures represent the final phase of withdrawal. Appropriately treated cases seldom progress to seizures, but in untreated cases— particularly those involving "downers"—this complication is frequent and can be life-threatening.

> A disheveled man in his fifties was found lying in an alleyway, grasping at his chest and complaining of pain. He was taken by ambulance to the emergency room of a county hospital, where he was diagnosed as having suffered a severe heart attack.
>
> Over the next 2 days, the patient's chest pain subsided. He was cooperative and fully alert. He carried on normal conversations, denying any previous history of serious illness, trauma, or alcohol

consumption. But because he had smelled of alcohol on admission, his story was considered suspect.

By the end of the second day, the man became agitated and verbally abusive with hospital staff. This was in marked contrast to his previous friendly demeanor. That evening he was found standing in his bed, undaunted by the leads from the heart monitor and the intravenous line going into his arm. Sweating profusely, he shouted out commands as though he were the captain of a ship and the hospital were an oceangoing vessel. He addressed hospital staff as ship's personnel. His eyes shifted about as though he were responding to visual hallucinations, and he spoke to imaginary persons, using graphic expletives and dramatic gestures. His pulse rate, blood pressure, and temperature were all elevated.

For his safety, the man was subdued and restrained in bed. Despite aggressive treatment of his delirium tremens, his condition worsened over the next 24 hours with the onset of pneumonia. He died on the fifth hospital day.

It was assumed that the man had been an alcoholic. When, having been hospitalized, he was abruptly cut off from drinking, he had gone into alcohol withdrawal (delirium tremens, or DTs). This, in combination with pneumonia was the cause of death. (Taylor, 1980)

The clinical presentations of drug withdrawal are variable. A typical situation, much like that of the preceding case, involves a person brought in for treatment (or confined to jail) in response to inebriation. After the symptoms of intoxication subside, over the next 12 to 36 hours, the stage is set for withdrawal.

Clinicians sometimes dismiss the possibility of drug withdrawal if all the characteristic symptoms are not present or if it is clear that the person has not completely stopped using drugs or alcohol. This is a mistake. Drug withdrawal can manifest as a single symptom, such as hallucinations, and it can develop after a reduction in the amount of drug consumed. Abstinence is not essential to drug withdrawal.

The severity of withdrawal reactions depends on the particular substance and the amount and duration of use. It is a widely held misconception that withdrawal from opiate drugs (such as heroin) is the most serious form of drug withdrawal. The death rate from "cold turkey" heroin withdrawals is extremely low; in contrast, withdrawal from barbiturates carries a significant mortality rate, even higher than that associated with alcoholic delirium tremens. Because many addicts fail to fit the stereotypical image of the "drugger," withdrawal symptoms may go unrecognized.

Finally, the clinician should be familiar with a particularly baffling form of drug withdrawal. Usually, the case involves a person who has ingested pills as a suicide attempt or is acutely intoxicated. The person is admitted to a treatment facility "drunk." Unknown to the clinician, such a person may have an extensive history of substance abuse that may include mixed use of benzodiazepines, pain medications, and alcohol. As the immediate effects of the overdose or intoxication wear off, the clinical picture begins to shift radically. Because the patient no longer has access to his or her supply of drugs, withdrawal symptoms displace the initial signs of intoxication. This shifting clinical presentation can leave the unsuspecting clinician quite bewildered.

Drug use is pervasive if not epidemic. The clinician is well advised to maintain a heightened suspicion of drug-induced mental disorders.

REFERENCES

Applebome, P. (1999, April 25) Always asking, what is this really about? *The New York Times*, p. 13.

Arya, D. (1996). Withdrawal after discontinuation of paroxetine. *Australian and New Zealand Journal of Psychiatry, 30*, 702.

Ban, T. (1976). Drug interactions with psychoactive drugs. *Diseases of the Nervous System, 36*, 164–166.

Discover (Staff writer). (1988, September 8). Muscling in on madness. *Discover*, p. 8.

Fox, G., Ebeid, S., & Vincenti, G. (1997). Paroxetine-induced chorea. *British Journal of Psychiatry, 170*, 193–194.

Gabel, T. (1998). Herbal medications, nutraceuticals, and anxiety and depression. In L. Miller & W. Murray (Eds.), *Herbal medicininals, a clinician's guide* (pp. 205–235). New York: Pharmaceutical Products Press.

Gelenberg, A. (1999, September). Neuroleptics and elevated prolactin. *Biological Therapies in Psychiatry* (newsletter), *22*, 38.

Gelenberg, A., & Mandel, M. (1977). Catatonic reactions to high-potency neuroleptic drugs. *Archives of General Psychiatry, 34*, 947–950.

Granacher, R. & Baldessarini, R. (1975). Physostigmine. *Archives of General Psychiatry, 32*, 375–380.

Greene, G., Patterson, S., & Warner, E. (1996) Ingestion of angel's trumpet: an increasingly common source of toxicity. *Southern Medical Journal, 89*, 365–369.

Haddad, P. (1997). SSRI discontinuation syndrome. *Journal of Clinical Psychiatry, 58*, 17–22.

Hall, R., Popkin, M., Stickney, S., & Gardner, D. (1978). Covert outpatient drug abuse: incidence and therapist recognition. *Journal of Nervous and Mental Disease, 166*, 343–348.

Hasan, S. & Buckley, P. (1998). Novel antipsychotics and the neuroleptic malignant syndrome: a review and critique. *American Journal of Psychiatry, 155*, 1113–1116.

Hoffman, B. (1977). Diet pill psychosis (letter). *Canadian Medical Journal, 116*, 351–355.

Holleman, M. (1998). Herbal medicine and drug abuse. In: L. Miller & W. Murray (Eds.). *Herbal medicininals, a clinican's guide* (pp. 227–235). New York Pharmaceutical Products Press.

Juergens, S. & Morse, R. (1988). Alprazolam dependence in seven patients. *American Journal of Psychiatry, 145*, 625–627.

Klawans, H., Moskovitz, C., Navsieda, P., & Weiner, W. (1979). Levodopa-induced dopaminergic hypersensitivity in the pathogenesis of psychiatric and neurological disorders. *International Journal of Neurology, 13*, 225–236.

Kline, M. & Jaggers, E. (1999). Mania onset while using dehydroepiandrosterone (letter). *American Journal of Psychiatry, 156*, 971.

Los Angeles Times (Staff Writer). (1988, September 5). Steroid addiction reported, Part II. (3).

Manschreck T. (1988, August). Cocaine abuse, medical and psychopathologic effects. *Drug Therapy, 18*, 26.

Marangell, L., Yudofsky, S., & Silver, J. (1999). Psychopharmacology and electroconvulsive therapy. In R. Hales, S. Yudofsky, & J. Talbott, (Eds.), *American psychiatric association textbook of psychiatry* (Third Edition). (pp. 1025–1132). Washington D.C.: American Psychiatric Press.

Markowitz, J., Carson, W., & Jackson, C. (1999). Possible dihydroepiandrosterone-induced mania. *Biological Psychiatry, 45*, 238–240.

Meyers, B. (1988). Psychological misinterpretations in the diagnosis of acute dystonia. *Psychosomatics, 29*, 224–226.

Pope, H. & Katz, D. (1987). Bodybuilder's psychosis. *Lancet, 1*, 863.

Renault, P., Hoofnagle, J., Park, Y., Mullen, K., Peters, M., & Jones, B. (1987). Psychiatric complications of long-term interferon alpha therapy. *Archives of Internal Medicine, 147*, 1577–1580.

Rozzini, R., Inzoli, M., & Trabucchi, M. (1988). Delirium from transdermal scopolamine in an elderly woman. *Journal of the American Medical Association, 260*, 478.

Shader, R. & Greenblatt, D. (1971). Uses and toxicity of belladonna alkaloids in synthetic anticholinergics. *Seminars in Psychiatry, 3*, 449–476.

Siris, S. (1985). Three cases of akathisia and "acting out." *Journal of Clinical Psychiatry, 46*, 395–397.

Sussman, N. (1999). The role of antidepressants in sexual dysfunction. *Journal of Clinical Psychiatry (Monograph Series), 17*, 9–14.

Taylor, R. (1980). Extracted from private clinical files.

Taylor, R., Maurer, J., & Tinklinberg, J. (1970). Management of "bad trips" in an evolving drug scene. *Journal of the American Medical Association, 213*, 422–425.

Wong, A., Smith, M., & Boon, H. (1998). Herbal remedies in psychiatric practice. *Archives of General Psychiatry, 55*, 1033–2044.

---- Chapter 9 ----

Somatization:
The Other Side of Things

Judge not according to appearance. —St. John

The focus of this chapter is somatization: the translation of psycho-logical conflicts into somatic symptoms. Since somatization presents clinically as "physical" symptoms, psychological masquerade would seem an unlikely concern. The problem arises because of the ten-dency to apply terms such as *psychosomatic* and *hysterical* prema-turely to bona fide medical disorders. In this age of psychological sophistication, the "psychologizing" of somatic symptoms can be overdone.

The critical first step in assessing "psychosomatic" cases is to con-firm that a medical evaluation has been done. The second involves looking for characteristic findings. If these are absent, the diagnosis of somatization should remain suspect. This chapter reviews the charac-teristic findings in three versions of somatization: simple somatiza-tion, somatization disorder (hysteria or Briquet's syndrome), and conversion disorder.

SIMPLE SOMATIZATION

From time to time most of us experience somatic symptoms without any demonstrable organic basis. Studies have shown that during any given week, as many as 60 to 80% of healthy individuals report vague somatic complaints (Kellner, 1987). The various demands of day-to-day living have a way (not clearly understood) of being expressed in somatic language. Perhaps it is merely a matter of stress making people more aware of minor aches and pains that otherwise might be ignored; or, perhaps, stress causes greater muscle tension, with resulting soreness and discomfort. Whatever the reason, many people who seek medical help suffer from somatization whose origins are psychosocial.

The basic guideline for evaluating somatic complaints is this: Well-defined somatic symptoms of increasing severity and more than a few days duration always deserve medical evaluation. The same is true of vague somatic symptoms if they persist and fail to conform to the patterns reviewed in this chapter.

There are four essential characteristics of simple somatization. First, there is no obvious organic basis. Second, the somatic complaints occur in a stressful context: a work or school problem, marital difficulty, a personal loss, or a major life transition. Often, when the stressful situation is identified and openly discussed, the symptoms quickly improve.

Temporariness is the third characteristic. The long-standing doctor joke "Take two aspirin and call me in the morning" captures an important principle that healers have taken advantage of for centuries: given time, the body heals itself psychologically as well as physically. Even if the stressful situation persists, the severity of simple somatization complaints often diminishes.

Finally, somatization complaints are more often than not, vague in nature. Even if encouraged to be more specific, the patient has difficulty pinpointing his or her complaints. When a person describes somatic symptoms in detail, simple somatization is not the most likely explanation.

In summary, if somatic symptoms occur in the absence of identifiable stress, if they persist, or if they are described in great detail, organic disease should be considered. (Also, if the person has a history of a medical disorder that caused similar symptoms, a recurrence must be ruled out.)

One word of caution: What appears at first to be a vague complaint often proves, with slight elaboration by the clinician, to be well defined. Take fatigue. This symptom may prompt clinicians to jump to a premature conclusion: "Fatigued? Yes. Well, how long have you been *depressed?*"

Fatigue does not always imply depression. When a patient complains of fatigue, he or she should be encouraged to elaborate.

CLINICIAN: What do you mean by the word *fatigued?*
PATIENT: I don't have any energy.

CLINICIAN: Say more.

PATIENT: At my job, I can't carry the heavy containers . . . mainly it's my left arm. Guess I'm just getting old.

In the course of this short hypothetical exchange, the initial, vague complaint of "feeling fatigued" has become weakness in the left arm, a very specific physical symptom and an unlikely expression of simple somatization.

Consider a second symptom.

PATIENT: I'm not my old self. I'm just not well.

CLINCIAN: Not well?

PATIENT: Yeah, I hardly ever get out of the house.

CLINICIAN: Why not?

PATIENT: I can't walk more than a few steps without getting out of breath. At home, I can't make it up the stairs without being winded.

What initially is described as unwellness becomes, with brief clarification, shortness of breath. Breathlessness is seen in various heart and lung conditions. It deserves a complete medical evaluation.

Organic diseases that cause people to feel apathetic, fatigued, or weak are at high risk for being characterized erroneously as "psychosomatic." Anemia is a good example. This is a common medical problem, especially among women. The most frequent cause is iron deficiency, often related to a cumulative loss of iron from menstrual periods. Other conditions, such as ulcers, hemorrhoids, and certain internal cancers can also lead to chronic blood loss and anemia. Regardless of the precise etiology, anemia can cause pallor, fatigue, lassitude, and breathlessness. Diagnostic mistakes arise when such symptoms are misconstrued as expressions of depression.

Hyperparathyroidism causes scattered complaints. The parathyroid glands (small, peashaped nodules located in the neck adjacent to the thyroid gland) play a central role in the body's regulation of calcium. In hyperparathyroidism, an excessive amount of parathyroid hormone is released, causing high concentrations of calcium in the blood and urine. The calcium precipitates in the kidneys as "stones" that produce shifting abdominal and back pain as they pass from the body. In addition, complaints of generalized aches and pains arise as calcium is rapidly mobilized from the bones. Approximately 25% of patients with hyperparathyroidism develop peptic ulcer, providing yet another source of somatic complaints. With the combined symptoms of muscle weakness, lethargy, and depression, a "psychosomatic" diagnosis may become irresistible.

Apathetic, depressed and losing strength, a 68-year-old widow explained her deteriorating condition as the product of loneliness. For 4 years, she had suffered from vague, intermittent upper-abdominal discomfort. After an evaluation by her internist, the woman was referred to a consulting psychiatrist who diagnosed her as moderately depressed.

During the course of further medical evaluation, however, a duodenal ulcer was detected. Follow-up blood studies showed an elevated serum calcium level, leading to a diagnosis of hyperparathyrcidism. At surgery a parathyroid adenoma (benign tumor) was removed. The woman recovered without complication and experienced prompt healing of her ulcer. Her symptoms of lethargy, weakness, and depression resolved without additional therapy. (Martin, 1979)

This case illustrates the importance of distinguishing muscle weakness from complaints of lethargy, apathy, or fatigue. Until proven otherwise, actual muscle weakness is a neurological problem.

When "psychological" symptoms dominate a case, there is a tendency to ignore somatic complaints, especially if they are somewhat vague. This is an unsound practice. The syndrome of hyperventilation provides an excellent example. It may start out as anxiety, but, as the anxious feelings build, the person starts to overbreathe and symptoms result from the blowing off of excessive carbon dioxide. The person becomes light-headed and experiences numbness and tingling around the mouth and in the fingers and toes. In more severe cases, chest pain and twisting muscle spasms of the wrists and ankles develop. (On rare occasions, the person may even hallucinate.) Understandably, such symptoms contribute to a vicious cycle of escalating anxiety.

When the full spectrum of symptoms is present, the organic nature of hyperventilation is easily recognized. In more typical cases, however, the clinician encounters an anxious person who gives a plausible reason for being upset. The somatic symptoms may be dismissed as part of the person's anxiety. It is important to recognize that once a person overbreathes to the extent of becoming symptomatic, continuous rapid or deep breathing is no longer necessary to sustain the chemical imbalance. A few sighing breaths every so often will do the trick.

Accompanied by her boyfriend, a 22-year-old woman sought emergency medical help for what she thought was a heart attack. Frightened and anxious, she complained of shortness of breath and chest pain. She also described a tingling sensation around her mouth and a feeling of light-headedness. The symptoms had come on soon after she discovered that her boyfriend had been with another woman. (Dubousky & Weissberg, 1978)

If a person is hyperventilating, symptom relief comes from reduced breathing. The patient should be encouraged to relax and breathe more slowly. Sometimes the person is too anxious to follow this direction. If so, he or she can be instructed to breathe in and out of a paper bag for a few minutes. This time-honored technique ensures the rebreathing of carbon dioxide; and, in most cases, it produces quick a and dramatic improvement.

Hyperventilation should be considered in all cases of acute anxiety. It is often a manifestation of an underlying medical condition. In a study of 30 patients with hyperventilation symptoms, 7 were found to have associated organic disorders (Pincus & Tucker, 1974). This possibility should go to the top of the suspect list if hyperventilation fails to respond to simple measures.

Hyperventilation can also be caused by panic attacks. The person suddenly becomes extremely anxious for no apparent reason. It is not uncommon for patients to go to emergency rooms out of fear they are having a heart attack. Some are convincing enough to be subjected to invasive cardiac testing. One study of 33 cardiac catheterization patients with *normal* coronary arteries found that one-third fit the criteria for panic disorder (Mukerjiv & Alpert, 1987).

After intravenous infusions of sodium lactate solution, 50% of panic disorder patients experience an attack, as compared to 9% of persons who have no history (Cowley & Roy-Byrne, 1987). This *biological marker*—along with evidence of significant genetic loading—strongly suggests a biological basis for panic disorder. Additionally, 80% of patients respond favorably to antidepressant medication. Within 4 weeks of continuous treatment, roughly half of patients are free of symptoms (Klerman, 1988).

Panic attacks are not always the product of panic disorder. They can be caused by hyperthyroidism, cardiac arrhythmias, complex partial seizures, hypoglycemia, and stimulant drugs (including caffeine). Consider the following case.

> One week after she and her husband had resigned as motel managers, a 55-year-old woman suffered an attack of severe anxiety associated with difficulty breathing, tightness in her throat, and a feeling of impending doom. She said she was acutely aware of her heart beating and that she felt things becoming unreal. The initial episode was followed by similar occurrences.
>
> The woman's husband said that during these episodes she was difficult to understand (on occasion she had bitten her tongue) and seemed unaware of what was going on around her. Sometimes she became so agitated that she fell to the ground. The attacks lasted anywhere from a few minutes to an hour.

When she sought help at an outpatient psychiatric clinic, she described four occasions over the previous 3 months when she had been taken by paramedic ambulance to emergency rooms. Her evaluations turned up nothing other than mild hypertension.

She had lost 60 pounds during that 3-month period (from 280 to 220 pounds). On examination, she was anxious but fully alert and coherent. She had difficulty concentrating and related a history of crying spells, feelings of low self-worth, and a fear of leaving her house. A Doppler flow study of her carotid arteries was normal. She had no history of psychiatric illness.

The patient received a diagnosis of "agoraphobia with panic attacks and concurrent depression." She was treated with imipramine 50 mg, increasing to 150 mg over a 2-week period, and diazepam 5 mg four times a day. She responded well. Her anxiety disappeared.

Three weeks later, her physician received a telephone call from the woman's husband telling him that she had developed right-sided weakness. Later, in the emergency room, this weakness was diagnosed as a "hysterical reaction." After further deterioration, she was admitted to a psychiatric unit. Two neurology residents concurred in their belief that the woman's anxiety and weakness were psychological symptoms!

For legal reasons, she was given an electroencephalogram (EEG) and Computed tomography (CT) scan. They demonstrated a left-sided frontoparietal mass (glioblastoma multiforme). Following surgical removal, the panic attacks disappeared. (Dietch, 1984)

This woman's "panic attacks" were complex partial seizures triggered by rapid tumor growth. The major clinical red flags included speech disturbance, tongue biting, falling to the ground, and loss of awareness during her "panic" episodes. Also, at age 55, the woman was much older than most patients having their first panic attacks.

As panic disorder is more widely discussed, the risk of applying this label prematurely increases. (*Eight* physicians examined this woman before the correct diagnosis was made.) Although somatic expressions of psychosocial stress are common, the clinician must guard against automatically interpreting cases of vague somatic complaints as simple somatization, particularly in the absence of the essential characteristics listed in Table 9.1.

TABLE 9.1 Essential Characteristics of Simple Somatization

No obvious organic basis
Associated with increased life stress
Symptoms limited to period of stress
Nonspecific, vague somatic complaints

SOMATIZATION DISORDER
(BRIQUET'S SYNDROME OR HYSTERIA)

Hysteria implies the psychological cause of physical symptoms. Because of loose application and outright abuse, the term has lost most of its usefulness. *Hysterical* has become more a pejorative adjective than an accurate clinical descriptor. A replacement— *Briquet's syndrome*, after the French physician who described the condition in 1859 was suggested (Woodruff et al., 1974), but the newer term failed to have any staying power, so we are left with *somatization disorder*, as listed in the fourth edition of the *Diagnostic and Statistical Manual of Mental Disorders* (DSM-IV) (American Psychiatric Association, 1987).

Manifestations of this condition first appear during the teen years. There are multiple physical complaints, some quite specific and many involving pain. Despite the absence of an organic basis, various diagnoses, hospitalizations, and treatments (including surgery) accumulate, along with an ever-growing list of "fired" physicians. The person becomes compulsively preoccupied with ill health; complaining about a myriad of physical symptoms, a way of life; a total absorption in physical symptoms and health professionals. Persons with this severe form of somatization invariably have thick medical charts and therapy records. The dramatic exaggeration of symptoms is another essential aspect, as is a history of significant interpersonal conflict, often of a sexual nature. In fact, one researcher maintains that the diagnosis is highly questionable in any person with good sexual adjustment (See Table 9.2).

> For several years, an unemployed 31-year-old divorced man complained of multiple psychiatric and somatic symptoms. During his divorce, he became depressed and on several occasions disappeared for extended periods. Each time, upon his return, his memory for what had transpired was hazy.

TABLE 9.2 Essential Characteristics of Somatization Disorder

No obvious organic basis
Extensive number of somatic complaints (minimum 13)
Onset during teens or early twenties
Dramatic elaboration of symptoms
History of chaotic interpersonal relationships, particularly with respect to sexuality

There had been nine psychiatric hospitalizations. On each occasion, he had undergone numerous procedures for his multiple somatic symptoms. No organic basis had ever been found. His extensive medical history dated back to age 12, when he was hospitalized for abdominal pain, thought to be appendicitis. On further evaluation, he was discharged without diagnosis or treatment. Five years later, he was hospitalized again, this time for long-lasting headaches. No organic cause could be determined. At age 30, a recurrent bout of abdominal pain led to another round of exhaustive but unproductive medical workups.

More recently, he had been operated on for gallstones, but his gallbladder turned out to be normal. Additionally, over the years, he had been evaluated for endocrine, cardiac, and respiratory problems and a variety of gastrointestinal complaints. There was no organic pathology. (On one occasion, however, at age 24, he had suffered severe pain from what proved to be renal stones.)

When interviewed, he listed more than 30 different physical symptoms, most of them described in exaggerated terms. For example, when asked if he had experienced fatigue, he responded: "Yes. Sometimes I have more energy than Carter has pills, but sometimes I don't have enough energy to pick up a pin."

He related a past history of embarrassment about sex. After being exclusively homosexual between the ages of 16 and 21, he gave in to pressure from his mother and started seeing women. Soon after, he married. The marriage was marked by turmoil. He found himself indifferent to sex and impotent much of the time.

Mentally, the man was oriented without delusions or hallucinations. He was described as "flamboyant," "enthusiastic," and "friendly." At times he was overly emotional and easily moved to tears or laughter without provocation. Surprisingly, he expressed a belief that most of his problems—mental and physical—had psychological causes. (Kaminsky & Slavney, 1976)

Although this example of somatization disorder contains the essential features—early onset, extensive number of somatic complaints, numerous normal medical evaluations, dramatic presentations, and a history of chronic sexual dissatisfaction—it also includes certain notable aberrations. First, the patient is a man. Most cases involve women. Second, this patient appeared to have some insight into the psychological nature of his problem. Much more characteristic would have been a complete unwillingness to entertain the possibility.

One other aspect of this case is worth emphasizing. There was nothing psychosomatic about this patient's renal stones. People who somatize also can become physically ill. It is an important point to keep in mind.

Certain diseases, by attacking multiple organ systems, cause an array of seemingly unrelated symptoms that can be confused with somatization disorder.

Shortly after the aircraft manufacturing firm for which he worked started laying off employees, a 32-year-old aeronautical engineer, father of three, consulted his family physician. He complained of transient episodes of double vision, dizziness, leg weakness, and "tingling" sensations in his legs over a 3-month period.

During this same time, the man was involved in two minor automobile accidents while driving alone in his car. On both occasions he sustained minor lacerations. As for his personal life, his marriage of 11 years was described as good. Other than infrequent arguments with his wife about money, they got along well.

Up to this point, the man had been in excellent health. He denied ever having fainting spells, seizures, or problems with speech. Two years prior, his father (with whom he had been quite close) had died from a stroke.

The man was intelligent. His memory was excellent. Early in the interview he expressed concern that his symptoms might be caused by the threat of losing his job. His physical examination, including a careful neurological assessment, revealed no abnormal findings. (Fuller, 1976)

Given the facts of this case, somatization disorder is an unlikely possibility. In his early thirties, the patient had no previous history of somatization. Furthermore, rather than rushing to the doctor with a dramatic elaboration of symptoms, he delayed for 3 months. His 11-year marriage appeared relatively stable, and his willingness to consider a possible psychological explanation suggested considerable psychological awareness. Based on these findings, a psychiatric consultant who had been asked to evaluate the case concluded that there was strong evidence *against* a diagnosis of somatization. The patient was discharged without a definitive diagnosis. A few months later, he developed flagrant neurological symptoms, including partial paralysis and sensory loss, from multiple sclerosis.

Multiple sclerosis (MS) is a degenerative neurological disease of undetermined etiology. It causes patchy destruction of the nerve coverings with resulting areas of "short circuiting" scattered through the nervous system. Diverse symptoms may include sensory changes, visual disturbances, selective weakness, altered speech, and increased emotionality. Characteristically, symptoms abruptly appear and then diminish or disappear, only to recur again months or even years later. Initially, temporary deficits in vision and other sensory modalities can be the only symptoms; with time, however, additional deficits develop. The person becomes progressively disabled. To date, no curative treatment exists.

Given its diverse and shifting clinical presentation, MS is a setup for "psychosomatic" explanations. Emotional lability and mood swings are common findings (Finger, 1998). One report described 19 patients with what is known as the "encephalitic" form of the disease. All of them first experienced psychiatric symptoms. Neurological signs and symptoms were either absent or overlooked (Felgenhauer, 1990).

> A high school student became increasingly apathetic and unable to concentrate. On a school excursion, she complained of an "electric current" shooting through her body. Her mind played tricks on her. She feared someone was going to slip a knife under her pillow. In public, she thought others were talking about her. Finally, she was admitted to a psychiatric hospital as a case of "acute schizophrenia" and described as incoherent, delusional, and depressed. A few days later, she became agitated. Although she improved on clozapine, she failed to recognize people who should have been familiar to her. During this hospitalization, she also complained of a brief period of decreased visual acuity. (Her mother recalled that, earlier, her daughter's eyelid had drooped for a few days.)
>
> Six months later, she seemed recovered, participating fully at school and preparing for finals, but 2 years after her psychiatric hospitalization, she developed spasticity in all her limbs, decreased sensation in her lower body, and ataxia. Her diagnosis was multiple sclerosis. (Felgenhauer, 1990)

Like MS, other "autoimmune" diseases produce a mystifying array of symptoms. These conditions are thought to result from a "memory lapse" on the part of the body's immune system. Early in embryonic development, the immune system normally memorizes the difference between the body's own cells and foreign invaders, such as bacteria and viruses. This enables it to selectively seek out and destroy agents of disease. For reasons not fully understood, in autoimmune diseases the immune system's ability to distinguish between "self" and "not self" fails. This essential surveillance system becomes confused and attacks the person's own body as though it were a foreign invader. The result is a spectrum of degenerative diseases that reflect the particular organ systems under siege. Psychiatric symptoms are frequently part of the clinical picture. They can arise from direct brain damage or secondarily, from support-system failure.

In a study of patients with systemic lupus erythematosus (SLE), roughly one-fifth of patients showed psychiatric symptomatology.

Intermittent somatic symptoms easily mistaken for somatization occurred. Joint pains (arthralgias) were present in 92% of cases; pleuritic pain in 54%, and fatigue and breathlessness in 32% (Feinglass, Arnett, Porsch, Zizic, & Steverns, 1976).

Cancer of the pancreas is often heralded by vague abdominal discomfort; it also causes severe depression. Researchers found that while one-third of pancreatic cancer patients (9 of 28) met the diagnostic criteria for major depression, none of nine patients with stomach cancer were similarly depressed (Joffe, Rubinow, Denicoff, Maher, & Sindelar, 1986). Although the exact mechanism is unknown, cancer of the pancreas has a special proclivity for causing depression early in the course of the disease. Patients often report a sense of impending doom. This morbid response, along with vague symptoms such as backache, loss of appetite, and fatigue, can easily be mistaken for simple depression.

> A 59-year-old woman developed insomnia, nervousness, and depression. She also complained of weakness, vague abdominal symptoms, loss of appetite, and a 10-pound weight loss. There was a history of crying spells and thoughts of something horrible happening. A complete physical examination, including gastrointestinal studies, failed to reveal any organic disease. She received a diagnosis of neurasthenia and anxiety neurosis.
>
> Two months later, after further weight loss and continuing abdominal pain, the woman was reexamined and found to have a hard mass on the left side of her abdomen. At surgery, carcinoma of the body of the pancreas was found. Because of its advanced stage of growth, the cancer was inoperable. The patient died at home a few weeks later. (Yaskin, 1931)

Abdominal discomfort, depression, and weight loss in a middle-aged or older person should raise the possibility of pancreatic cancer. Whereas somatization disorder seldom appears after the age of 30, cancer of the pancreas typically occurs after the age of 50.

When vague somatic complaints accompany fatigue and depression, two other conditions must be considered. The first is fibromyalgia (fibrositis). Some rheumatologists claim that this is the most common condition they see. Patients complain of early morning stiffness, fatigue, and daytime drowsiness (regardless of how many hours they sleep at night). They also suffer from depression. When examined, these patients have tenderness points, particularly over various bony prominences (Kirmayer, Robbins, & Kapusta, 1988).

The second condition is chronic mononucleosis (Epstein-Barr disease). Some persons who contract "infectious mono" (caused by the

Epstein-Barr herpesvirus), afterwards suffer recurrent bouts of fatigue, vague somatic complaints, depression, low-grade fever, and environmental allergies. These patients have elevated antibody titers to the Epstein-Barr virus, but many individuals with similar titers fail to report these symptoms (Hellinger et al., 1988).

Both fibromyalgia and chronic mononucleosis occur more commonly among women than men. There are reports of favorable responses to low-dose antidepressant medication, but much remains to be understood about these two conditions and their treatments.

CONVERSION DISORDER

Conversion disorder (formerly called *hysterical conversion neurosis*) involves the sudden, dramatic onset of a "neurological problem" that, when fully evaluated, proves to have no organic basis. Since the time of Freud, the most widely accepted explanation for conversion symptoms posits the translation of repressed psychological conflict into somatic language. It is assumed that the person finds the conflict more acceptable when it is expressed indirectly in physical terms.

Unlike somatization disorder, conversion disorder presents as a single, prominent symptom complex rather than multiple diverse complaints. It can manifest as muscle weakness, paralysis, or sensory loss; characteristically, it has an abrupt or even explosive, onset. Conversion reactions can be superimposed on somatization disorder. Both conditions are far more common among women than men. As shown in Table 9.3, there are three clinical types of conversion disorder.

In *loss of function* cases, the person suddenly loses sensation, sight, hearing, or ability to move an arm or leg. This type of conversion characteristically appears in individuals of limited psychological sophistication and educational background. (Interestingly, these demographics represent a striking change from the turn of the century, when Freud and other investigators described conversion hysteria in a sophisticated, well-educated clientele.)

When carefully evaluated, the conversion deficit proves to be only a rough approximation of what is predicted neuroanatomically. The

TABLE 9.3 Types of Conversion Disorder

Loss of function
Pseudoseizure
Pain reaction

person says he or she cannot move his or her leg, yet when the examiner diverts the person's attention, the leg moves. A sensory deficit fails to fit the anatomical distribution of nerves, the loss being described over a square or circular area of the body instead of along the lines of nerve distribution. In the absence of neurological inconsistencies, the diagnosis of conversion disorder is always questionable. Approximately one third of conversion cases eventually turn out to have medical causes. (Reid & Wise, 1995)

> A young man—previously an acrobat and dancer in the circus— enlisted in the army during peacetime. Compared to his traveling life with the circus, he found his new lifestyle monotonous and the discipline of military life a rude awakening. He thought about deserting but decided otherwise.
>
> Without warning, he became unable to walk and could not feel anything in his legs. He had no previous history of this problem. In the face of this catastrophic event, he appeared surprisingly unconcerned. He was hospitalized and officially discharged from the army on a doctor's certificate of disability.
>
> His symptoms could never be reconciled with any organic deficit. Gradually, he regained function in his legs and experienced a return of normal sensation. Within a few months, he left the hospital fully recovered. His diagnosis was conversion reaction. (Kolb, 1977)

Pseudoseizure is a second type of conversion disorder. The person suddenly collapses on the floor or makes violent thrashing movements. Inevitably, the episode is quite dramatic, and it hardly ever occurs in the absence of other people.

In many of these cases, even a passing familiarity with true seizures leads the observer to suspect a nonorganic origin. For example, the person, while appearing to have a grand mal seizure, may show signs of consciousness, such as speaking in a faint voice or responding to verbal commands. It is important to keep in mind that certain bona fide seizures (complex partial) can have atypical manifestations. All shifts in consciousness or behavior that recur in episodic fashion should be evaluated neurologically. The clinician should be especially suspect of "conversion" cases that include a history of loss of bladder control, self-injury, or occurrence when the person is alone. While common in cases of organic epilepsy, these findings are uncharacteristic of conversion. (The reader will recall that in the previous case of multiple sclerosis thought to be hysterical, the man had injured himself in two minor automobile accidents while driving alone. This was compelling evidence against a diagnosis of conversion disorder.)

The third type of conversion disorder manifests itself as a *pain reaction*. These cases are particularly difficult to evaluate. Medical specialists have at their disposal sophisticated testing procedures for differentiating organic from psychogenic pain. Usually, this is not a legitimate area of assessment for the nonspecialist. Even when an organic basis is not found initially, if pain persists or recurs, it should be reevaluated. Pain is an elusive phenomenon, one whose organic basis sometimes remains unidentified for long periods despite intensive investigation.

Invariably, conversion disorder—regardless of type—is associated with significant interpersonal conflict. In fact, the conversion symptom often provides at least a partial resolution. This may be symbolic. For example, a long-suffering woman confronted repeatedly with her husband's infidelity becomes paralyzed in her right hand, rendering her unable to pull the trigger of the gun with which she has fantasized killing him. Sometimes the conversion resolution is more literal. A man confronted by the desire to tell off his tyrannical boss (but realistically unable to do so) becomes mute and thus unable to act out his conflicted desire.

In addition to resolving conflict, psychiatric symptoms produce secondary gain; that is, the person derives an additional advantage of personal attention from having become "ill." The role of "medical patient" affords a person certain privileges not otherwise available and sometimes tips the interpersonal balance in his or her favor.

It is unusual for a person to have a single episode of conversion disorder. In the absence of such, the clinician should be skeptical even when an initial neurological evaluation fails to turn up an organic cause. Similarly, the clinician should seriously question a diagnosis of conversion disorder that does not include the essential characteristics outlined in Table 9.4.

After returning home from church, a 16-year-old girl complained of a severe headache and nausea. She went into the bathroom to take her medication (Fiorinal®) and afterwards was discovered by her parents,

TABLE 9.4 Essential Characteristics of Conversion Disorder

No obvious organic basis
Sudden, dramatic onset in the middle of interpersonal
    conflict or some other high-stress situation
Single prominent physical symptom

unconscious, lying on the floor. There was no previous history of similar episodes. She was rushed to a nearby hospital, where, after a few hours, she regained consciousness. A neurologist diagnosed a conversion reaction.

(At this juncture, even when rendered by a neurologist, the diagnosis of conversion reaction was inappropriate. The fact that the patient lost consciousness in the absence of anyone else and without previous history makes the diagnosis of conversion risky indeed.)

Subsequently, the patient was admitted to a psychiatric hospital. She gave a 2-year history of headaches. No neurological basis had been established. She had been followed by a physician and treated with Fiorinal® (butalbital, aspirin, and caffeine), from which she obtained partial relief. Her headaches were unilateral and were associated with nausea, blurred vision, and unsteadiness. Her friends said that during these headaches she walked as though she were intoxicated.

The hospital staff described the patient as attractive and intelligent, depressed at times but genuinely concerned about her condition. She talked openly with her psychologist about competing with her sister. She described how good it felt to receive the special attention that she got from her mother when her headaches first started. Her Minnesota Multiphasic Personality Inventory (MMPI) showed a "conversion V" (allegedly seen in persons prone to conversion reactions). But based on her behavior on the unit, the nursing staff consistently described her as a "healthy, normal teenager."

Further neurological evaluation led to the correct diagnosis: "migraine headaches, basilar type." (LaWall & Ooommen, 1978)

Basilar migraine—an unusual variant of common migraine—is characterized by a "sick" headache, usually one-sided, with unsteadiness and visual disturbances. It is primarily seen in adolescents, usually girls. This case illustrates the importance of resisting the diagnosis of conversion in the absence of essential characteristics. Although no organic basis had been found, other findings strongly argued against conversion disorder. The patient had multiple symptoms including headache, nausea, blurred vision, and unsteadiness. Furthermore, no escalation in the conflict with her sister or other stressful situation could be identified that would account for the present reaction. Another factor arguing against conversion was the patient's psychological awareness.

The diagnostic difficulties encountered in dealing with the symptom of pain (including headache) are considerable. In a study of 250 patients with protracted head pain, after repeated negative medical consultations, 25% turned out to have a causative organic disorder

(Friedman & Frazier, 1973). Most clinicians are well advised to avoid labeling pain symptoms as conversion disorder.

This chapter has covered three forms of somatization, with the objective of familiarizing the reader with their essential characteristics. The clinician should concentrate on identifying inconsistencies that argue against somatization. As demonstrated in the various case histories, failure to detect organic disease alone is a fragile basis on which to base a diagnosis of somatization. The casual use of terms like *psychosomatic* or *hysterical* is fraught with peril.

REFERENCES

American Psychiatric Association (1987). *Diagnostic and statistical manual of mental disorders (DSM-IV)*. Washington, DC: American Psychiatric Association.

Cowley, D. & Roy-Byrne, P. (1987). Hyperventilation and panic disorder. *American Journal of Medicine, 83,* 929–937.

Dietch, J. (1984). Cerebral tumor presenting with panic attacks. *Psychosomatics, 25,* 861–863.

Dubousky, S. & Weissberg, M. (1978). *Clinical psychiatry in primary care.* Baltimore: Williams & Wilkins Co., 203.

Feinglass, E., Arnett, F., Porsch, C., Zizic, T., & Steverns, M. (1976). Neuropsychiatric manifestations of systemic lupus erythematosus: diagnosis, clinical spectrum and relationship to other features of the disease. *Medicine, 55,* 323–339.

Felgenhauer, K. (1990). Psychiatric disorders in the encephalitic from of multiple sclerosis. *Journal of Neurology, 237,* 11–18.

Finger, S. (1998). A happy state of mind, a history of mild elation, denial of disability, optimism, and laughing in multiple sclerosis. *Archives of Neurology, 55,* 241–250.

Friedman, A. & Frazier, S. (1973). Critique of the psychiatric treatment of chronic headache patients. In *Proceedings of the 5th World Congress of Psychiatrists.* New York: American Elsevier.

Fuller, D., M.D., Professor of Psychiatry, University of Texas at San Antonio Medical School. Personal communications, 1976.

Hellinger, W., Smith, T., Van Scoy, R., Spiker, P., Fougacs, P., & Edson, R. (1988). Chronic fatigue syndrome and the diagnostic utility of antibody to Epstein-Barr early antigen. *Journal of the American Medical Association, 260,* 971–973.

Joffe, R., Rubinow, D., Denicoff, K., Maher, M., & Sindelar, W. (1986). Depression and carcinoma of the pancreas. *General Hospital Psychiatry, 8,* 241–245.

Kaminsky, M. & Slavney, P. (1976). Methodology and personality in Briquet's syndrome: a reappraisal. *American Journal of Psychiatry, 133,* 58–88.

Kellner, R. (1987). Hypochondriasis and somatization. *Journal of the American Medical Association, 258,* 2718–2722.

Kirmayer, L., Robbins, J., & Kapusta, M. (1988). Somatization and depression in fibromyalgia syndrome. *American Journal of Psychiatry, 145,* 950–954.

Klerman, C. (1988). Overview of the cross-national collaborative panic study. *Archives of General Psychiatry, 45,* 407–412.

Kolb, L. (1977) *Modern clinical psychiatry.* Philadelphia: W. B. Saunders Co., 520.

LaWall, J. & Ooommen, K. (1978). Basilar artery migraine presenting as conversion hysteria. *Journal of Nervous and Mental Disease, 166,* 809–811.

Martin, J. (1979). Physical disease manifesting as psychiatric disorders. In G. Usdin & J. Lewis (Eds.). *Psychiatry in general medical practice* (pp. 337–351). New York: McGraw-Hill.

Mukerjiv, V. & Alpert, M. (1987). Panic disorder: a frequent occurrence in patients with chest pain and normal coronary arteries. *Angiology, 38,* 236–240.

Pincus, J. & Tucker, G. (1974). *Behavioral neurology* (pp. 183–187) New York: Oxford University Press.

Reid, W. & Wise, M. (1995). *DSM-IV training guide.* Levittown, Pennsylvania: Brunner/Mazel.

Woodruff, R., Goodwin, D., & Guse, S. (1989). *Psychiatric diagnosis* (4th ed.). New York: Oxford University Press.

Yaskin, J. (1931). Nervous symptoms as earliest manifestations of carcinoma of the pancreas. *Journal of the American Medical Association, 96,* 1664–1668.

Chapter 10

The Old and the Young

They say an old man is twice a child.   —William Shakespeare

Although the basic principles for detecting psychological masquerade are generally applicable regardless of a patient's age, there are certain nuances relative to children and older adults. They are the focus of this chapter.

AGING AND ORGANIC MENTAL DISORDERS

Old age, increasingly commonplace, carries with it an added risk of masquerading medical conditions. Key to their recognition is rejection of the image of aging as synonymous with senility. It is simply not true. One author has recommended "prophylactic injections against the notion that old age involves imbecility" (Comfort, 1980). Old age by itself is never an adequate explanation for mental decline or behavioral problems.

Additionally, it is important to understand that all "senility" is not the same. Of particular importance is the fact that many cases are reversible; they only *mimic* dementia. They are caused by correctable medical problems. This is why the proper identification of psychological masquerade in the elderly is so very important.

IRREVERSIBLE DEMENTIAS

At present true senile dementia is irreversible; however, with the tremendous strides being made in the neurosciences, this may change in the near future. Roughly 2% of persons at age 65 suffer from irreversible dementia. Among those who have reached 80 years of age, the number rises tenfold to 20% (Mace & Robins, 1991). Two forms of irreversible dementia account for 60% of all cases— Alzheimer's disease, 50%, and multi-infarct dementia, 10% (Adams, Victor, Ropper, 1997).

Alzheimer's Disease

Research studies suggest that Alzheimer's disease (or dementia of the Alzheimer's type-DAT) is identical to the presenile dementia that sometimes strikes persons in midlife. It is simply a matter of some people developing the illness earlier than others. The precise cause of this dementing disease, which involves widespread, progressive destruction of brain cells, remains unknown. Clinically, people with Alzheimer's disease present with failing memory and disorientation. Initially, these deficits can be so subtle that only in retrospect are they recognized as signaling the onset of dementia. Relentlessly, they grow more pronounced and are joined by other symptoms. Appointments may be forgotten, stories repeated, and mistakes made more often. These people may lose their way in their own neighborhoods. Depression and anxiety surface. There is less spontaneity. Facial expressions are less animated. Activities and friends hold increasingly less interest. Apathy settles in, only to be interrupted periodically by unexplained panic or hyperexcitability.

As Alzheimer's disease progresses, the person has difficulty reading. In conversations, finding the right word becomes increasingly problematic. Good judgment slips away. Mobility decreases, characterized by unsteadiness and a shortened gait. Much later, bowel and bladder control are compromised.

Early in the evolution of Alzheimer's disease, it can be mistaken for reactive depression. The growing memory deficit also sets the stage for paranoid reactions. Eventually, full-blown delusional thought and hallucinations emerge. As the condition progresses, evidence for organicity builds until its neurological basis becomes obvious.

Multi-infarct Dementia

Multi-infarct dementia is associated with arteriosclerotic narrowing of the blood vessels. This increases the risk of arterial blockage and the resulting death of small areas of the brain. (The term *infarct* refers to dead tissue arising from arterial insufficiency.) Usually, people who develop multi-infarct dementia suffer from high blood pressure. The symptoms accompanying multi-infarct dementia are virtually indistinguishable from Alzheimer's, but the two conditions take somewhat different clinical courses. Whereas Alzheimer's disease proceeds as a gradual deterioration, multi-infarct dementia progresses in stepwise fashion. Clinical recognition depends on the identification of core features of brain syndrome that are often overshadowed by depression, anxiety, and paranoia.

There is no corrective treatment for theses two forms of irreversible dementia, but early recognition is important to the patient and his or her family for planning purposes. When these irreversible dementias are correctly identified rather than being mistaken for crazy behavior or "getting old," families can be educated on how to anticipate and cope with future problems.

REVERSIBLE DEMENTIAS

Approximately 10% of all cases involving symptoms suggestive of senile dementia result from potentially correctable medical disorders (Cummings, Benson, & LoVerne, 1980). Accurate diagnosis represents the difference between recovery and eventual irreversibility. In these cases, misinterpretation of psychological changes as expressions of "senility" can lead to an unnecessary tragedy. (See Table 10.1)

Drug Intoxication

The most common form of reversible dementia is drug intoxication. Older persons consume more than their share of both prescription and over-the-counter medications—substances to which they are supersensitive. Small amounts can cause major problems.

As a general rule, the older a person is, the more sensitive he or she is to the effects of medications. People over the age of 80 are twice as reactive as those under age 60 (Hurtwitz, 1969). Even a drug as seemingly innocuous as acetaminophen (Tylenol®) can cause adverse effects such as confusion and hallucinations. With the unexplained onset of mental or emotional decline in an elderly person, medications are the number one suspect.

Many medications, especially psychoactive drugs, exert prolonged effects in the aging body. Several factors contribute to this delayed metabolism. Owing to age-related decline in cardiac efficiency, circulation time lengthens in older people, so that it takes longer for

TABLE 10.1 Causes of Reversible Dementia

Intracranial conditions
  Meningiomas
  Subdural hematomas
  Hydrocephalus
  Epilepsy
  Multiple sclerosis
  Wilson's disease

Systemic illnesses
  Pulmonary insufficiency
  Cardiac arrhythmia
  Severe anemia
  Polycythemia vera
  Uremia
  Hyponatremia
  Hepatic encephalopathy
  Porphyria
  Hyperlipidemia

Deficiency states
  B$_{12}$ deficiency
  Pellagra
  Folate deficiency

Endocrinopathies
  Addison's disease
  Myxedema
  Hypoparathyroidism
  Hyperparathyroidism
  Recurrent hypoglycemia
  Cushing's disease
  Hyperthyroidism

Drugs
  Disulfiram
  Lithium carbonate
  Phenothiazines
  Phenytoin
  Benzodiazapines
  Barbiturates
  Clonidine
  Methyldopa
  Propranolol hydrochloride
  Atropine and related compounds

TABLE 10.1 (*continued*)

Heavy metals
    Mercury
    Arsenic
    Lead
    Thallium

Exogenous toxins and industrial agents
    Trichloroethylene
    Toluene
    Carbon disulfide
    Organophosphates
    Carbon monoxide
    Alcohol

Infections
    General paresis
    Chronic meningitis
    Cerebral abscess
    Cysticercosis
    Whipple's disease
    Progressive multifocal leukoencephalopathy
    Encephalitis

Collagen-vascular and vascular disorders
    Systemic lupus erythematosus
    Temporal arteritis
    Sarcoidosis

Source: Adapted from Cummings, Benson, & LoVerne, 1980. Reversible dementia. *Journal of the American Medical Association, 243*, pp. 2434–2439.

medications to pass through the body's "breakdown stations"—the kidneys and liver. Also, these organs themselves undergo aging changes. The kidneys become less effective filters, and the liver produces less of the enzymes essential for drug metabolism. A final factor relates to a relative increase in body fat that goes with getting older. This makes for a prolonged response to psychoactive drugs, since most of these substances are stored in the body's fat reserves. From these storage depots, medications are slowly released, as with time-release capsules.

A twice-widowed man in his middle eighties, known to his friends and family for his zestful approach to living, became apathetic and withdrawn. He sat in a chair for days on end, showing little interest in food, friends, or recreational pursuits. Earlier, on several occasions, he had parked his car and forgotten where it was. When, for the third time, he reported it stolen, the police threatened to revoke his license.

His local doctor thought his problem was old age, but he referred the man for more extensive evaluation. Although generally coherent, he appeared confused at times. No evidence of physical disease was discovered.

Initially, the man denied taking any medications, but further inquiry revealed that after the death of his first wife (many years before), he had taken a butabarbital tablet nightly for sleep. When, upon his second wife's death, his sleeplessness returned, a second sedative was prescribed for him (Quaalude, methaqualone). His current problems, as it turned out, stemmed from his continued use of both medications.

Despite strong protests from the old man, his sleeping medications were discontinued. Within 10 days his zest for life had returned, and his confusion completely cleared. He started socializing again and had no further incidents of misplacing his car. (Comfort, 1980)

In part, because of their widespread use, certain medications are notorious for producing psychological masquerades in the elderly. Anti-inflammatory drugs cause depression and, more rarely, psychosis. Many of the diuretics, because of their potassium-depleting effect, are associated with fatigue, apathy, and depression. Older persons are often overmedicated with anxiolytics and sedatives. Many of these drugs have prolonged actions, thereby setting the stage for significant buildup over a few days with resulting drowsiness and listlessness. This problem can be minimized by using medications that have no active metabolites such as the benzodiazepine oxazepam (Serax®).

Cimetidine (Tagemet®) is widely prescribed for stomach hyperacidity, dyspepsia, and ulcers. Even small amounts have caused delirium and psychosis in older persons.

In nursing homes and hospitals, older persons frequently receive neuroleptic medication for agitation. Drug-induced parkinsonism may go unappreciated. The person becomes stiff and unable to move normally. Stooped posture, a halting slow gait, and drooling develop; spontaneity and normal facial expression are lost. Upon cessation of the drug, these complications quickly disappear.

Digitalis (and its various derivatives) has been a cornerstone in the management of heart failure. Even though it has been replaced to some extent by newer preparations, this venerable remedy is still widely used. The problem with digitalis is that the dose required for a therapeutic response is close to being toxic. Even when serum levels of digitalis are within a therapeutic range, various mental and emotional aberrations are possible. One report described two men treated with digoxin (digitalis derivative), both in their 70s, who, despite "nontoxic" levels, became extremely tearful. When the medication was reduced, the tearfulness disappeared (Eisendrath & Sweeney, 1987).

As noted earlier, older persons are particularly vulnerable to anticholinergic agents. Any therapeutic benefits are often outweighed by the side effects.

> A 74-year-old man, tremulous and rigid, was diagnosed as having Parkinson's disease. Despite treatment with antiparkinsonian medications, his memory deteriorated and he began to have difficulty finding the right words to express himself. He became disoriented and developed paranoid delusions and hallucinations. Eventually, he fell into a severe depression with uncontrollable crying spells.
>
> After 2 years, he was referred to a special clinic for Parkinson's disease. The preliminary impression was that he now suffered, additionally, from "cortical dementia, probably of the Alzheimer's type." Further neuropsychological testing, however, suggested drug intoxication. The patient's anticholinergic medication was tapered off over the next 8 days. Within a week he showed a dramatic improvement in memory and mood. His wife described him as a "new man." (Kurlan & Como, 1988)

For the elderly, there are no "minor" tranquilizers! The medications they take, particularly sedatives, often put them at risk for mental dysfunction

Subdural Hematoma

A subdural hematoma is a collection of blood in the space just beneath the dura, the brain's outermost covering. Traumatic injury to the head that tears the small veins traversing the subdural space is the most common cause. Symptoms, which can be primarily mental or behavioral, arise from increased intracranial pressure and from encroachment of surrounding brain tissue by the expanding blot clot.

Accidental falls put older people at risk for subdural hematomas. A problem with alcohol substantially compounds this risk. Given a history of abrupt change in an older person, the clinician should always inquire about accidents or falls. The possibility of a subdural hematoma should not be dismissed simply because the patient does not remember a fall or a blow to the head. In a study of 75 cases, one out of three patients lacked any recollection of head trauma (Stuteville & Welch, 1958). Even when a person cannot recall a previous injury, bruising about the head or eyes can tell the story.

In contrast to acute subdural hematomas, the chronic variety evolves slowly and is more subtle in its clinical presentation. Chronic subdural hematomas become symptomatic over a period of days to weeks. Symptoms are varied but can include social withdrawal, disinterest, intellectual decline, or psychosis. Headache is a frequent finding. Neurological deficits—such as weakness in the arms, legs, or muscles of the face—sometimes signal the organic nature of this condition, but such signs are not invariably present.

> An elderly man, active and in good health, occupied himself with gardening and odd-jobbing for his neighbors. Just prior to Christmas, while digging under an apple tree, he struck his head on a low-hanging branch. Although he felt dazed, he quickly recovered without loss of consciousness. The following day, walking home from a neighbor's house, he fell over in the road. Later, an observer reported seeing the old man get to his feet and walk on, appearing somewhat unsteady on his feet.
>
> Over the next few days, the man became disorganized, drowsy, and "completely unlike his former self." He also lost control of his bladder.
>
> Three weeks later, he was admitted to a hospital and found to have right-sided facial weakness. Arteriography showed a large subdural hematoma that was surgically evacuated. The man had an excellent recovery without residual problems. (Pygott & Street, 1950)

Treatment outcomes for chronic subdural hematomas are gratifying. One study of 52 elderly patients showed that 75% were restored to their prior level of functioning following surgery. (Raskind & Glover, 1972)

Normal-Pressure Hydrocephalus

Another masquerader to watch for among the elderly is normal-pressure hydrocephalus. This neurological condition results from an excess of cerebrospinal fluid. Typically, it shows up in the seventh and eighth decades of life. Although several diseases can cause a similar problem, most cases have no specific identifiable etiology. Corrective surgery involves the implanting of a shunt for draining off excess fluid.

Psychiatric symptoms, especially apathy, may be the first sign. With time, forgetfulness and day-to-day shifts in the ability to concentrate emerge, along with a peculiar pattern of walking. This "magnetic gait" reflects difficulty in initiating each step. It is as though the person's feet were stuck to the floor. The person tries to adapt by widening his or her stance and taking slow, short steps.

The third classic symptom of normal-pressure hydrocephalus is loss of bladder control. When cognitive decline is found in association with difficulty walking and urinary incontinence, normal-pressure hydrocephalus must be considered. If detected early, this condition can be successfully treated. The earlier the diagnosis, the more favorable the outcome.

> A 58-year-old man became delusional, insisting he had given his wife a serious illness. He also thought his neighbors were talking about him and meant to do him harm. After he was admitted to a hospital, it was established that he had been suffering from depression for the preceding 8 months. His memory was poor, and he was unable to concentrate even for short periods. His walking was labored and unsteady.
>
> The results of a series of neurological studies, including an electroencephalogram (EEG), brain scan, and skull x-rays), proved to be normal. A neurologist and a psychiatrist concluded that there was no organic brain disease. They felt that the man was having a psychotic depression.
>
> Over the next six months, he was treated with haloperidol (an antipsychotic) and imipramine (an antidepressant). His symptoms appeared to improve, but a year later he was readmitted when his ability to walk became seriously compromised. During this hospitalization, he was treated with electroconvulsive therapy (ECT) and discharged again without the appropriate diagnosis.
>
> Within 2 months, he returned; this time he was acutely agitated and paranoid, having impulsively attempted suicide with an overdose of pills. His memory was severely impaired, as was his ability to think abstractly. Findings from a battery of neurological studies were consistent with a diagnosis of normal-pressure hydrocephalus. Following a surgical shunting procedure, the man was 80 to 90% his normal self a year later. (Price & Tucker, 1977)

Schizophrenic-like symptoms have been reported in normal-pressure hydrocephalus. Allegedly, surgical shunting ameliorated the "schizophrenia" (Lying-Tunnell, 1979). This is an intriguing finding, suggesting the possibility of a special hydrocephalic subcategory of schizophrenia.

Losing One's Senses

Older people have diminished sensory acuity. As hearing or vision declines, the aging person may become depressed in response. Paranoid thinking is another common reaction to sensory loss. Paranoia becomes a way of trying to make sense (albeit irrationally) of situations in the absence of normal sensory input. *Paraphrenia* is a term applied to old-age paranoia that occurs in the absence of a history of schizophrenia. Several studies have suggested that diminished hearing plays an important causative role (Eisdorfer, 1980).

Failing sight can also precipitate psychiatric symptoms. Evidence for this comes from studies of elderly persons who undergo cataract surgery. Following surgery, the person's eyes are covered with black patches. This state of iatrogenic blindness often leads to rapid-onset brain syndrome.

It is important to keep in mind that the aging body gradually loses some of its ability to signal the presence of disease. For example, the characteristic symptoms of pneumonia—fever, chills, increased respiratory rate, and pain on breathing—may be quite muted or even absent in an elderly person. Instead, the person may simply become lethargic and incoherent. This absence or softening of symptoms has the potential to mask serious medical conditions such as heart attack, heart failure, and pulmonary insufficiency. Whereas in a younger person the resulting symptoms make such conditions readily identifiable, in an older person psychological or behavioral changes (from secondary brain failure) may be the only observable manifestation. This is why it is imperative for a clinician to pursue even the most innocuous-appearing physical complaints in an older person.

> A 75-year-old widow lived alone. Although she was said to have eccentric religious beliefs, she had never been psychotic—never, that is, until she began to express obvious religious delusions and became agitated and paranoid. When she was found trying to set her house on fire because of "instructions from Jesus Christ," she was admitted to a psychiatric unit.
>
> Her heart rate was rapid (160 beats per minute). An electrocardiogram (ECG) showed supraventricular tachycardia, thought to be causing congestive heart failure. After 3 days of treatment with digoxin, her heart rate slowed to 86 beats per minute and her symptoms of heart failure improved. Simultaneously, she became lucid again. By the following week, her acute psychosis had resolved completely, leaving in its place an aging woman with a slightly eccentric personality. (Clark, 1970)

Vitamin B₁₂ Deficiency (Pernicious Anemia)

Vitamin B$_{12}$ deficiency is found in roughly 3 to 10% of patients over age 65 (Carethers, 1988). The most common cause relates to the failure of the stomach lining to produce a substance known as *intrinsic factor*. (Understandably, B$_{12}$ deficiency sometimes occurs in persons who have undergone partial or full removal of the stomach.) Vitamin B$_{12}$ is stored in the liver. Once it is no longer produced in the stomach, the reserves are gradually depleted. This accounts for the rather insidious onset of symptoms. Sometimes this disease is nutritional in origin. Strict vegetarians or elderly persons living on "tea and toast" are particularly susceptible.

Eventually, people with B$_{12}$ deficiency develop obvious neurological deficits such as numbness and tingling in their fingers and toes as well as severe imbalance when walking. Blood testing reveals a characteristic anemia, but psychiatric changes can occur first, giving rise to the possibility of psychological masquerade.

> After 8 days of peculiar behavior, a 47-year-old woman was evaluated medically. Quite out of character, she had become preoccupied with religious themes. She commented that "Jesus has hold of my soul." She believed that Jesus had commanded her to board a spaceship. An electroencephagram (EEG) study showed theta-wave slowing in the posterior and temporal areas of the brain.
>
> Despite the absence of anemia or neurological symptoms, the woman was treated with B$_{12}$ injections. A month later, her EEG revealed a return to normal alpha rhythm. Her psychiatric symptoms had completely cleared. (Evans, Edelsohn, & Golden, 1983)

Pseudodementia

What looks like dementia is not always the real thing. Pseudodementia is a *neurological* masquerade—depression masquerading as dementia. It is critically important to avoid mislabeling a patient as having Alzheimer's disease, particularly if he or she is suffering from a readily treatable condition such as depression. It is estimated that 10 to 20% of depressed elderly patients show substantial cognitive deficits that can be mistaken for dementia. To further complicate the clinician's task, Alzheimer's patients commonly become severely depressed.

There are several important differentiating points (Reynolds, 1988; Wells, 1979). Pseudodementia tends to come on rather rapidly, in contrast to the gradual onset of dementia. Furthermore, whereas a depressed (pseudodemented) patient frequently complains of losing his or her mind or being unable to think, a person with Alzheimer's disease usually tries to cover up the problem by minimizing the deficits. With respect to problem solving, the truly demented patient makes obvious mistakes; the depressed patient, in contrast, often responds with near misses or says she does not know.

CHILDREN AND ORGANIC MENTAL DISORDERS

As a general rule, any significant psychological or behavioral symptom in a child occurring for the first time or associated with physical illness should be thoroughly evaluated medically. In the absence of significant stress or a specific precipitating event, mental aberrations in children are more likely organic than psychological.

Declining School Performance

A child's school performance is a sensitive indicator of overall well-being. With the exception of cases of reactive depression, substantial decline in schoolwork should receive a full medical evaluation. In one report of children with neurological disease (all of whom had initially been given psychiatric diagnoses), declining school performance showed up early in every case (Mark & Gath, 1978). As a clinician, you are putting yourself on thin ice when—*without* a neurological evaluation—you explain declining school performance in terms of family dynamics.

> A 12-year-old Yugoslavian-born child was brought up in Iceland by his aunt until his parents (who had emigrated to the United States several years earlier) called for him. Although the boy had some initial difficulty with language, after the first 6 months he did well in school until, mysteriously, his school performance plummeted.
>
> At first this change was attributed to cultural shock. The boy was started in counseling and given psychiatric medications; still, his academic work continued to decline.
>
> Another 6 months passed before a neurological consultation was requested. Based on the presence of spastic movements and EEG and spinal fluid findings, a diagnosis of subacute sclerosing panencephalitis was made, a condition for which, unfortunately, there was no known cure.
>
> Over the next 3 years, the child became severely demented and suffered frequent seizures before eventually succumbing to this tragic condition. (Laufer & Taranth, 1979)

This slow virus infection is always fatal. In this case, its initial clinical manifestation was a dramatic decline in school performance.

Childhood Psychosis

Before the age of 12, psychotic symptoms are relatively rare. When a child does develop hallucinations, delusions, or bizarre behavior, organic mental disorder is the most likely explanation. One form of childhood organic psychosis is autism (Ornitz & Ritvo, 1976). Although the exact cause has yet to be established, there is little doubt as to its organic origin. Appearing virtually from birth, it is characterized by highly stereotypical behavior and is associated with significant genetic loading and neurobiological abnormalities (as reflected in EEGs and CT scans; Volkmar & Cohen, 1988).

Autistic children exhibit four kinds of abnormalities: speech disruption, peculiar responses to stimulation, disturbed relatedness, and peculiar movements. They fail to acquire meaningful speech, remaining either mute or limited to strange, high-pitched sounds. In those few instances where speech does appear, it is usually late in onset and has notable peculiarities. The child may repeat phrases over and over again in echo-like fashion (echolalia). Normal rhythm and tone are missing and there is a mechanical quality to what limited speech exists.

Autistic children respond inappropriately to their immediate environment. For example, there may be no observable reaction to sounds or normally compelling sights. Periods of intense staring from which nothing can distract the child are typical. It is as though an invisible barrier were raised between the child and the outside world. As if to overcome this insulation, the child resorts to self-stimulating activities, such as endless whirling or head rolling. The autistic child also may walk on his or her toes for extended periods. Body rocking is common, as is a peculiar kind of hand flapping. At times these aberrations of movement are replaced by extended periods of "frozen" postures.

Most physical contact with other persons is shunned. There is a decided preference for constancy that is threatened by the presence of other people. Not surprisingly, normal social skills fail to evolve, including the ability to smile.

Usually, autism is fully manifest by the age of 3. Treatment is limited, but proper diagnosis helps to avoid inappropriate therapy and unwarranted parental guilt. Furthermore, once it is recognized that the child's autistic problem is not psychological, a more realistic management program can be instituted.

A host of other organic conditions—including brain tumors, central nervous system infections, and drug intoxications—can cause childhood psychosis. The important point to remember is that psychotic symptoms in children should never be interpreted as psychological without a careful assessment for possible organic mental disorder.

Childhood Seizures

As with seizures in adults, if gross motor movements characterize a child's seizures, the problem is usually recognized as neurological. There are those childhood seizure disorders, however, that manifest predominantly as behavioral changes. The symptoms seen in complex partial epilepsy (temporal lobe) are similar to those described for adults in Chapter 7. This disorder should always be suspected in children experiencing unexplained shifts in consciousness, especially when these are combined with semipurposeful movements and a preceding aura.

Petit mal epilepsy occurs predominantly in children. The seizures are characterized by sudden, brief lapses in consciousness during which the child momentarily stops what he or she is doing. If an episode comes on while the child is talking, he or she stops in midsentence. If the period of "absence" is quite brief, the child may resume talking where he or she left off. With longer attacks, a degree of confusion or bewilderment persists after consciousness returns. When attacks of petit mal epilepsy follow one another in rapid-fire fashion (so that the child never quite recovers from one seizure before the onset of the next), the condition is called *status epilepticus*, an allusion to its sustained nature. It is not difficult to envision how a child experiencing status petit mal becomes disoriented and acts bizarrely.

Although most attacks of petit mal arise spontaneously, they sometimes have specific precipitants. Music, light, even reading and emotional stress have been known to trigger seizures in predisposed children. In one version, the child for no apparent reasons falls to the ground or floor in a sudden drop attack. Due to their dramatic nature, these seizures are sometimes misconstrued as hysterical or feigned.

> For several years, a 9-year-old girl frequently passed out just as she was leaving home for school. Although initially concerned, her parents eventually decided that their daughter was faking these attacks. Her family physician also concluded that she was staging the attacks in order to avoid going to school. His diagnosis was school phobia.

After several years, the child was referred for a complete neurological workup. A detailed history disclosed that her fainting episodes occurred only on sunny days. With the aid of EEG studies, it was determined that bright light precipitated these seizures. Each morning, when the child stepped out her front door into the morning sunlight, she lost consciousness and fell to the ground. (Livingston, Pauli, & Bruce, 1980)

Psychiatric Symptoms and Movement Disorders

The combination of psychiatric symptoms and abnormal movements occurs in children as well as adults. Wilson's disease is a prime example. It results from a genetic error that leaves dysfunctional the body's system for transporting copper. As a result, there is a destructive "plating-out" of copper in various body tissues, mainly the liver and brain.

Approximately 20% of cases initially manifest as psychiatric symptoms such as anxiety, depression, mania, or paranoid thinking. In other cases, the psychiatric changes emerge in conjunction with abnormal movements—tremors, jerkiness, or subtle twisting of the extremities. Sometimes, symptoms of hepatitis are also present, because of the toxic effects of excessive amounts of copper in the liver.

As Wilson's disease progresses, the person's facial expression becomes increasingly vacant. Emotional control is tenuous, giving rise to episodes of inappropriate crying or laughing. Full-blown psychosis is common.

For 2 years, school officials described the child as "emotionally disturbed." In addition, she evidenced a noticeable lack of coordination in physical education activities. The persistence of her emotional problems led to her admission to a child psychiatric unit, where she was treated for childhood schizophrenia. But the increasing severity of her jerky movements resulted in a neurological consultation. A slit-lamp eye examination showed a characteristic "golden ring" in her corneas. Laboratory tests confirmed the diagnosis of Wilson's disease.

Unfortunately, by the time the correct diagnosis was made, her condition was far advanced. Despite treatment with a chelating agent (for the elimination of excessive body copper), the child died a month later. (Malamud, 1975)

Early detection of Wilson's disease is critical; otherwise, the patient is condemned to a premature death.

Tourette's syndrome (TS) is another movement disorder associated with numerous behavioral changes. First reported in 1885 by Gilles de la Tourette, the French neurologist after whom it was named, it is an uncanny disorder that makes a person appear possessed. Nervous tics and jerky movements combine in various combinations with compulsive, often explosive behaviors, including involuntary utterances that vary from indecipherable growls to outbursts of "dirty" words.

Typically, TS has its onset in childhood. It may begin with excessive eye blinking, followed by facial tics and grimacing. With time, these involuntary movements are joined by compulsive behaviors. The child feels compelled to touch or smell things or to repeat commonplace activities such as squatting, hopping, or jumping. In roughly 50% of TS patients, uncontrollable vocalizations appear. Initially, they may be mistaken for coughing or throat clearing, but eventually they often evolve into unmistakable verbalizations of dirty words (coprolalia). The TS patient struggles against this compulsion. He or she may cover his or her mouth or run from the situation. When unsuccessful in his or her attempt to suppress the urge, the result is an embarrassing flood of graphic expletives ("fuck, shit, cock . . .").

Research on TS has found excessive amounts of brain dopamine. This could account for the favorable response to haloperidol (and other dopamine blocking agents). Treatment, however, is not without its drawbacks. Patients report feeling slowed down physically and mentally. In his book *The Man Who Mistook His Wife For A Hat*, Oliver Sacks describes a man named Ray who had accommodated to his TS well enough to be a weekend jazz drummer. He had become well known locally for his wild musical improvisations. Nine years of treatment with haloperidol had dramatically changed his life for the better, but his drum playing suffered. Finally, he worked out a compromise with his physician. Ray took the medication on weekdays but discontinued it for his weekend jazz performances so he could "let fly" (Sacks, 1987).

Luckily, most cases of TS are milder in severity. A study of 142,636 children enrolled in public and private school turned up 41 cases; only 3 had an "impairing, diagnosable disorder." Most of these children experienced tics and other relatively minor alterations in movement. Roughly half suffered from obsessive-compulsive tendencies. Family histories of TS or tics were common (Caine, 1988). Inappropriate referrals for traditional psychotherapy are often given to persons with TS. One study found that the initial symptoms were most often mistaken for anxiety. (Golder, 1977).

The Problem of Inattention and Hyperactivity

Attention-deficit hyperactivity disorder (ADHD) is characterized by two core dysfunctions: inattention and hyperactivity/impulsivity. For these symptoms to qualify for this diagnosis, they must occur often and in a fashion that causes significant impairment or distress. This is a common psychiatric disorder in children. It leads to poor school performance, erratic and explosive behavior, and poor social relations, and it has been associated with increased risk for delinquent and criminal behavior (Greenhill, 1998).

Hyperactivity is not invariably present in ADHD (Edelbrock, Costello, & Kessler, 1984). In DSM-IV, this version of the disorder is classified as "ADHD, predominantly inattentive subtype." (American Psychiatric Association, 1987) Children with this type of ADHD, however, may be at greater risk than those with full-blown ADHD. There is some evidence that they have more school difficulty, more unhappiness, and greater risk for long-term social problems. Girls are overrepresented in this group without hyperactivity, making them more likely to go unrecognized (Berry, Shaywitz, & Shaywitz, 1985).

The clinician screening for ADHD would do well to concentrate on confirming that the child cannot sustain normal attention for more than a few minutes, *even when engaged in pleasurable activity*. In the absence of such a deficit, a diagnosis of ADHD is highly questionable.

Many children with attention deficits respond, paradoxically, to stimulants such as methylphenidate (Ritalin®). Attention span improves and hyperactivity diminishes. But this treatment remains controversial. Although there is little question that the diagnosis of ADHD has been applied too liberally. Dramatic improvements in school and social performance often result from medication treatment when it is restricted to children who meet strict criteria.

Adjusting the dose of methylphenidate (or other stimulants) can be a delicate balancing act—not enough, and the child's condition remains unimproved; too much, and the child becomes tremulousness, sleepless, fearful, and even paranoid.

> A 6-year-old boy lived with his mother and infant sister in a government-subsidized high-rise apartment. His mother said he constantly "got into things". After an episode during which the child covered himself and the entire apartment with baby powder, his mother took him to see a psychiatrist.
> The history (along with his interview) showed that the boy often failed to listen and had trouble complying with directions. As a result, he failed to complete most assignments. At preschool he was distractible,

defiant, and impulsive. He got into fights and often spoke out of turn. In the psychiatrist's office, despite being friendly and outgoing, the boy proved difficult to interview because of his distractibility and hyperactivity.

Shortly after he was diagnosed as having ADHD and started on methylphenidate, his teacher complained that he was acting erratically. For extended periods he appeared "spacy," like a "zombie." Abruptly, he would snap out of it, only to go into a rage. At other times, he cowered in a corner of the classroom, anxiously describing insects and spiders that no one else could see. His school performance rapidly deteriorated.

His mother took him to another clinic for a second opinion. It was concluded that he was having a toxic reaction to the methylphenidate. The dosage was lowered. His erratic behavior disappeared and his schoolwork improved significantly, as did his personal relationships at home and at school. (Meller & Lyle, 1987)

It was originally thought that ADHD was limited to childhood. It was assumed that affected children eventually grew out of this condition. As it turns out, this is not always true. Persistence into adulthood has been well described (Wender, 1987).

ADHD has received considerable publicity, but it is important for clinicians to keep in mind that it does not account for all cases of hyperactivity.

A 7-year-old boy's schoolwork showed a marked decline. His teachers described him as irritable and forgetful. After being evaluated by a neuropsychologist, he was diagnosed as having ADD. Luckily, because of other somatic symptoms, a full neurological assessment was undertaken to assess his history of headaches, lack of coordination, and joint pain. A positive Lyme disease test was the result. With antibiotic treatment, the symptoms of "ADD" resolved and the boy's grades improved. Over the course of several years, when attempts were made to stop antibiotics, the original symptoms returned. With resumption of treatment, they disappeared again. (Fallon, Kochevar, Gaito, & Nields, 1998)

Lyme disease is a tick-borne illness caused by a spirochete. Although the greatest incidence is in the Northeast, upper Midwest, and Pacific coastal states, it is now reported throughout the country. The early phase includes a rash and mild flu-like symptoms. After this, the disease may remain quiescent for many months or even years. In other cases, the infestation disseminates rapidly throughout the body. Of these patients, 15 to 40% manifest psychiatric/neurological symptoms, such as mood alteration, confusion, compulsive behavior, psychosis, panic attacks, and even personality changes. In children, the most common "psychological" changes are oppositional behavior, irritability, and anxiety.

Other Considerations

Sensory deficits, such as impairment of hearing or vision cause behavioral disturbances in children. Because there is no basis for comparison, the child may never complain. Hearing and vision should be routinely tested in children with psychiatric symptoms. The clinician can grossly screen for problems by having the child visualize printed words on a wall across the room. A whisper when the child is not looking, if not responded to, provides evidence of a hearing deficit. These simple screening procedures, however, should not substitute for standardized testing of vision and hearing when there is suspicion of a sensory deficit.

Bulimia affects women primarily. It commonly begins in adolescence. Characteristically, there are secret episodes of binge eating over which the person feels no sense of control. In addition, self-induced vomiting, laxatives, and diuretics are sometimes used as aids to weight control. Through all of this the person often holds steadfastly to a distorted view of her actual weight.

I bring up the subject of bulimia because it is often complicated by serious medical problems of the patient's own making. For example, some bulimics resort to syrup of ipecac as a means of inducing vomiting. Because it is effective, cheap, and available without a prescription, ipecac is a likely candidate. The problem is that it is highly toxic to skeletal and cardiac muscle. As the person uses ipecac more and more, it works less well, resulting in greater absorption of the syrup itself, until toxic levels are reached.

One report described a 19-year-old bulimic woman who used ipecac so extensively that, eventually, she walked in a waddling gait and could not hold her hands above her head for more than a few seconds. This condition was due to severe muscle weakness. She also suffered from cardiac enlargement, with resulting shortness of breath (Friedman, Seine, Roberts, & Fremouw, 1987).

Another complication of bulimia is the depletion of body stores of magnesium and potassium. Hypomagnesemia arises from chronic use of diuretics and laxatives. Roughly a quarter of bulimic patients have this complication. The symptoms include restlessness, decreased concentration, and poor memory. Bulimics are also susceptible to potassium loss from overuse of diuretics. Apathy, depression, and fatigue are common. If the potassium loss is too great, life-threatening cardiac arrhythmias are a possibility.

Some 20% of bulimic women are chemically dependent, and they are susceptible to the side effects of the various drugs they use (Mickley, 1988). Diet pills, if used for extended periods, have been known to cause increasing suspiciousness and even paranoid psychosis.

In short, what starts out as bulimia may evolve into medical complications that are easily overlooked unless the clinician is vigilant.

To summarize, with respect to children, looking for psychological masquerade begins with the assumption that significant behavioral or psychological symptoms in a child (not under significant stress) is most likely an organic problem. With the exception of reactive depression, a striking decline in school performance is virtually always an indicator of organicity. Psychotic symptoms—whenever they appear in children—demand a thorough medical evaluation. The clinician should be sensitive to the association of abnormal movements and "psychological" symptoms and should be continuously on the lookout for lapses or "spells" indicative of a seizure disorder. Children with visual or hearing problems develop behavioral problems out of stress and frustration. The integrity of basic sensory modalities should always be confirmed in child psychiatric cases. Finally, bulimia, with all its potential complications, is a prime candidate for psychological masquerade.

REFERENCES

Adams, R., Victor, M., Ropper, A. (1997). Principles of Neurology (6th Edition). New York: McGraw Hill.

American Psychiatric Association (1987). Diagnostic and Statistical Manual of Mental Disorders (DSM-IV). Washington D.C.: American Psychiatric Association.

Berry, C., Shaywik, S., & Shaywitz, B. (1985). Girls with attention deficit disorder: a silent minority? A report on behavioral and cognitive characteristics. *Pediatrics, 76*, 801–809.

Caine, E. (1988). Tourett's syndrome in Monroe County school children. *Neurology, 38*, 472–475.

Carethers, M. (1988). Diagnosing vitamin B_{12} deficiency, a common geriatric disorder. *Geriatrics, 43*, 89–112.

Clark, A. (1970). Ectopic tachycardias in the elderly. *Gerontologica Clinica, 12*, 203–212.

Comfort, A. (1980). *Practice of geriatric psychiatry.* New York: Elsevier.

Cummings, J., Benson, F., & LoVerne, S. (1980). Reversible dementia. *Journal of the American Medical Association, 243,* 2434–2439.

Edelbrock, C., Costello, A., & Kessler, M. (1984). Empirical corroboration of attention deficit disorder. *Journal of the American Academy of Child Psychiatry, 23,* 285–290.

Eisdorfer, C. (1980). Paranoia and schizophrenic disorders in later life. In E. Busse, D. Blazer (Eds.), *Handbook of geriatric psychiatry* (pp.329–337). New York: Van Nostrand Reinhold.

Eisendrath, S. & Sweeney, M. (1987). Toxic neuropsychiatric effects of digoxin at therapeutic serum concentration. *American Journal of Psychiatry, 144,* 506-507.

Evans, D., Edelsohn, G., & Golden, R. (1983). Organic psychosis without anemia or spinal cord symptoms in patients with vitamin B_{12} deficiency. *American Journal of Psychiatry, 140,* 218–221.

Fallon, B, Kochevar, J., Gaito, A., & Nields, J. (1998). The underdiagnosis of neuropsychiatric Lyme disease in children and adults. *Psychiatric Clinics of North America, 21,* 693–703.

Friedman, A., Seine, R., Roberts, T., & Fremouw, W. (1987). Ipecac abuse: a serious complication in bulimia. *General Hospital Psychiatry, 9,* 225–228.

Golder, G. (1977). Tourette syndrome. *American Journal of Diseases of Children, 131,* 531–534.

Greenhill, L. (1998). Diagnosing attention-deficit/hyperactivity disorder in children. *Journal of Clinical Psychiatry, 59 (Supplement 7),* 31–41.

Hurtwitz, N. (1969). Predisposing factors in adverse reactions to drugs. *British Medical Journal, 1,* 536–539.

Kurlan, R. & Como, P. (1988). Drug-induced Alzheimerism. *Archives of Neurology, 45,* 356–357.

Laufer, M. & Taranath, S. (1979). Acute and chronic brain syndromes. In J. Noshpitz (Ed.), *Basic handbook of child psychiatry* (Vol.2, pp. 381–402). New York: Basic Books.

Livingston, S., Pauli, L., Bruce, I. (1980). Neurological evaluation of the child. In H. Kaplan, A. Freedman, B. Sadock (Eds.), *Comprehensive textbook of psychiatry,* III. 2461–2473.

Lying-Tunnell, V. (1979). Psychotic symptoms in normal pressure hydrocephalus. *Acta Psychiatrica Scandinavia, 59,* 415–419.

Mace, N. & Robins, P. (1991). Brain disorders and the causes of dementia. In *The 36-hour day* (pp. 363–373). New York: Warner Books.

Malamud, N. (1975). Organic brain disease mistaken for psychiatric disorder: a clinicopathologic study. In D. Benson & D. Blumer (Eds.), *Psychiatric aspects of neurological disease* (pp. 287–307). New York: Qrune & Stratton.

Mark, S. & Gath, A. (1978). *Psychological disorders of children.* Baltimore: Williams & Wilkins.

Meller, W. & Lyle, K. (1987). Attention deficit disorder in childhood. *Primary Care, 14,* 745–759.

Mickley, D. (1988). Evaluating common eating disorders—ten questions to ask your patient. *The Female Patient, 13,* 33–36.

Ornitz, E. & Ritvo, E. (1976). The syndrome of autism: a critical review. *American Journal of Psychiatry, 133,* 609–621.

Price, T. & Tucker, G. (1977). Psychiatric and behavioral manifestations of normal pressure hydrocephalus. *Journal of Nervous and Mental Disease, 164,* 51–55.

Pygott, F. & Street, D. (1950). Unsuspected treatable organic dementia. *Lancet, 1,* 1371.

Raskind, R. & Glover, B. (1972). Chronic subdural hematoma in the elderly: a challenge in diagnosis and treatment. *Journal of the American Geriatrics Society, 20,* 330–334.

Reynolds, C., Hoch, C., Kupter, D., Buysse, D., Houck, P., Stack, J., & Campbell, D. (1988). Bedside differentiation of depressive pseudodementia from dementia. *American Journal of Psychiatry, 145,* 1099–1103.

Sacks, O. (1987). *The man who mistook his wife for a hat and other clinical tales.* New York: Touchstone.

Stuteville, P. & Welch, K. (1958). Subdural hematoma in the elderly. *Journal of the American Medical Association, 168,* 1445–1449.

Volkmar, F. & Cohen, D. (1988). Neurobiologic aspects of autism. *New England Journal of Medicine, 318,* 1390–1392.

Wender, P. (1987). *The hyperactive child, adolescent, and adult.* New York, Oxford University Press.

Wells, C. (1979). Pseudodementia. *American Journal of Psychiatry, 136,* 895–900.

Chapter 11

Putting It to the Test: A Summary and 15 Test Cases

Look to the essence of a thing, whether it be a point of doctrine, of practice, or of interpretation. —Marcus Aurelius

Psychological symptoms are not always best explained psychologically. Certain organic disorders cause symptoms similar to those associated with psychological reactions. Anxiety, mania, depression, paranoia—and a host of other "psychological" symptoms—can be either psychological responses to problems in living or reflections of mechanical breakdown in the brain itself.

These masquerading organic mental disorders present a diagnostic challenge to the clinician. In psychiatric clinic settings, roughly one out of every ten patients has a causative organic disorder. Clinical success in detecting psychological masquerade requires, above all, a "porous" mental set that resists premature diagnostic closure. Active clinical suspicion is the essential starting point. Such suspicion is refined by clinical familiarity with brain syndrome, an expression of global brain dysfunction, whose four core deficits are:

Disorientation
Recent memory impairment
Diminished reasoning
Sensory indiscrimination.

Although brain syndrome usually involves more than one of these core deficits, clinical detection of any one of them constitutes presumptive evidence of an organic mental disorder. But the clinician intent on detecting psychological masquerade cannot not rely solely on recognition of brain syndrome. There are other important clues, constituting two types of evidence. *Alerting* clues sensitize the clinician to the possibility of an organic mental disorder; even stronger in their clinical importance are *presumptive* clues. If present, they (like symptoms of brain syndrome) must be considered indicative of organicity until proven otherwise. In the presence of psychiatric symptoms, alerting clues include the following:

No history of similar symptoms
No readily identifiable cause
Age 55 or older
Coexistence of chronic disease
Use of drugs.

Presumptive clues are:

Head injury
Change in headache pattern
Visual disturbances
Speech deficits
Abnormal body movements
Sustained deviations in vital signs
Changes in consciousness.

Optionally, the clinician can use three simple screening tests: Write a Sentence, Draw a Clock, and Copy a Three-Dimensional Figure. These tests can be quickly administered. They provide supplemental information about brain functioning.

The search for clues to organic mental disorders need not be intrusive or excessively time consuming. In the course of an interview, many questions related to psychological masquerade will be answered. Those that remain unanswered can be inserted at appropriate points along the way or at the end of the interview.

The clinician greatly enhances his or her chances of detecting psychological masquerade if he or she can avoid the most common clinical errors:

Mistaking symptoms for their causes
Getting seduced by the story
Equating psychosis with schizophrenia (or functional psychosis)
Relying (unnecessarily) on limited information.

The range and subtlety of clinical manifestations of organic mental disorders are considerable as illustrated by cases of brain tumors (particularly of the frontal and temporal lobes), seizures, endocrine disorders, and AIDS. Of various masquerading conditions, drug-induced masquerades are the most common. With respect to psychological masquerade, drugs (including medications) are always suspect. Taken alone or in combination, few medications are without risk of causing organic mental disorder. Even medications used to treat psychiatric conditions are perpetrators of "psychological" symptoms in the form of adverse reactions. Both drug intoxication and drug withdrawal can cause bizarre symptoms easily misconstrued as schizophrenia.

The translation of psychological conflicts into somatic symptoms is called *somatization*. This explanatory concept, while often helpful, must be used with caution. Many cases initially thought to be somatization prove to be organic. When the characteristic clinical features of conversion disorder, simple somatization, and somatization disorder are absent, a psychosomatic explanation becomes doubtful.

Old age does not imply senility. Aging *per se* is inadequate as an explanation for psychiatric symptoms. Although conditions such as Alzheimer's disease and multi-infarct dementia are irreversible, their accurate recognition can be invaluable for purposes of planning. It also avoids inappropriate referrals and misdirected therapies. Of even greater importance, a number of conditions easily mistaken for irreversible dementia, if recognized early and properly treated, are correctable. Psychiatric symptoms appearing in a person's later years should be thoroughly evaluated medically. Sensory deficits, especially impaired hearing and decreased visual acuity, can cause psychiatric symptoms, as can accidental falls (for which older people are at special risk). Medications are always prime suspects.

As for children, any rapid change in personality or mood (especially if the child appears physically ill) should be considered organic. Other common indicators of possible organicity include psychotic symptoms and substantial declines in school performance.

Seizures and disorders of movement mimic psychological reactions in children. The key to their recognition is to avoid being distracted by accompanying psychiatric symptoms.

Finally, with the dramatic increase in eating disorders among adolescent girls, the clinician should be on alert for the various medical complications that can arise.

PUTTING IT TO THE TEST

I have selected fifteen clinical cases as a final exercise. Although most of them are examples of psychological masquerade, some are not. It is left to you, the reader, to decide. Your task, if you are game, is to review each case and to answer the following questions:

> What findings, if any, raise the suspicion of an organic mental disorder?
> Is the evidence strong enough to merit further medical evaluation?
> Based on the evidence, do you think this case was a psychological reaction or an organic mental disorder?

Once you have answered these questions to your satisfaction, turn the page and compare your answers with the facts of the case.

CASE HISTORY #1: THE TRANSFER

An aging woman in her early seventies was transferred from a nursing home to a hospital for treatment of a urinary tract infection.

Initially, she was managed on a medical service, but within a short time, psychiatric consultation was requested because she was "disturbing the rest of the ward." The examining psychiatrist found her disoriented to time and place. In addition, her general awareness fluctuated widely from one interview to another. At times she referred to objects and people in the hospital as though she were at home.

The patient had been taking several medications, one of which was the antipsychotic agent chlorpromazine. When the psychiatric consultant was unwilling to increase the medication to control the woman's "psychosis," the medical staff insisted she be transferred to the psychiatric unit. (DeVaul, 1976)

DISCUSSION: CASE HISTORY #1

Here we have an *elderly* woman taking *medications*, who, upon being examined is found to have at least one core manifestation of brain syndrome, *disorientation*. She also evidences a *fluctuating level of consciousness*. The psychiatric consultant resists the medical staff's insistence that the woman is schizophrenic and simply needs more antipsychotic medication.

After the patient was transferred to the psychiatric unit, all her medication were discontinued. Ten days later, she was alert and oriented, stating that "she felt better than she had in years."

An interesting additional note: the woman left the hospital to live with her sister instead of returning to the nursing home!

Medications are always suspect!

Condition: Drug-induced organic mental disorder.

CASE HISTORY #2 WORKAHOLIC

A highly successful businessman, age 45, with no previous psychiatric history, became obsessed with his work. Eventually, he was working so much that he managed only 2 to 3 hours of sleep a night. Impulsively, he would sometimes go on uncharacteristic spending sprees beyond his means. Although he felt extremely productive and claimed he was doing the work of five men, his boss felt otherwise. The quality of his work was down, as reflected in poor business decisions. Finally, when the man complained of headaches, his boss insisted he seek help. (Jamieson & Wells, 1979)

DISCUSSION: CASE HISTORY #2

This patient had *no previous history* of similar psychiatric symptoms. His poor business decisions could have indicated *a deterioration in simple problem-solving skills*. But the most compelling evidence for organicity was the *recent onset of headaches*.

When examined medically, the man was found to have severe papilledema (a sign of increased intracranial pressure). Four malignant masses were discovered in his brain, presumably spread there from another site. Eleven months later, he died of cancer.

Condition: Organic mental disorder secondary to metastatic cancer.

CASE HISTORY #3: THE DESPONDENT LADY

Shortly after the announcement of her only child's engagement, a 53-year-old married woman became irritable and began to overeat compulsively. Previously she had been in good health, without history of trauma, alcoholism, or drug abuse.

As the wedding approached, the woman became more and more withdrawn. She refused to have anything to do with the wedding preparations. Eventually, she lost her job because of her inability to concentrate. On occasion, her friends observed her obsessively counting out loud to herself. Later, she became obsessed with the fear of dying and had great difficulty sleeping.

When she became depressed and entertained thoughts of taking her own life, she was hospitalized in a psychiatric facility. Treatment with various psychiatric medications over 6 months produced no change; in fact, her condition worsened. She had an episode of catatonia with mutism, after which she appeared disoriented. Her walking became unsteady, and she began to urinate on herself. (Rosen & Swigar, 1976)

DISCUSSION: CASE HISTORY #3

The stressful life situation is there: A mother, "losing" her only child to marriage becomes depressed and consequently is fired from her job. Other findings, however, suggest that this explanation might be too easy.

First, this is a 53-year-old woman with *no previous history of psychiatric problems*. In addition to her becoming depressed, she *loses her ability to concentrate* to the point where she can no longer do her job.

Time and treatment, which usually alter the course of reactive depression favorably, failed to benefit this woman. The evidence for an organic mental disorder became overwhelming when she developed *catatonia, mutism, disorientation, and urinary incontinence*. But despite these symptoms, the woman was treated with electroconvulsive therapy for depression. It was only after other neurological signs appeared that a pneumoencephalogram was done and revealed normal-pressure hydrocephalus.

Neurosurgical shunting produced a gradual improvement, but residual symptoms—unsteadiness, decreased spontaneous speech, and intermittent disorientation—persisted, presumably due to irreversible brain damage sustained prior to treatment.

A final note: early in the course of her disease, this woman experienced a strong sense of impending death. Although certainly not a universal finding in organic diseases, the fear of imminent destruction often accompanies life-threatening organic mental disorders.

Condition: Organic mental disorder secondary to normal-pressure hydrocephalus.

CASE HISTORY #4: "OUT OF THIS WORLD"

"What a curious feeling!" said Alice. "I must be shutting up like a tele-scope!"

And so it was indeed: she was now only 10 inches high, and her face brightened up at the thought that she was now the right size for going through the little door into that lovely garden. First, however, she waited for a few minutes to see if she was going to shrink any fur-ther: she felt a little nervous about this; "for it might end, you know," said Alice to herself, "in my going out altogether, like a candle. I won-der what I should be like then?"

A while later . . .

"Curiouser and curiouser" cried Alice. (She was so much surprised, that for the moment she quite forgot how to speak good English). "Now I'm opening out like the largest telescope that ever was! Goodbye, feet!" (For when she looked down at her feet, they seemed to be almost out of sight, they were getting so far off.) "Oh, my poor little feet, I wonder who will put on your shoes and stockings for you now, dears? I'm sure I shan't be able! I shall be a great deal too far off to trouble myself about you: you must manage the best way you can"—"but I must be kind to them," thought Alice, "or perhaps they won't walk the way I want to go! Let me see. I'll give them a new pair of boots every Christmas." (Carroll, 1951)

DISCUSSION: CASE HISTORY #4

Of course this is not an actual case history. It is a quotation from Lewis Carroll's *Alice in Wonderland.* I have included it because of Alice's graphic description of her unusual perceptual experiences. She is suddenly seized by *bizarre visual distortions,* alternating between seeing herself as extremely small and then extremely large. During this experience, a sense of fear comes over her momentarily and she has *trouble speaking.*

A history of sudden *changes in consciousness,* if presented by a patient, constitutes presumptive evidence of organicity. Alice's problem smacks of the perceptual changes commonly seen during the initial aura of complex partial seizures. Similar perceptual distortions are associated with certain rare forms of migraine, a condition suffered by Lewis Carroll himself.

Condition: Organic mental disorder secondary to complex partial seizure (?) migraine (?)

CASE HISTORY #5: DOWNHILL

A 22-year-old male graduate student was referred to the student health service by a professor. Over the preceding semester, the student's grades had declined dramatically. He found himself unable to concentrate and had little initiative. He had difficulty falling asleep and felt "down" much of the time. These symptoms came on shortly after he broke up with his male lover, who subsequently enrolled in college in another state.

Although the young man admitted to the passing thought of suicide, there was little evidence that this was a serious consideration. On examination, he was alert and showed no abnormalities with respect to speech, vision, or movement. Other than weekend beer drinking, he denied the use of medications or drugs. There was no history of serious injury or disease. His answers to questions revealed an intact, above-average intelligence. (Taylor, 1969)

DISCUSSION: CASE HISTORY #5

This is depression resulting from a significant personal loss. It is a psychological reaction. The student's poor academic performance reflects his loss of initiative, a common finding in reactive depression. *There is no presumptive evidence of an organic mental disorder.* The absence of such findings in conjunction with an identifiable precipitant argues against an organic mental disorder.

The student was in weekly psychotherapy sessions for 2 months. He worked through his personal loss and resumed most of his social activities. His school performance improved greatly.

Condition: Psychological reactive depression.

CASE HISTORY #6: SUPERNATURAL

Suddenly, she would be "seized by a horrible feeling of terror." The "spells" came over this 44-year-old woman irrespective of what she was doing. Initially, she would detect a strange odor, "a horrible smell—not a real smell—somewhat like the smell of burning hedges." At times she felt she was choking on this unpleasant odor.

Although she rarely lost consciousness, on one occasion she fell to the floor. For a short while after these spells, she was unable to respond but could hear conversations. There were times when she felt an unusual sensation in her abdomen. (MacRae, 1954)

DISCUSSION: CASE HISTORY #6

Episodic attacks of *shifts in consciousness, olfactory hallucinations, and the inability to speak* must be considered organic.

When this woman was evaluated neurologically, she was found to be of normal intelligence without memory deficit or disorientation. Visual testing, however, revealed that she was functionally blind in her right eye. She had also lost the sense of smell in her right nostril. These findings, along with her clinical history, suggested the possibility of a tumor. At surgery, a sizable meningioma was removed from the right temporal and frontal areas. Six months later the woman reported that she had not experienced any more attacks. It should be noted that the woman's vague awareness during her seizures could easily have been mistaken for a hysterical reaction.

Condition: Organic mental disorder secondary to a right frontotemporal meningioma.

CASE HISTORY #7: SATAN'S WORK

She had been in excellent health, an active high school student and a competitive swimmer. Suddenly, she changed. She took copious notes on her family's conversations and on various television programs, making comments no one else could understand. At times, her speech was jumbled. After 3 days of this strange behavior, she developed chills and felt that "Satan is taking me over." Her parents drove her to the hospital. She was treated with neuroleptic medication without any improvement. Her speech became more slurred, until finally she stopped speaking altogether. Her temperature was 102° F. After being observed walking with a limp, she was transferred to the psychiatric service of a university hospital. (Wilson, 1976)

DISCUSSION: CASE HISTORY #7

A healthy high school student *abruptly becomes psychotic.* She develops a *speech deficit, begins to limp, and has a fever of 102°F with chills.* The real question is why she was ever admitted to a psychiatric service! Her condition should have been recognized as neurological.

Shortly after her admission, spinal fluid taken from a spinal tap showed white cells, indicative of a central nervous system infection. Her elctroencephalogram (EEG) showed changes consistent with this diagnosis. It was presumed that she had contracted herpes simplex encephalitis, a viral infection with a particular predilection for the limbic system.

Condition: Organic mental disorder secondary to herpes simplex encephalitis.

CASE HISTORY #8: SUSPICIONS

After 6 months of alleged sobriety, a 45-year-old woman was admitted to the hospital when she became unable to care for herself. Her husband insisted she had not started drinking again. He had no explanation for why she had neglected her housework and stumbled about the house. On occasion, she had lost her way in the neighborhood. She had also been involved in several minor automobile accidents.

While being interviewed, the woman claimed that her husband was trying to have her committed so that he could continue his affair with a neighbor's wife. When asked the date, she was off by 10 days. Later, after her admission to a hospital ward, she wandered away and was unable to find her way back.

On mental status examination, her hands were tremulous. She made several errors in serial subtractions and was able to recall only one out of three objects after 5 minutes. (Horvath, 1979)

DISCUSSION: CASE HISTORY #8

Difficulty walking, with a *recent history of automobile accidents* and *losing her way* in the neighborhood made a psychological explanation highly unlikely. The argument for organicity is strengthened by her *disorientation and problem with recent memory*.

After several days of hospitalization, a large quantity of proprietary sedatives containing bromides was found in the woman's locker. A blood test for bromide showed a level that accounted for her cognitive deficits. Several days later, once the bromide had been excreted from her system, the woman was bright and alert.

Condition: Organic mental disorder secondary to bromide intoxication.

CASE HISTORY #9: MYSTERY WOMAN

A patrol policeman, making his nightly rounds, discovered a middle-aged woman in a deserted parking lot. She was disheveled and had no possessions other than the clothes she wore. She did not speak spontaneously but did follow simple instructions and attempted to answer questions. She had no idea of who or where she was. (Gregory, 1968)

DISCUSSION: CASE HISTORY #9

This woman is *mute*. Her untidiness as well as the fact that she appears lost suggests *cognitive impairment*. On this basis, she should receive a thorough medical examination.

This was done but revealed no evidence for organicity. The woman was having a psychological reaction known as *dissociation*. Her inability to remember where or who she was turned out to be a psychological defense against facing up to her problems. Closer evaluation showed that, in fact, she was not disoriented and her memory was intact. Another indicator of the psychological nature of the problem was disorientation to self. While disorientation to time and place is a hallmark of brain syndrome, disorientation to self is quite rare in organic conditions.

The fact that further evaluation did not confirm this as a case of psychological masquerade does not detract from the importance of entertaining the possibility. Looking for masquerading conditions will inevitably turn up a few false positives.

Condition: Psychological reaction, dissociative disorder.

CASE HISTORY #10: STOPS AND STARTS

For 5 years, a middle-aged man had periods of peculiar behavior, lasting a few minutes to several hours. Gradually, they increased in frequency until they were occurring four or five times a week. The man's behavior varied from one episode to another but was always strikingly different from his usual self.

On one occasion, he wandered aimlessly about the place where he worked for more than 2 hours. Eventually, he removed his shirt and stared silently at the people around him. At home, during another attack, he abruptly stopped chopping wood and then walked through his neighborhood, glassy-eyed, holding an ax in a threatening manner. When he was finally taken to a hospital, his speech was indistinct, and he exhibited grotesque movements.

He had no recollection of these periods. Others related how they seemed to occur more often after excessive exertion or toward the end of the morning. (Romano & Coon, 1942)

DISCUSSION: CASE HISTORY #10

Unexplained *shifts in consciousness* and *memory disturbance*, plus, on at least one occasion, *disturbed speech* and *abnormal body movements* add up to organicity. The fact that these attacks came on after excessive exertion and during the morning hours provides an important clue to the etiology.

Eventually, a fellow employee (whom the patient threatened with a knife during one of these attacks), having observed numerous episodes at work, wrote out a detailed description. He described the man as quite pale, unsteady on his feet, and sweating profusely.

Laboratory studies confirmed that these episodes correlated with severe drops in the patient's blood sugar, the product of an insulinoma, an insulin-producing tumor.

Condition: Organic mental disorder secondary to hypoglycemia resulting from an insulinoma.

CASE HISTORY #11: A THING FOR LIGHT POLES

A 67-year-old retired x-ray technician moved to Las Vegas, Nevada, to be closer to her son. She was bright, active, and independent. Adjustment to her relocation went well until she started having strange urges. She had never experienced anything like it before. When she passed light poles on the street, she was overcome with the desire to swing herself around the pole and climb it!

Other changes followed. When she left her house, she felt compelled to crawl through the window rather than going out the door. Although fully aware of how peculiar her behavior was, she had a hard time resisting. She also started having memory lapses and found herself having to buy a newspaper in order to keep up with what week or month it was. Occasionally, after being out shopping, she had trouble finding her way home. She felt nervous about what was happening. Her intellect, however, did not seem to suffer. She had no headaches or difficulty walking, and she continued to lead an independent life. (Giarrantano, 1988)

DISCUSSION: CASE HISTORY #11

An older woman undergoes the stress of moving to a new home where she is alone and in a strange place. Is that enough to account for her peculiar symptoms? Not really. Perhaps so if it were a matter of her becoming mildly depressed or anxious, but not when she abruptly starts to have irresistible urges to climb light poles and crawl through windows along with telltale *signs of brain syndrome.*

Although it is true that the ability to remember things normally shows some decline with age, old age itself does not cause *memory lapses* where chunks of what has happened disappear. She also was *disoriented to time and space.*

It is not clear why this woman failed to seek help earlier. Perhaps it was her independent nature; perhaps it was her need to deny that anything was wrong. Whatever the case, she suffered in silence for almost a year. Finally, after volunteering as a foster parent, she underwent a mandatory physical examination. She mentioned the changes she had been having and was referred to another doctor who, upon hearing her story, sent her to a neurologist. It was only then that a diagnosis was made of a right-sided frontal lobe tumor (most likely a meningioma). The tumor was sizable, but after preliminary cooling, it was successfully removed.

Nine years later, at the age of 76, the woman was a volunteer teacher and a foster grandparent. Her only problem was a slight speech impediment that lingered after surgery.

Condition: Organic mental disorder secondary to a frontal lobe tumor.

CASE HISTORY #12: A RULER'S RUIN

He was a man of considerable power, ruling over a vast empire. Although other countries were constant threats to him, it was not a foreign power that eventually brought him down.

In the middle of his life, the ruler suffered painful, debilitating episodes every few years without warning or cause. He became giddy, talking and pacing nonstop. His ideas came in torrents; before one was finished, another took a different tangent. At night his condition worsened. He became confused; he heard voices and saw things that were not actually present. Upon awakening he would insist on seeing the queen to make certain she had not been abducted. On occasion he became totally exhausted and fell into despair. His muscles weakened so that he could not walk or even speak. He also experienced strange fits of pain. Doubled over in agony, he could not stand to be touched (not even by the bedclothes) without crying out in pain.

During one of his most severe attacks, royal physicians debated behind closed doors whether or not he would ever recover his mental faculties. Word leaked out that the ruler was gravely incapacitated. Political forces aligned themselves for a takeover, but suddenly he recovered—temporarily. Several years later, he became "violently insane." Secret arrangements were made for his wife to assume power. He remained psychotic with only brief intervals of lucidity until he died, 9 years later. (Macalpine & Hunter, 1969)

DISCUSSION: CASE HISTORY #12

This is the true story of the tragic life of King George III, who ruled England during the Seven Years' War, when an empire was won, and during the Revolutionary War, when the American colonies were lost.

In 1941, a leading psychoanalyst, Dr. Manfred Guttmacher, wrote a book entitled *America's Last King: An Interpretation of the Madness of George III* (Guttmacher, 1941). He offered his expert opinion that the King's problems could be fully explained psychologically: "His five manic attacks were precipitated by political and domestic events that pierced his very vulnerable defenses and caused him to decompensate." Guttmacher went on to speculate how the King lost his mental balance "when he found himself impotent and unable to act."

Dr. Guttmacher was wrong. He failed to pay enough attention to clues of organic mental disorder. The King suffered *visual and auditory hallucinations*. He became *confused*, more so at night. He manifested a *severe somatic pain syndrome*, incompatible with hysteria or conversion disorder. In addition, he experienced *muscle weakness* that *prevented him from walking* and *compromised his speech*.

The King's problem was a psychological masquerade. Although, to be certain, he had plenty to deal with, his condition was not the result of a stressful life. Most likely he suffered from porphyria, a genetic metabolic disease, resulting from the lack of a certain enzyme. The buildup of porphyrins causes brain dysfunction and severe attacks of abdominal pain. One-third of people with this form of porphyria are admitted to mental hospitals, usually with the mistaken diagnosis of schizophrenia or bipolar disorder.

Condition: Organic mental disorder secondary to porphyria.

CASE HISTORY #13: GOING CRAZY

A 10-year-old girl abruptly became hostile, anorexic, and unable to sleep. After a few days she was muttering irrational phrases and "seeing" things. Within 3 weeks she stopped speaking altogether and was incontinent of urine and feces. A psychiatrist and a neurologist examined her; both considered her psychotic. Treatment with several different neuroleptics proved of no benefit.

Three months after the onset of her symptoms, the girl was admitted to a child and adolescent psychiatric service where she was aggressive, hyperactive, and emotionally labile. There were frequent unprovoked episodes of shouting or crying. She resisted all attempts by staff to relate to her.

With the exception of periodic bouts of tonsillitis, she had been in good health. There was no previous psychiatric history. (Matarazzo, 1996)

DISCUSSION: CASE HISTORY #13

The *abrupt change* in a 10-year-old *without previous psychiatric history* tells a powerful story. These two facts alone demand a relentless search for a causative medical condition. With the onset of *visual hallucinations* and *urinary and fecal incontinence*, the case for organic mental disorder is essentially made.

The patient's white blood cell count was elevated. An examination of her throat revealed the source of infection: inflamed tonsils and adenoids. The swollen glands were removed surgically. Three days post-op, the patient started to speak again. Within 10 days, normal hygiene was established. A month later, she was writing and drawing again, and was playing normally with other children. Her mother said she was back to normal. Her speech, however, remained slightly impaired, and there was some residual disorganization in her EEG. She was treated with adrenocortieotropic hormone(ACTH) and prophylactic penicillin. One year later her EEG had normalized and she was reportedly doing well mentally and physically.

It was thought that antibodies stimulated by the infection of her tonsils and adenoids had attacked her brain. (This is the same mechanism underlying the *paraneoplastic encephalitis* associated with certain cases of cancer.) Removing the site of infection interrupted the stimulation of antibodies, allowing for partial brain recovery. The addition of ACTH (an anti-inflammatory hormone) completed the treatment.

Condition: Autoimmune encephalitis associated with tonsillitis.

CASE HISTORY #14: A MILKMAN'S STORY

A 41-year-old milkman underwent a major personality change. In contrast to his usual assertive and energetic self, he became tentative and passive. He slept a lot and appeared apathetic. He began to make mistakes at work, and in a 6-month period he was involved in four road accidents. During the prior 23 years, he had not had any accidents. He had no major medical problems and was without any psychiatric history.

Finally, (2 years later), he was referred to a neuropsychiatric service for evaluation. Although generally alert, he appeared disoriented at times. He confabulated and repeated himself. After 5 minutes he was unable to recall a name and address. Based on the man's inconsistent performance and his seeming lack of concern, a tentative diagnosis of hysteria was made. (Hotopf, Pollock, & Lishman, 1994)

DISCUSSION: CASE HISTORY #14

Midlife psychological changes happen, but *four driving accidents* in 6 months in a man with a stellar, 23-year driving record does not fit the pattern. Similarly, *mistakes at work (cognitive decline)* suggest more than a midlife crisis. The mental status examination cannot be dismissed as pointing to "hysteria," at least not justifiably. The man is *disoriented* and has a *disturbance of recent memory* severe enough to cause him to make up answers (confabulate). These findings, when considered in the larger context of the patient's personality change, declining work performance, and history of accidents make a good case for organic mental disorder.

Over the next 8 years, this man underwent a steady deterioration. His cognitive ability was profoundly compromised. With respect to speech, he became dysphasic. He had severe ataxia and was incontinent of urine. Eventually, he was diagnosed as having multiple sclerosis.

Condition: Organic mental disorder secondary to multiple sclerosis.

CASE HISTORY #15: HOMICIDAL MANIAC

A young man in his late twenties was transported to a psychiatric hospital after threatening to kill his father with a knife. The father said the episode was unprovoked. His son had a history of alcohol dependence (and other drug use), with at least one episode of delirium tremens, but he did not appear intoxicated when he confronted his father. His knife-wielding behavior was out of character.

On the psychiatric unit, he was paranoid and obsessed with the thought that his father was out to steal his money. After being diagnosed as having "schizophrenia and antisocial personality with alcohol and drug abuse," he was started on antipsychotic medications. The treatment proved of little benefit. (Tardiff, 1998)

DISCUSSION: CASE HISTORY #15

After 2 months in the hospital with little improvement in his "schizophrenia," the patient became increasingly lethargic, disoriented, and forgetful. He was unable to concentrate, even for short periods. He contracted pneumonia, and—despite intensive treatment—died. Before his death, an HIV test was positive. An autopsy showed evidence of encephalitis.

An initial episode of schizophrenia at age 29, although possible, is unlikely. In this case, other than paranoid thought, there was no supporting evidence for this diagnosis. The behavior that got the man into the hospital—pulling a knife on his father—*was out of character for him and, apparently, not the product of intoxication.* But it is easy to see how the assumption was made that his behavior had something to do with his alcoholism, perhaps another episode of DTs. Once in the hospital, as the "alcoholic" explanation became increasingly questionable, the paranoid psychosis remained to be explained. Schizophrenia became a handy substitute. The loose use of the term *schizophrenia* underlines many a clinical mistake.

Drug use always raises the possibility of HIV infection. Persons who "shoot up" and share needles are at high risk. AIDS is a common cause of psychological masquerade.

Condition: Encephalitis secondary to HIV infection.

REFERENCES

Carroll, L. (1951). *Alice in wonderland and other favorites*. New York: Washington Square Press.

DeVaul, R. (1976). Acute organic brain syndrome: clinical considerations. *Texas Medicine, 72*, 51–54.

Giarrantano, S. (1988). Personal communication.

Gregory, I. (1968). *Fundamentals of psychiatry* (Second Edition; pp. 352–358). Philadelphia: W. B. Saunders.

Guttmacher, M. (1941). *America's last king, an interpretation of the madness of George III*. New York: C. Scribner & Sons.

Hotopf, M., Pollock, W, & Lishman, W. (1994). An unusual presentation of multiple sclerosis. *Psychological Medicine, 24*, 525–528.

Horvath, T. (1979). Organic brain syndromes. In A., Freeman, R., Sack, P., & Berger, (Eds.), *Psychiatry for the primary care physician* (p. 228). Baltimore: Williams & Wilkins.

Jamieson, R. & Wells, C. (1979). Manic psychosis in a patient with multiple metastatic brain tumors. *Journal of Clinical Psychiatry, 40*, 280–283.

Macalpine, I. & Hunter, R. (1969). *George III and the mad business*. New York: Pantheon Books.

MacRae, D. (1954). Isolated fear: a temporal lobe aura. *Neurology, 4*, 497–505.

Matarazzo, E. (1996). Organic psychosis linked to chronic tonsillitis and subsequent encephalitis: a probable autoimmune process. *Biological Psychiatry, 40*, 292–294.

Romano, J. & Coon, G. (1942). Physiologic and psychologic studies in spontaneous hypoglycemia. *Psychosomatic Medicine, 4*, 283–300.

Rosen, H. & Swigar, M. (1976). Depression and normal pressure hydrocephalus. *Journal of Nervous and Mental Disease, 163*, 35–40.

Tardiff, K. (1998). Unusual diagnoses among violent patients. *Psychiatric Clinics of North America, 21*, 567–576.

Taylor, R. (1969). Extracted from private clinical files.

Wilson, L. (1976). Viral encephalopathy mimicking functional psychosis. *American Journal of Psychiatry, 133*, 165–170.

Annotated Bibliography

Adams, R., Victor, M., & Ropper, A. (1997). *Principles of neurology (6th Ed.).* New York: McGraw-Hill.

This is an up-to-date general neurology text with excellent chapters on delirium and dementia.

Angell, M., & Kassirer, J. (1998). Alternative medicine—the risks of untested and unregulated remedies. *New England Journal of Medicine, 339,* 839–841.

This essay reminds us that alternative medicines have their share of adverse effects. A substance promoted as an immune booster has estrogenic effects. "Natural" dietary supplements turn up contaminated with heavy metals and digitalis. With respect to psychological masquerade, alternative medicines, like conventional medicines, are always suspect.

Anonymous (1950). Death of a mind: a study in disintegration. *Lancet, 1,* 1012–1015.

In Chapter 3, I quote extensively from this article. If I could recommend but a single reference to give the clinician a feeling for the emergence of brain syndrome, this would be it. Written by a sympathetic, personally involved, keen observer, this presentation poignantly communicates the struggle of a deteriorating mind.

Benson, D. F. (1978). Amnesia. *Southern Medical Journal, 71,* 1221–1227.

Written by an outstanding behavioral neurologist, this article characterizes amnesia as the impaired ability to learn despite normal immediate and long-term memory and the preservation of other cognitive abilities. Though brief, it is fully packed with information on the various presentations of defective recent memory.

Benson, D. F., & Blumer, D. (Eds.). (1975). *Psychiatric aspects of neurological disease.* New York: Grune & Stratton.

Various authors cover the mental concomitants of physical disease, dementia, disorders of verbal expression, personality changes with frontal and temporal lobe disorders, organic brain syndromes, temporal lobe epilepsy, and spontaneous and drug-induced movement disorders seen in psychotic patients. The opening chapter by the late Norman Geschwind, entitled, "Some Common Misconceptions," serves as an excellent introduction to psychological masquerade. The final chapter includes a series of cases of "organic brain disease mistaken for psychiatric disorder."

Chan, B. (1999). Delirium: making the diagnosis, improving the prognosis. *Geriatrics, 54*, 28–30, 36, 39–42.

This is an informative look at delirium in older persons. It describes a basic approach to the diagnosis and management of this medical emergency and reviews distinctions between dementia, delirium, and depression. Under a miscellaneous category of potential causes, the author discusses changes in environment, urinary retention, and sensory deprivation.

Comfort, A. (1980). *Practice of geriatric psychiatry,* New York: Elsevier.

A well-written presentation of psychiatric problems among the elderly, this book includes chapters on the assessment of "senility" and "organic cementing processes." The first chapter is a must. In a few pages, the author does a masterful job of introducing the subject of psychiatric symptoms among the aged, with special emphasis on those arising from medical disorders. "Of all old people who present with a 'psychiatric' problem, between 10% and 30% owe their illness to an undiagnosed medical condition, or to the effects of medication, or to both."

Cummings, J. L. (1988). Organic psychosis, *Psychosomatics, 29*, 16–26.

Cummings focuses on specific delusional syndromes reported in organic psychoses, including Capgras syndrome, lycanthropy, and parasitosis. He drives home the point that Schneiderian first-rank symptoms are not restricted to schizophrenia. They occur in organic mental disorders as well.

Dilsaver, S. (1992). Differentiating organic from functional psychosis. *American Family Physician, 45*, 1173–1180.

This article emphasizes the fact that "psychosis is not pathognomonic of psychiatric illness." Rather, it is a syndrome that can arise from a broad array of medical disorders. Much of the article is spent on the differentiating aspects of functional and organic psychoses.

Gelenberg, A. J. (1976). The catatonic syndrome. *Lancet, 1*, 1339–1341.

In a brief, but highly informative look at one particular psychological masquerade the author describes cases of catatonia resulting from Parkinson's disease, viral encephalitis, brain tumors, epilepsy (petit mal), diabetes, and psychoactive drug intoxication.

Hooper, J., & Teres, D. (1986). *The three-pound universe.* New York: G. P. Putnam's Sons.

This is the book you want to read if you are looking for a relatively pain- less way to review the way the brain works. You get a sense of the writers' somewhat offbeat style by the titles of various chapters: "Caligula's Brain—The Neurology of Violence," "Anatomy of Hallucination: Prophets of the Void," and "The Hanged Man: Altered States of Consciousness."

Illowsky, B., & Kirch, D. (1988). Polydipsia and hyponatremia in psy- chiatric patients. *American Journal of Psychiatry, 145,* 675–683.

These authors review "water intoxication" and its various manifestations, including confusion, lethargy, and psychosis. This strange syndrome has been found in association with schizophrenia, affective disorders, organic brain syndrome, anorexia nervosa, and personality disorders.

Jacobson, S. (1997). Delirium in the elderly, *Psychiatric Clinics of North America, 20,* 91–110.

Jacobson covers the causes, diagnosis, and treatment of delirium. She emphasizes that delirium, especially if it is not recognized early, can become dementia. Among the elderly, delirium may be the only clue to an undiagnosed life-threatening condition, such as myocardial infarction.

Jenike, M. (1988). Psychoactive drugs in the elderly: antipsychotics and anxiolytics, *Geriatrics, 43,* 53–65.

Jenike discusses reasons for the increased susceptibility of older persons to side effects of psychoactive drugs, covering antipsychotic medications, anxiolytics, and sleeping medications.

Katon, W., Sheehan, D., & Uhde, T. (1988). Panic disorder: a treat- able problem, *Patient Care, 22,* 148–173.

This discussion of the different faces of panic disorder underscores an abrupt onset as its most distinctive feature and describes the overwhelm- ing feeling of unreality that people undergoing panic attacks often feel. Good descriptions of how patients, sensing they are going to die or lose their minds, often frantically skip from one health provider to another in search of relief. Phobias, depression, and substance abuse may emerge if effective intervention is not forthcoming.

Lawall, J. (1976). Psychiatric presentations of seizure disorders. *American Journal of Psychiatry, 133,* 321–323.

Lawall offers a look at the various ways seizure disorders are mistaken for psychological reactions. He comments on temporal lobe epilepsy as well as grand mal and petit mal seizures and provides three illustrative case histories to "demonstrate some of the principles to keep in mind in diagnosing epilepsy with predominantly psychiatric symptoms."

Lishman, W. (1997). *Organic psychiatry: the psychological consequences of cerebral disorder (3rd Ed.)*, Oxford: Blackwell Scientific Publications.

This is the most comprehensive single volume on organic mental disorders—a truly encyclopedic presentation. It is an excellent resource for the clinician wanting to review in detail specific diseases that give rise to organic mental disorders. Filled with case examples, it is elaborately documented. This is a one-of-a-kind, exhaustive resource.

Maletzky, B. (1973). The episodic dyscontrol syndrome. *Diseases of the Nervous System, 34,* 178–185.

Relying heavily on his clinical study of 22 persons with episodic dyscontrol, the author discusses this controversial syndrome of violence. Two illustrative case histories are included.

Marangell, L., Yudofsky, S., & Silver, J. (1999). Psychopharmacology and electroconvulsive therapy. In R. Hales, S. Yudofsky, & J. Talbott (Eds.). *APA Textbook of psychiatry (3rd Ed.)*, Washington, DC: American Psychiatric Press (vol. 27, pp. 1025–1132).

A thorough, up-to-date review of psychopharmacology.

Marsh, C. (1997). Psychiatric presentations of medical illness. *Psychiatric Clinics of North America, 20,* 181–204.

This overview defines organic mental disorders as mental symptoms judged to be the direct physiological consequence of a general medical condition. It lists various DSM-IV categories, including delirium, dementia, amnestic disorder, other cognitive disorders, and disorders due to a general medical condition.

Moss, R., D'Amico, S., & Maletta, G. (1987). Mental dysfunction as a sign of organic illness in the elderly. *Geriatrics, 42,* 35–40.

This article focuses on three masqueraders found in older adults: vitamin B_{12} deficiency, hypothyroidism, and normal-pressure hydrocephalus. Emphasis is on the early onset of psychiatric symptoms in B_{12} deficiency, before neurological or hematological changes appear. With respect to thyroid disease, the authors point out the limits of routine thyroid function tests. They miss subclinical hypothyroidism in 50% of cases. Regarding normal-pressure hydrocephalus, they underscore the frequent occurrence of apathy and the difficulty shifting from one task to another.

Newton, H. (1995). Common neurologic complications of HIV-1 infection and AIDS. *American Family Physician, 51*, 387–398.

Newton provides a good overview of AIDS dementia complex.

Perry, S., & Jacobsen, P. (1986). Neuropsychiatric manifestations of AIDSspectrum disorders. *Hospital and Community Psychiatry, 37*, 135–142.

This is a review of functional and organic mental symptoms related to AIDS. Psychological reactions in response to serious disease are to be expected, but organic mental disorders secondary to opportunistic infections, malignancies of the brain, and direct viral invasion of the nervous system are also common complications. The authors include several illustrative case histories.

Pincus, J. H., & Tucker, G. J. (1985). *Behavioral neurology (3rd Ed.).* New York: Oxford University Press.

The chapter entitled "Disorders of Intellectual Functioning" considers several organic conditions seen in children, including autism, minimal brain damage, and nutritional disorders. The concluding chapter, "Distinguishing Neurological and Psychiatric Disorders," contains particularly helpful information on hyperventilation, headache, and hysteria.

Ramachandran, V. S., & Blakeslee, S. (1998). *Phantoms in the brain.* New York: William Morrow (Quill).

This is a an engaging exploration of masquerading neurological conditions. Chapter 9, "God and the Limbic System," is a real tour de force.

Rapoport, J., & Fiske, A. (1998). The new biology of obsessive-compulsive disorder: implications for evolutionary psychology. *Perspectives in Biology and Medicine, 41*, 159–175.

The authors make an engaging case for a biological substrate of obsessive-compulsive disorders, offering a good review of the circuitry in the basal ganglia capable of short-circuiting and causing secondary OCD symptom. They include an excellent discussion of recent findings suggesting an autoimmune basis for certain cases of OCD (a neuropsychiatric equivalent of Sydenham's chorea).

Reite, M. (1998). Sleep disorders presenting as psychiatric disorders. *Psychiatric Clinics of North America, 21*, 591–607.

Reite discusses sleep disorders that most commonly present as psychiatric cases: delayed sleep phase syndrome, sleep behavior disorders, sleep apnea, and narcolepsy. He includes a case of homicidal somnabulism in which a killer is acquitted on the basis of his sleep disorder.

Rhawn, J. (1996). *Neuropsychiatry, neuropsychology, and clinical neuroscience (2nd Ed.)*. Baltimore: Williams & Wilkins.

This book contains a comprehensive review of brain evolution and brain anatomy and function.

Rossman, P. L. (1969). Organic diseases resembling functional disorders. *Hospital Medicine, 5*, 72–76.

Rossman offers a discussion based on a study of 130 patients whose initial symptoms led to various psychiatric diagnoses but who subsequently were found to have organic diseases. The author stresses the futility of trying to match psychiatric symptoms to certain organic diseases. For example, in his study, he found that hyperthryoidism masquerades as four different symptoms: anxiety, psychoneurosis, personality disorder, and depressive reaction. This article highlights the need for an approach to psychological masquerade based on general principles rather than a cookbook listing of all diseases that can masquerade.

Sachs, O. (1998). *The man who mistook his wife for a hat and other clinical tales*. New York: Touchstone Books.

This extraordinary writer/neurologist provides us with an exquisite exploration of unexpected perceptual and cognitive aberrations arising from breakdowns in the brain. Through a series of true cases, the author describes the workings of aphasia, agnosia, and compulsion. An extraordinary book.

Saravay, S., & Koran, L. (1977). Organic disease mistakenly diagnosed as psychiatric. *Psychosomatics, 18*, 6–11.

The authors discuss their experiences on a psychiatric consultation service, where 4% of all referrals were instances of organic illness masquerading as psychological reactions. Although 4% may seem like a low figure, it is impressive when you consider that these referrals were made by physicians. The article contains four illustrative case histories.

Schatzberg, A., Cole, J., & DeBattista, C. (1997). *Manual of clinical psychopharmacology (3rd Ed.)*. Washington, D.C.: American Psychiatric Press.

This is an outstanding, readable compendium of psychiatric medications with good discussions of their benefits and adverse effects.

Stephenson, J., & Ohirich, E. (1988). The major complications associated with eating disorders and their pathophysiology. In K. Clark, R. Parr, & W. Castelli (Eds.), *Evaluation and management of eating disorders*. Champaign, Illinois: Life Enhancement Publications.

This work covers most of the medical problems associated with bulimia and anorexia. It gives the reader a solid grounding in medical complications that can be overshadowed by the more dramatic symptoms of an eating disorder.

Stoudemire, A., & Fogel, B. (Eds.) (1993). *Psychiatric care of the medical patient*, New York: Oxford University Press.

This is a comprehensive text. There are two particularly relevant sections. Section III, Neuropsychiatry, covers dementia, delirium, sleep disorders, and traumatic brain injury. Section IV takes a look at specific disorders, including endocrine diseases, respiratory and cardiac conditions, and sexual impotence.

Tardiff, K. (1998). Unusual diagnoses among violent patients. *Psychiatric Clinics of North America, 21*, 567–576.

After making the point that most violence does not result from specific medical disorders, the author reviews a variety of cases of biologically based violence. He emphasizes that while medical and neurological signs are often present, sometimes all the clinician has to go on are psychiatric symptoms. The somewhat rare cases of violence arising from medical disorders are important to keep in mind, since they are often treatable.

Waugh, E. (1957). *The Ordeal of Gilbert Pinfold*, Boston: Little, Brown and Company.

This is a semiautobiographical, fictional account of a successful but nerve-racked middle-aged novelist who sets out on a recuperative trip to Ceylon. As a result of his overindulgence in self-prescribed medications, the gentleman soon finds himself in a terrifying world of barking dogs, wild jazz bands, loud revival meetings, and threatening voices of strangers. The reader sees the world through the eyes of a man caught up in the throes of the paranoid confusion of organic brain syndrome. Good reading.

Woodruff, R., Goodwin, D., & Guze, S. (1989). *Psychiatric diagnosis (4th Ed.)*, New York: Oxford University Press.

A "no-nonsense," "just-the-facts" treatment of the major psychiatric diagnoses, this book provides an excellent discussion of psychiatric diagnoses including somatization disorder (hysteria) and brain syndrome. In a time when many psychiatric texts have become voluminous (and often extraneous), this "little" volume remains an excellent practical reference.

Index

Note: Page numbers followed by letters *f* and *t* indicate figures and tables, respectively.

$ *Springer Publishing Company*

Psychosocial Interventions in the Home: Housecalls

Nancy A. Newton, PhD
Kadi Sprengle, PhD, Editors

This book provides a comprehensive introduction to home-based psychosocial interventions. The editors examine current treatment models and programs designed to meet the needs of children, adolescents, adults, and the elderly. In-depth presentations of clinical cases from a variety of mental health populations and first person accounts from clients and caregivers illustrate the realities of this work, ranging from families in crisis to acute and chronic stages of mental illness. Several chapters by experts in their respective areas provide guidelines for dealing with constraints particular to managed care, mental health law, assessment and treatment interventions, and training and supervision for professional and paraprofessional home-based caregivers. Psychologists and social workers in home care will find this a valuable resource.

2000   312pp.   0-8261-1339-7   hard   www.springerpub.com

536 Broadway, New York, NY 10012-3955 • (212) 431-4370 • Fax (212) 941-7842

Springer Publishing Company

Primary Care Psychiatry and Behavioral Medicine

Brief Office Treatment and Management Pathways

Robert E. Feinstein, MD, and Anne A. Brewer, MD

"The material is practical, thorough, and well-written. It is a valuable addition to the library of every physician working in the outpatient setting."
—**Robert E. Rakel**, MD, Professor
Department of Family and Community Medicine,
Baylor College of Medicine

This volume provides primary care physicians with a desk reference to psychiatric and behavioral conditions they are likely to encounter in office-based practice. Each chapter focuses on a specific psychiatric disorder or on behavioral factors that predispose or follow upon a medical illness. For each disorder, the authors provide a description of the condition, its prevalence, its course and indicators, and then treatment issues including pharmacology, psychological interventions, and medical considerations. The text is chock-full of tables and figures that allow the reader to easily look up questions or concentrate on just one condition.

Partial Contents: Introduction • Psychosocial Aspects of Primary Care: Theoretical Considerations, *P. M. Rabinowitz* **Psychiatric Disorders in Primary Care** • Anxiety Disorders, *R.E. Feinstein* • Psychological Disorders of Childhood and Adolescence, *M. Hart and S. Kaye* • **Behavioral Medicine in Primary Care** • Cardiovascular and Psychosocial Risk Factors Reduction: Office Based Interventions, *R.E. Feinstein et al.* • Women's Health Through the Reproductive Cycle: Premenstrual Syndrome, Post-Partum Disorders and Menopause, *E.C. Caligor and M. Ormont* • Death & Dying, *A.A. Brewer and J.V. Connelly* • **Psychosocial Treatments in Primary Care** • Consulting and Counseling in Primary Care, *L. Prunofsky and R.E. Feinstein* • Crisis Intervention in Office Practice, *R.E. Feinstein and L. Carey* • Family Counseling, *A.A. Brewer and C. Creech* • Behavioral Counseling and Medical Adherence, *R.E. Feinstein and J. Pachman*

1998   528pp.   0-8261-1224-2   hardcover   www.springerpub.com

536 Broadway, New York, NY 10012-3955 • (212) 431-4370 • Fax (212) 941-7842

Springer Publishing Company

Telemedicine and Telehealth
Principles, Policies, Performance and Pitfalls

Adam William Darkins, MD, MPH, FRCS
Margaret Ann Cary, MD, MBA, MPH

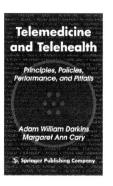

"The most comprehensive resource on telehealth. Clearly a must read for those who feel telehealth can rebuild the physician-patient relationship."
—**Charles Safran,** MD
Chief Executive Officer
Clinician Support Technology

"This is the thinking person's gateway to the world of telemedicine...these authors set the stage for nearly everyone involved in planning or evaluating a telemedicine program, policy, or research project."

—**Douglas A. Perednia,** MD
Founder and President
Association of Telemedicine Service Providers

Telemedicine and telehealth are changing the face of health care delivery and becoming a multi-billion dollar industry. The authors provide practical insights and advice on transforming telemedicine programs into successful clinical services.

Contents: Introduction • Definitions of Telemedicine and Telehealth and a History of the Remote Management of Disease • Telehealth: A Patient Perspective • Telehealth and Relationships with Physicians • Using Telehealth to Make Health Care Transactions • Telehealth Services • Regulatory, Legislative and Political Considerations in Telehealth • The Market for Telehealth Services • Contracting for Telehealth Services • The Business of Telehealth • The Management of Telehealth Services • Choosing the Right Technology for Telehealth • Other Important Influences on Health Care that Affect the Future of Telehealth • References • Glossary of Terms and Abbreviations

2000   328pp.   0-8261-1302-8   hard   www.springerpub.com

536 Broadway, New York, NY 10012-3955 • (212) 431-4370 • Fax (212) 941-7842

$\boxed{\text{S}}$ *Springer Publishing Company*

Making Collaborative Connections With Medical Providers

A Guide for Mental Health Professionals

L. Kevin Hamberger, PhD, Christopher Ovide, EdD, and Eric L. Weiner, PhD

"A helpful primer on collaboration for the wide range of therapists who are considering working closely with primary care physicians. This practical book will help!"

-William Doherty, PhD
Dept. of Family and Social Services,
University of Minnesota

This book provides detailed, concrete, and practical information on successful collaborations between physicians and mental health service providers. The authors draw on their experience working with physicians on referrals in a variety of clinical settings and specialties. Mental health professionals will find important basic skills such as how to present their credentials to medical providers; negotiate through the referral process; follow through after a referral; and report back to physicians on cases. This is a valuable guidebook for clinical psychologists, family therapists, social workers and others who want to establish more effective collaborations with medical colleagues.

Contents: Introduction: The Purpose and Scope of this Book • Understanding Culture: Similarities Between Physicians and Mental Health Providers • Cross-Cultural Differences Between Mental Health Professionals and Physicians • Getting Known: Negotiating the Medical Community • First Contacts • Continuing Collaboration • Training Physicians to Collaborate: The Collaborative Family Conference • Summary and Future Directions • References

1999   160pp.   0-8261-1258-7   softcover www.springerpub.com

536 Broadway, New York, NY 10012-3955 • (212) 431-4370 • Fax (212) 941-7842